DISCOVER COLUMBUS

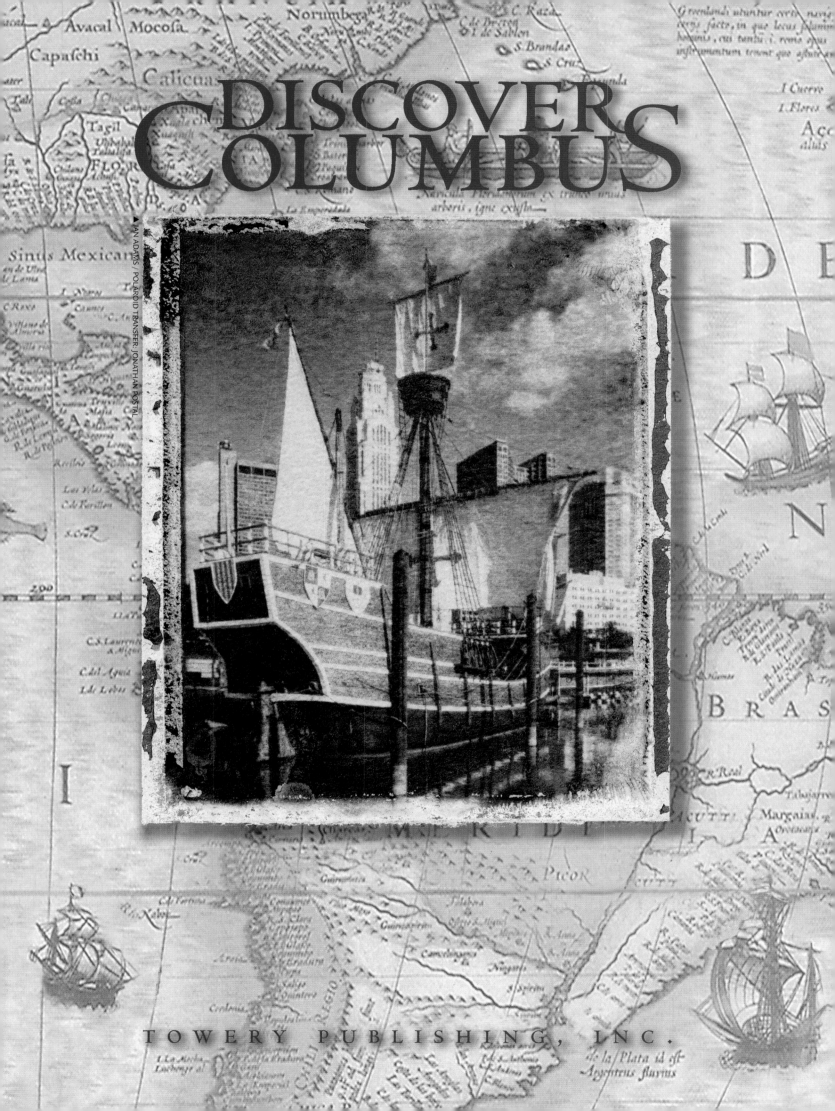

TOWERY PUBLISHING, INC.

DISCOVER COLUMBUS

By Mike Harden & Brooke Wenstrup

Profiles in Excellence by
Mark Bernstein

Art Direction by
Bob Shatzer & Jonathan Postal

URBAN
TAPESTRY
SERIES

TOWERY
PUBLISHING, INC.

LIBRARY OF CONGRESS CATALOGING-IN-PUBLICATION DATA

Harden, Mike
    Discover Columbus / by Mike Harden and Brooke Wenstrup ; Profiles
in excellence by Mark Bernstein ; captions by Mike Harden ; art
direction by Bob Shatzer and Jonathan Postal.
      p. cm. — (Urban tapestry series)
    Includes index.
    ISBN 1-881096-51-3
    1. Columbus (Ohio)—Civilization. 2. Columbus (Ohio)—Pictorial
works. 3. Business enterprises—Ohio—Columbus. 4. Columbus
(Ohio)—Economic conditions. I. Wenstrup, Brooke (Brooke Ann),
1957- . II. Bernstein, Mark (Mark Douglas), 1950-   Profiles in
excellence. c1997. III. Title. IV. Series.
F499.C75H37 1997
977.1'57—DC21   97-35155

Towery Publishing, Inc., 1835 Union Avenue, Memphis, TN 38104

PUBLISHER: *J. Robert Towery*
EXECUTIVE PUBLISHER: *Jenny McDowell*
NATIONAL SALES MANAGER: *Stephen Hung*
MARKETING DIRECTOR: *Carol Culpepper*
PROJECT DIRECTORS: *Mary Hanley, Jim Tomlinson*
EXECUTIVE EDITOR: *David B. Dawson*
MANAGING EDITOR: *Michael C. James*
SENIOR EDITORS: *Lynn Conlee, Carlisle Hacker*
EDITORS/PROJECT MANAGERS: *Lori Bond, Jana Files*
STAFF EDITORS: *Mary Jane Adams, Susan Hesson, Brian Johnston*

ASSISTANT EDITORS: *Pat McRaven, Jennifer C. Pyron, Allison Ring*
CREATIVE DIRECTOR: *Brian Groppe*
PROFILE DESIGNERS: *Laurie Beck, Kelley Pratt, Ann Ward*
DIGITAL COLOR SUPERVISOR: *Brenda Pattat*
DIGITAL COLOR TECHNICIANS: *Jack Griffith, Darin Ipema,*
   Jason Moak
PRODUCTION RESOURCES MANAGER: *Dave Dunlap Jr.*
PRODUCTION ASSISTANTS: *Geoffrey Ellis, Enrique Espinosa,*
   Robin McGehee
PRINT COORDINATOR: *Beverly Thompson*

CONTENTS

W ITH A FLAMBOYANT NAUTICAL
crown, Felicia Graham, Miss
Columbus 1991, marked the quincenten-
nial of Christopher Columbus' departure
for the New World.

C OLUMBUS MAY HAVE THOUGHT THE *Santa Maria* a slow and clumsy ship, but today's lighted replica—framed against a downtown landscape—lends the vessel a majesty the mariner never glimpsed.

By Mike Harden

AMING A LANDLOCKED MIDWESTERN CITY IN HONOR OF AN explorer who didn't really discover America may seem like one of the country's great paradoxes, but it set a precedent for other inland cities called Columbus. Here, in the Ohio incarnation of Columbus, residents seem to relish such enigmas. Native son James Thurber captured the soul of the city perfectly when he pointed out that "Columbus is a town in which almost anything is likely to happen, and in which almost everything has."

Vital and growing—while much of big-city America east of the Mississippi and north of the Sun Belt founders in a morass of urban devolution—Columbus is nonetheless viewed by its bicoastal detractors as a sort of Velveetaville lost in the high corn of one of those flyover states with too many vowels.

For instance, several years ago, when American Electric Power (AEP) decided to transplant 300 employees from the Big Apple to Buckeye country, it was not without much corporate hand-holding and gentle reassurance. If you don't like Columbus after a year, AEP promised unsettled employees, we will pay you to move back to Gotham. After 12 months of discovering that Columbusites were neither the Clampetts nor the Cleavers, only a dozen packed their bags.

A GIFT FROM THE PEOPLE OF GENOA— birthplace of the great explorer— this statue of Columbus looks out from City Hall upon the lazy Scioto River, ever reminding passersby where this Ohio town got its name.

NE OF THE FIRST MISCONCEPTIONS NEWCOMERS MUST PUT ASIDE HAS TO do with Ohio State football, the only local religion that emphasizes hooting, howling, and incomprehensible outbursts. Football is no mere sport in Columbus. It's a secular crusade, a part of our collective world view, that consumes the whole of autumn and—if the gods are kind—a portion of New Year's Day. On the November afternoon when Ohio State and Michigan meet—be it in Columbus or Ann Arbor—it is possible to roll a bowling ball down the main corridors of the city's shopping malls without hitting a soul.

Though most Columbus residents couldn't name all of the city's council members if you put a gun to their heads, they can, without hesitation, recite the names of the Buckeye starting backfield, recall all the school's Heisman Trophy winners, and even tell you the score of the infamous 1950 "Snow Bowl" (Michigan won it, 9-3, on a blocked punt). All that novices need to remember to get on with Buckeye fans is that Ohio Stadium is called the Shoe, the coach is Coop, and otherwise mature adults sometimes weep, unashamedly, when Michigan wins.

But football isn't the only game in town—it isn't even the only game in the Shoe. The Columbus Crew, of Major League Soccer, draws thousands out to Ohio Stadium. George

FAMOUS IN YEARS PAST FOR HER eccentric hats and lively manner, Carmen Miranda would surely have wept in envy at this nautical chapeau (OPPOSITE) or the game-day antics of the Ohio State University's mascot, Brutus Buckeye (BELOW).

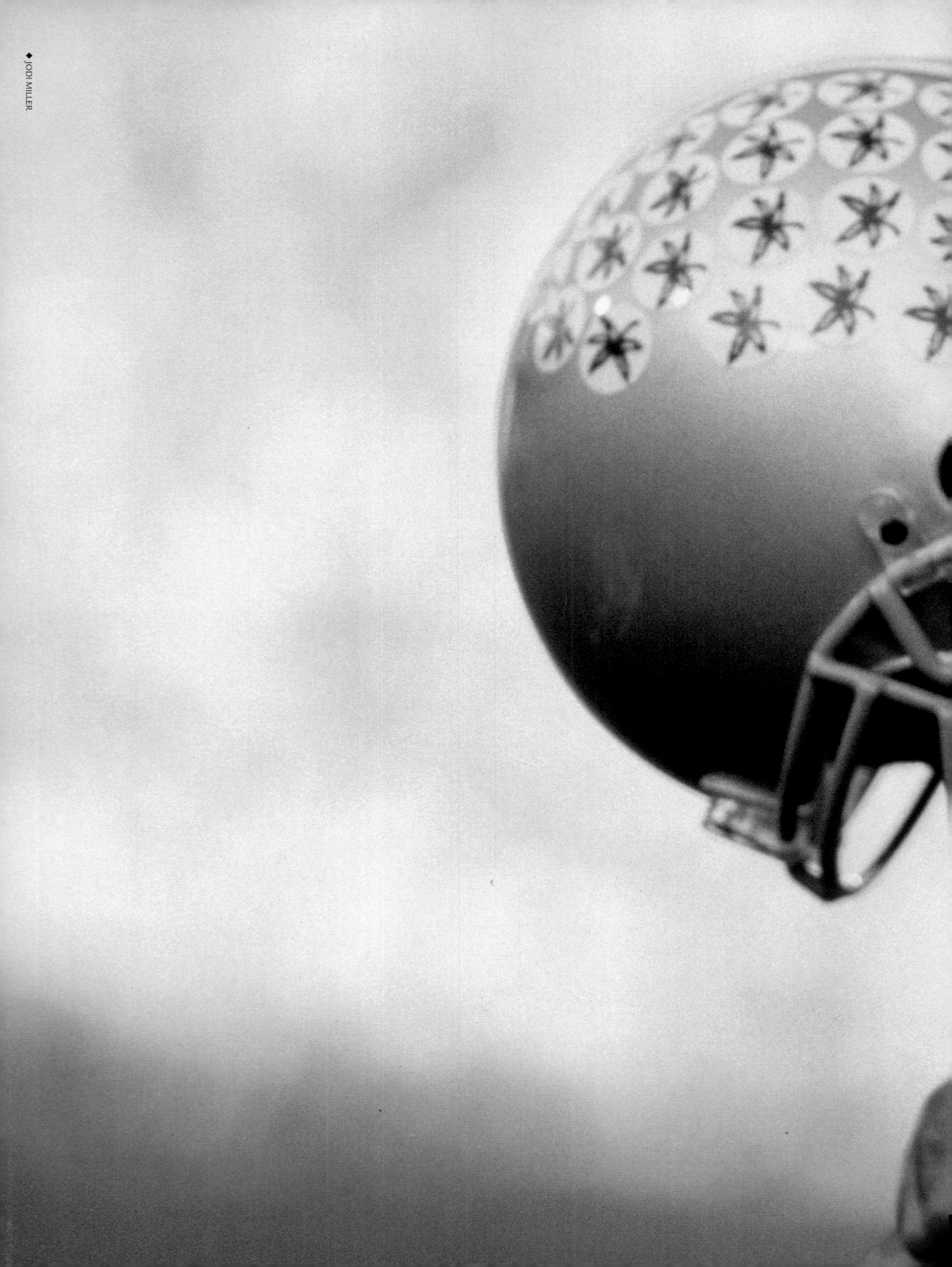

JODI MILLER

D URING A MOMENT OF QUIET REFLEC-
tion in a sea of autumn mayhem, an
Ohio State football player pauses while
90,000 fans look on (PAGES 12 AND 13). Even
though soccer has in recent years taken
Columbus by storm, football—and all the
hype that goes along with it—continues to
be the city's secular religion.

Steinbrenner's New York Yankees have their
first-line farm club, the Columbus Clippers, at Cooper Stadium. The Clippers,
who from time to time in their relatively
brief tenure in the city have been known to
outdraw major-league franchises, are the
latest heirs to the city's strong baseball tradition, a tradition that goes all the way
back to the Columbus Blue Birds
and the Co-
lumbus Elite
Giants of the
old Negro National League.

The city recently landed a National
Hockey League franchise, which will begin
play in 2000. And there's minor-league
hockey (The Chill) and professional women's
basketball (The Quest). Luring professional
sports teams to Columbus has been no easy
feat, and when past efforts to land a pro
franchise have come up short, pun-
dits have inevitably started
writing about how the
city suffers from a
bit of an inferi-
ority complex.
Thurber once
again hit the
proverbial nail
on the noggin when
he observed, "In the early
years of the nineteenth century, Columbus won out,
as state capital, by only one
vote over Lancaster, and
ever since then has had the
hallucination that it is being followed, a curious

municipal state of mind which affects, in some way or other, all those who live there."

Residents of Cleveland and Cincinnati, cities that once were larger (though no more), have sniffed at their midstate rival. After all, we were the city that—for decades—had only one skyscraper to break the horizon, a forlorn spire of concrete and high steel called the LeVeque Tower. (Columbus has come a long way since the days when the big thrill was to fork over a quarter to be admitted to the skyscraper's observation deck and stare through binoculars at inmates in the yard of the nearby Ohio Penitentiary.)

Columbus is the 16th-largest city in the nation, yet has long been gnawed by the suspicion that it is secretly viewed by its larger metropolitan sisters the way a Times Square streetwalker might look at Grant Wood's *American Gothic.*

Happily, the continuing vitality and growing sophistication of the city, along with a rich and variegated cultural plurality, are helping to melt away much of our civic self-consciousness. We are a great city to call home.

F OR DECADES, THE SPIRE OF THE historic LeVeque Tower visibly dominated the skyline, but today it takes its place among a promenade of sister skyscrapers.

ROGER BICKEL

Lucas Sullivant, one of the city's founding fathers, grasped that truth immediately when he first came to Central Ohio to survey what was, essentially, the promised land of the Revolution—a vast sprawl of unbroken frontier designated as the reward for those who had fought in the cause of the nation's founding. Sullivant arrived to find a twice-glaciated, billiard-table terrain whose owners—variously the Shawnee, Mingo, Wyandot, Miami, and Delaware tribes—were not quite ready to relinquish claim to the land they considered their birthright. Only after General "Mad Anthony" Wayne negotiated the Treaty of Greenville in 1795 with a dozen of the Ohio country's main tribes (they ceded land claims and promised peace for $20,000) did relative calm come to Central Ohio.

The first settlers of Columbus cleared a patch of bottomland on the west bank of the Scioto River, and soon found their new environs far less forgiving than were the native tribes from whom they had wrested it. Swamp- and marshland bred disease. Cholera and typhus epidemics cut a swath through the new settlers; hastily plotted graveyards were soon filled. The heartiest survived, though. They had come to Central Ohio to conquer the land, and took some satisfaction from having at least fought the untamed terrain to a draw.

The early settlers, largely of German, Scotch, Irish, and English descent, had a first-things-first idea of how Columbus ought to be built. In the 1812 deal that lured the state capital to Columbus, city fathers promised a statehouse and a prison. The latter seemed to take priority, it being generally conceded that the populace first needed protection from convicts who had already proven their criminality, as opposed to state legislators who were only beginning to exercise their skill at it.

Luring the legislature to Columbus in 1816 did little to aid early growth. What the city needed was a link to the world outside Central Ohio. Once Columbus was connected by canal (1831), by the National Road (1831), and by rail (1850) to the four points of the compass, it truly began to develop.

A Union hub during the Civil War, Columbus was the site of one of the largest Confederate prison camps in the North. More than 2,200 sons of Dixie perished in Camp Chase on the west side of town—most of them victims of disease brought on by the deplorable sanitary conditions of the camp. Though a Camp Chase visitor today can look upon orderly rows of individually carved stones, truth is, the dead were all interred in a mass grave, much to the chagrin of families in the South who—even to this day—appeal to have their ancestors' remains exhumed and returned.

Descendants of the city's German settlers today celebrate their heritage by donning lederhosen and other traditional garb for the annual Oktoberfest (above).

A filigree of ice glazes the scene at Cedar Falls in the Hocking Hills (opposite). Although most of the nearby trees are actually hemlocks, the area's first citizens mistook them for cedars—thus the name.

Though Columbus lacks the deep taproot of ethnicity that exists in neighboring communities like Cleveland or Pittsburgh, the melting-pot mix of the city has flourished for 150 years as wave after successive wave of immigrants and migrants have settled here. African-Americans steadily trekked into the city from the South, Ohio being a major terminus of the Underground Railroad before and during the Civil War. The Germans dominated in the last half of the 19th century, settling largely to the south of the capital, building breweries along the Scioto, and practicing every vocation from violin making to the crafting of stained-glass windows.

Another wave of immigration occurred when Italian-Americans settled a little north of downtown and west of the Ohio Penitentiary in an area christened Flytown. Many labored in the mills and factories that fringed the Flytown area, but a good number took on the limestone quarrying work at Marble Cliffs and formed the core population of San Margarita.

One of the largest boons to population growth came with the inroad migration to Columbus from Kentucky, West Virginia, and southern Ohio. As coal mines played out, became hostage to labor strife, or were given over to mechanized mining, a tremendous urban migration of Appalachians took place. They took jobs with General Motors, Westinghouse, North American-Rockwell, and Western Electric. Neither universally beloved nor understood in their new surroundings, they nursed homesickness with frequent weekend excursions back to home country.

Still, these migrants comprise a significant portion of the urban population that has never been politically numbered nor has held much sway in the affairs of the city. As to being misunderstood, a *Washington Post* travel writer (Christopher Corbett), who visited Columbus in 1990, noted of the substantial Appalachian population: "Over on Parsons Avenue there are genuine hillbillies fresh out of the wilds of West Virginia and Kentucky, driving real American cars held together with Bondo and bailing wire and eating biscuits and gravy."

The *Washington Post* notwithstanding, Appalachians not only turned the industrial engines of this city for decades, but they have also entwined its fabric with their music, their culture, and a genuine friendliness that would be brushed off as a prelude to panhandling if demonstrated in New York or Washington, D.C.

THE "PILLBOX HAT" OF THE GREEK Revival Ohio Statehouse (ABOVE) was barely in place when the structure was crepe draped to accommodate the body of a slain President Abraham Lincoln in 1865. At nearby Camp Chase, located on the city's west side, more than 2,200 Rebel soldiers are interred in Yankee soil (OPPOSITE).

IF THERE EXISTS WITHIN COLUMBUS A HALLMARK NATURAL RESOURCE THAT SETS IT aside from other metropolitan areas of similar size, it is probably gumption—that peculiarly American stew of imagination, tenacity, bootstrap ambition, and innovation. In short, we're good at producing entrepreneurs. ✷ Battelle, one of America's largest private research firms, developed xerography right here in Columbus.

A fresh graduate of Ohio State in the early 1960s, young businessman Les Wexner decided that working women needed a shop where they could clothe themselves without sinking the budget. He started The Limited.

R. David Thomas, a former army cook, launched Wendy's International in Columbus. The city is also headquarters to White Castle Systems, which has been making hamburgers across the United States for more than 75 years.

The diversity of the city's economy makes it virtually recession-proof. Two of Columbus' largest employers are government (local, county, state, and federal) and insurance (five dozen insurers are headquartered here). With government and insurance at the top, you have an economy built upon the rock of life's only two guarantees: death and taxes.

As for the third-largest employer, the Ohio State University is a city of 50,000 students within a city, contributing both jobs and a legion of consumers of goods and services.

FORMER ARMY COOK R. DAVID Thomas (OPPOSITE) is the burgher of burgers in the city where he launched his world-famous fast-food chain. Named for his daughter Wendy, the locally based enterprise boasts nearly 5,000 restaurants across the globe.

Locals young and old get a glimpse of Central Ohio's agrarian roots during a demonstration of early farming equipment (LEFT).

AT THE END OF THE GREAT DEPRESSION, THE OHIO WRITERS' PROJECT, A Works Progress Administration program, concluded its efforts to paint a portrait of the state with the publication of a 600-page hardback titled *The Ohio Guide*. The book's chapter on Columbus listed annual events in the city that might intrigue the vacationer, or pique the curiosity of tourists. Search though they did, the writers could come up with only six events for Columbus. Half of them were agrarian extravaganzas or meetings, such as the Ohio State Fair, Ohio Farmers Week, and Future Farmers of America's annual convention.

As the city has matured and grown less agrarian, its tastes have become more discerning, more cosmopolitan. Too, the infusion of new Columbus residents—from transplanted New Yorkers to somewhat lost Los Angelenos—has helped enhance the civic appetite for opera, ballet, and the symphony.

Columbus kick-starts each new month with a gallery hop in the Short North arts district. Singles mingle at the Columbus Museum of Art's First Thursday gathering each month. German Village, America's largest privately funded neighborhood restoration, showcases blocks of restored brick homes built in the mid- to late 19th century by German immigrants. Victorian Village, sandwiched between the southern fringe of Ohio State and downtown's Short North, offers an extravaganza of architectural gingerbread on restored, turn-of-the-century homes.

MUSIC IS A VIBRANT PART OF THE city's tapestry, and a rosined bow can lead to anything from Bach to bluegrass. Suggesting a Wagnerian wistfulness, German Village, a neighborhood just south of the State Capitol, features renovated 19th-century homes, shops, and restaurants (OPPOSITE).

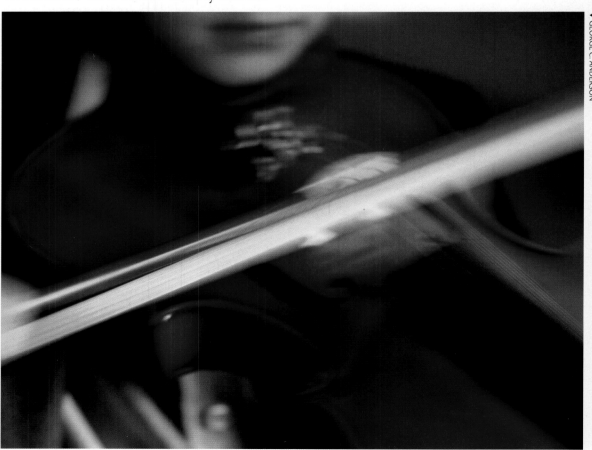

For the history buff, the Ohio Historical Center awaits, with craftsmen demonstrating 19th-century trade skills. For the patron of the arts, the Wexner Center on the Ohio State campus always features something to tantalize locals and visitors alike.

A short-sleeve, out-of-doors bent to local residents makes sure that ample use is always

Another 4-H Mary tends her little lamb at State Fair time (above). Plenty of hard work and a little luck may bring a blue ribbon her way: great news for Mary, but a yawner for the lion king at the Columbus Zoo (opposite).

made of the Columbus Metroparks system, the Franklin Park Conservatory, the Columbus Zoo, and the blossoming riverfront area, where a replica of Christopher Columbus' *Santa Maria* is tied up.

Columbus is a literary city. We are the nation's ninth-largest book market, and we're ahead of Los Angeles in public library usage. Thurber House, the restored boyhood home of James Thurber, routinely brings to the city some of the nation's best writers through its Evenings with the Authors series.

Columbus is a musical city. We like jazz, bluegrass, country, and classical, and we're continually shuffling the marquees of the Ohio Theatre, Palace Theatre, and Veterans Memorial Auditorium to make room for the next headliner to play the city. True to our midwestern, agrarian roots, the State Fair is still extremely popular—one of the largest in the nation, featuring Mary's little lambs, butter sculptures, blue-ribbon pies, tractor pulls, and just about any kind of food that can be eaten on a stick. The fair is a feast of absolute superlatives: biggest, fastest, toughest, prettiest, scariest, tastiest, even strangest.

It should tell Columbus something about itself that, though we've become much more cosmopolitan and sophisticated over the past two decades, we still like the State Fair. We still go a little crazy each autumn when the Shoe is standing-room-only and The Best Damned Band in the Land plays *Buckeye Battle Cry*. We have not lost our capacity for awe, our ability to be entertained and intrigued by the simplest of pleasures. We are still a little wide-eyed-in-Babylon about some of the insanity that goes on in big-city America, even though we are a part of big-city America.

We are proud enough of what we have become to get annoyed when someone from, say, New York asks, "Columbus? Which one?" We grew so weary of interlopers casting cow-town aspersions on us that we finally jumped on the bandwagon and began selling Mootown T-shirts at the airport.

When the grit and the gridlock and the orange construction barrels get to be a little much, we know we can jump on the interstate and in 10 or 15 minutes be sitting under a tree along a rural ribbon of two-lane blacktop, watching the wind ripple the high corn and sniffing the perfume of freshly cut alfalfa.

It is, in the heart of the heartland, the best of all possible worlds. ✳

In Central Ohio, the fruits of agriculture are as bountiful as its roots are deep. At the annual Farm Science Review—a veritable fashion show of new equipment—experienced farmers and those who may one day succeed them gather to marvel at what makes John Deere dear (LEFT).

APPROXIMATELY 500,000 CELEBRANTS ooh and aah as the Red, White & Boom! Fourth of July fireworks celebration fills the night sky with brilliant flashes, cleverly choreographed to patriotic and classical music. After the smoke settles and the scent of cordite fades, homebound revelers create a light show of their own as they snake out across city freeways.

A WHITE-COLLAR CITY WITH BLUE-collar sensibilities, Columbus is a major business hub whose tall towers are soaring testimonials to a virtually recession-proof economy.

S OME BEAMS WE BEND FOR ART
(ABOVE); others we rivet for commerce (OPPOSITE). Among America's 25
largest cities, Columbus is one of the few
towns located north of the Sun Belt and
east of the Mississippi River that is still
in a growth spurt.

I f Chicago is the City of Big Shoul- ders, then Columbus is the City of Hard Hats. The town's dynamic knack for reinvention and renewal may have been what attracted Nationwide Insur- ance founder Murray Lincoln, who chose to establish his corporate headquarters here in 1926. The company today directs its thriving business from offices in Na- tionwide Plaza, a three-tower complex that anchors the north end of downtown (OPPOSITE).

Built in 1980, the AAA four-diamond, Mobil three-star Hyatt Regency Columbus (LEFT) is the gateway to the Short North arts district, which features a number of shops and museums, as well as a monthly gallery hop.

Located across from the Ohio State-house, the Vern Riffe Center for Government & the Arts (RIGHT), stands as a tribute to state government leader Vern "Mr. Speaker" Riffe, who died in 1997.

CRITICS MAY ARGUE THAT THE Columbus Convention Center looks as if an earthquake jarred its foundation, but no one can dispute that the Peter Eisenman-designed, zigzag structure has helped foster a dramatic renewal of the Short North district.

T HE SCIOTO RIVER, AS SEEN FROM THE Franklin County Veteran's Memorial Auditorium (OPPOSITE), is said to have been named by the first dwellers in Franklin County—Native Americans. In the Delaware language, Scioto means "many deer." Today, the river beckons many folks, not the least of whom are these fishermen, dunking dough balls for carp south of downtown (ABOVE).

T HE FOUNTAIN AT THE PARK OF ROSES
intrigues frolicking children. The
park is one of many in the city that lure
cyclists and joggers, fishermen and lovers.

COLUMBUS NATIVES OF A CERTAIN AGE, now graying at the temples and long of tooth, recall learning the couplet, "In 1492, Columbus sailed the ocean blue." Seen here, dwarfing a racing shell, is the *Santa Maria*, a replica of one of the explorer's three vessels from his late-15th-century voyage (PAGES 50 AND 51).

C OLUMBUS MAY BE A LANDLOCKED city, but locals love their aquatic frolics and take to the water like Labrador puppies.

IN RECENT YEARS, CYCLING HAS GAINED speed as a popular sport in Columbus, and a number of bike paths and contests challenge the limits of local athletes (ABOVE). After a hard workout, a pair of pedalers stop to enjoy the familiar, cryptic smile and Mediterranean eyes painted in a mural on a Short North building (PAGES 56 AND 57).

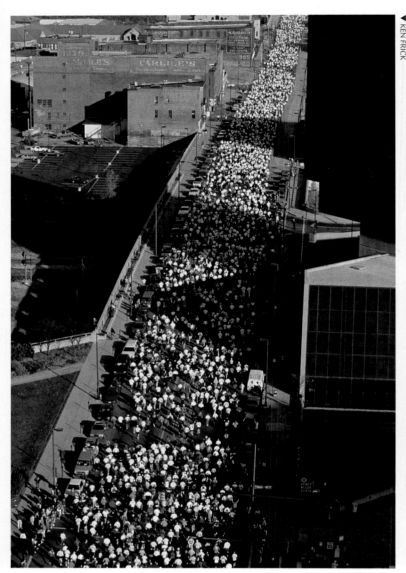

Columbusites don't need a marathon to run, as any downtown pedestrian trying to navigate lunch-hour joggers will attest. However, the annual Columbus Marathon always provides a good excuse to head for the finish line.

HILE A LOCAL SWIMMING COACH preaches no pain, no gain to her pupil (ABOVE), these youngsters splash their cares away at the Wyandot Lake water park near the Columbus Zoo (OPPOSITE).

The Columbus Clippers, the New York Yankees' Class-AAA farm team, draw the faithful out night after night to Cooper Stadium. Today's team is heir to a local baseball tradition that goes all the way back to the Negro National League Columbus Blue Birds and the Columbus Elite Giants.

I n Columbus, the thrill of the chill means more than just winter fun. Flying fists are routine when the Chill is on the ice, but if you stick around long enough, a hockey game will eventually break out.

P EOPLE OFTEN WONDER IF COLUMBUS Crew heartthrob Brian McBride is really as nice as he seems. Sure, unless you happen to be in his way and on an opposing Major League Soccer team (PAGES 66 AND 67).

Columbusites are fanatic about their hometown athletes, whether they're heading a soccer ball, going in for a layup, or celebrating with a teammate.

But the players themselves aren't the only game in town: This drum major knows that halftime is his chance to strut his stuff (RIGHT).

DISCOVER COLUMBUS

NOTHING DRAWS A CROWD LIKE AN Ohio State football game, and youngsters often dream of one day being the tuba player who dots the *i* in the Script Ohio, or making the play that sends Brutus Buckeye prancing. But few jobs are as coveted as that of drum major. Fill those shoes and you get to lead The Best Damned Band in the Land out of the tunnel for *Buckeye Battle Cry*.

▲ BRAD FEINKNOPF

I F YOU'RE GOING TO GET ON IN COLUMBUS, you have to know that Coach John Cooper is referred to as Coop, that the stadium is called the Shoe, and that many high schoolers live to be a Buckeye someday. Here, Coop leads the team onto the field (TOP), and Stanley Jackson, quarterback and 1997 cocaptain, keeps his eye on another victory (OPPOSITE).

THE BUCKEYES PLAY FOR GLORY IN a stadium whose dedication was attended by the likes of Knute Rockne and John Heisman. Time and again, fans prove that neither rain nor snow nor dark of a Michigan victory can keep them away from their anointed team.

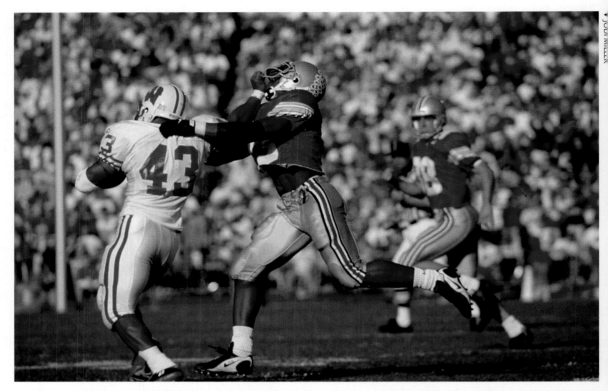

THE BUCKEYE BAND BEATS OUT A victory tattoo, the Ohio State equivalent of a rain dance. On autumn Saturdays, the Buckeye flag flies all over Columbus—not much below the American flag.

N ATIVE SON JACK NICKLAUS, ALSO known as the Golden Bear, put Columbus on the map in PGA circles when he began his legendary professional career (OPPOSITE). Back home, he made a permanent mark on the local landscape by designing the Muirfield Village Golf Club in nearby Dublin (ABOVE).

R AIN OR SHINE (USUALLY RAIN), THE Memorial Tournament at Muirfield Village Golf Club has drawn crowds of all ages since 1976. Some folks claim the event has been cursed with inclement weather because the course was built on an old Indian burial site.

COLUMBUS BOASTS PLENTY OF GREENS and greenery. There are several golf courses throughout the city for those who enjoy the sport Mark Twain called "a good walk spoiled" (OPPOSITE).

Although horticulturists adore the Franklin Park Conservatory & Botanical Garden, most golfers would consider the 88-acre wonderland to be the mother of all roughs (ABOVE).

S UBURBAN WESTERVILLE'S INNISWOOD
Metro Gardens offers a fine place
to test one's capacity for silent
contemplation.

I NSPIRED BY GEORGES SEURAT's *A Sunday Afternoon on the Island of La Grande
Jatte,* this clever tableau suggests nature
imitating art imitating nature.

▲ GEORGE C. ANDERSON

CREATED BY SCULPTOR JAMES T. Mason, the topiary rendition of Seurat's *Sunday Afternoon* takes its place on the grounds of the former School for the Deaf, now known as Deaf School Park. Mason's display, which covers nearly one acre, features approximately 50 topiary "people," the tallest of which is 12 feet high.

G REATER COLUMBUS OFFERS A NUM-ber of locales that inspire serenity and peace. Countless visitors are lured to Logan County's enchanting Castle Mac-O-Chee, built by Colonel Donn Piatt in the 1870s (OPPOSITE). In nearby Westerville, the 91-acre Inniswood Metro Gardens—the former estate of Mary and Grace Innis, founders of Ohio's first garden club—is noted for its rose and herb gardens, a woodland rock collection, and an 800-volume library of books relating to horticulture (LEFT). And north of Columbus in Marion is the Harding Memorial, which marks the final resting spot of Warren G. Harding, the last Ohio son to call the White House home (RIGHT).

T HEY MAY BE LOCATED IN DIFFERENT counties, but you'd hardly know it. The whorled rosinweed and blazing stars at Prairie Road Fen State Nature Preserve (OPPOSITE) compete for attention with the tall grass and prairie plants of the Bigelow Cemetery Prairie State Nature Preserve (ABOVE).

Franklin Park Conservatory (TOP) beckons us to stop and smell the proverbial roses. However, in a game of horticultural one-upmanship, the best place to do that is at the Park of Roses (BOTTOM). Of course, the Inniswood Metro Gardens offers its own colorful collection of the thorny beauties (OPPOSITE).

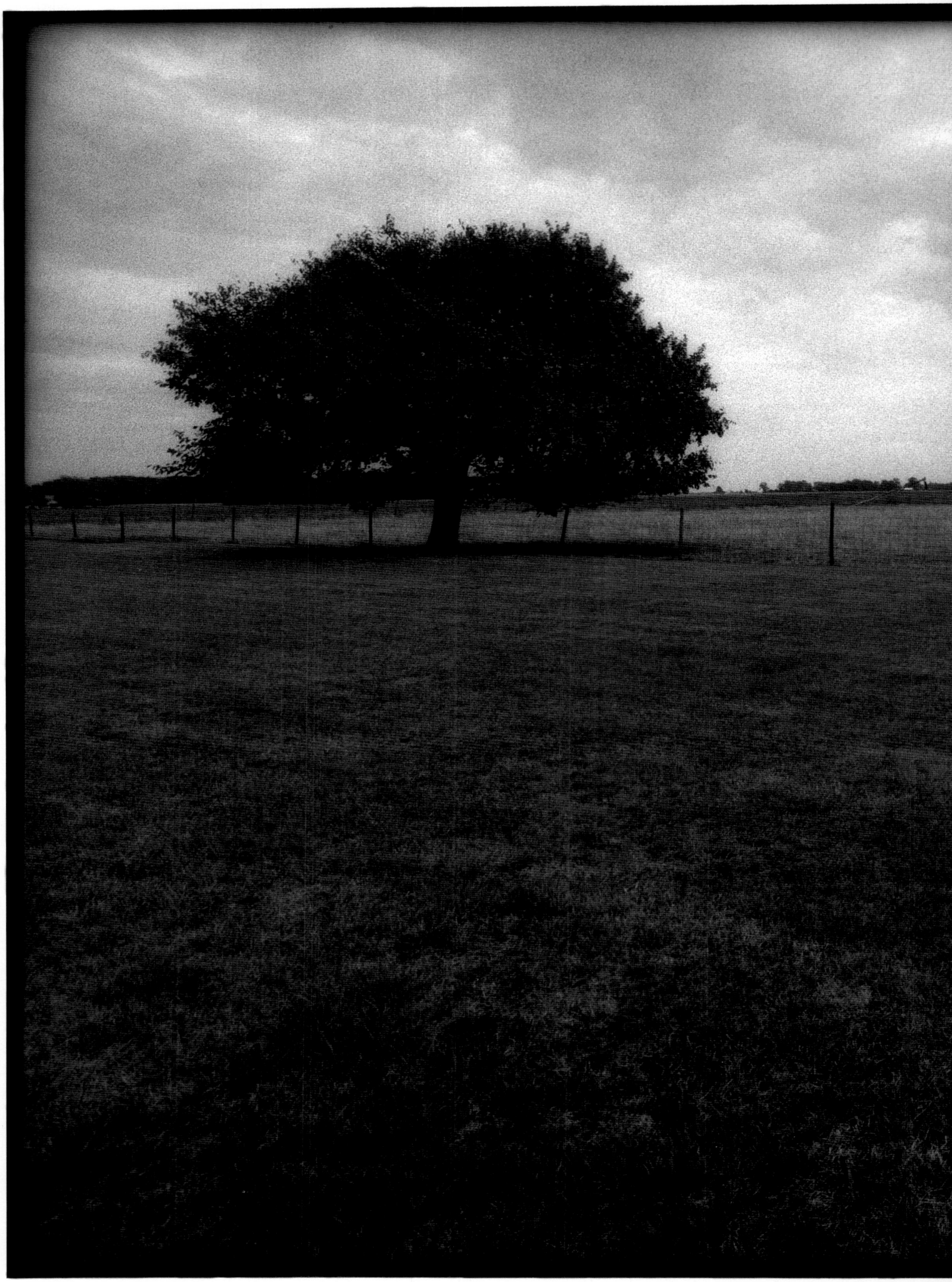

▲ GEORGE C. ANDERSON

W HILE ONE BOY CASTS HIS LINE AND
waits at Chestnut Ridge Metro
Park (ABOVE), another lucky angler
shows off his not-so-menacing catch
of the day (OPPOSITE).

C ONSTRUCTED IN 1826 AS A FEEDER lake for Ohio's canal system, Buckeye Lake, located east of Columbus, was down on its heels in the late 1970s (PAGES 98 AND 99). The 3,300-acre body of water is today enjoying a renewal and revitalization as a popular retreat for boaters, swimmers, anglers, and bird-watchers.

ON ALUM CREEK RESERVOIR IN nearby Delaware, Ohio, boaters savor the placid pleasures of an easy harbor (ABOVE), while the statue of Christopher Columbus looks out on a landlocked city that christened itself in his honor (OPPOSITE).

OHIO WINTERS CAN BE BRUTAL, BUT
the antidote for February's cabin
fever is spring at Inniswood Metro Gardens (ABOVE) or summer at Ash Cave in
the Hocking Hills, south of Columbus
(OPPOSITE).

C ENTRAL OHIO HAS LONG RELIED ON agribusiness as a primary contributor to the economy. Commemorating that heritage is Slate Run Living Historical Farm, located within the Columbus Metroparks system. Opened in 1981, the venue re-creates farm life in the 1880s, offering hands-on experiences with livestock and a shot at milking the old-fashioned way.

MOST CREATURES KNOW THAT FOUR
legs are better than two when it
comes to navigating traffic in Greater
Columbus, but that doesn't stop the
city's legion of runners from going the
distance—even on the coldest of days.

Locals commemorate the area's Native American heritage in numerous ways, including this powwow at the Fort Hayes Career Center (RIGHT). The event gave students at the alternative school a chance to glimpse the dress and customs of those who first called the Ohio country home.

As part of the community's Art in Public Places Project, the Dublin Arts Council commissioned this limestone likeness of Chief Leatherlips, which resides in Scioto Park (OPPOSITE). One of the signers of the Treaty of Greenville, a peace accord between local Native Americans and the U.S. government, Chief Leatherlips was tomahawked to death by tribesmen who opposed the agreement.

Long ago, when the coal mines of Hocking County played out, many natives traveled to Columbus in search of employment. Today, city-weary weekenders often return to the area to hike and camp at Conkle's Hollow State Nature Preserve (PAGES 112 AND 113) and enjoy the beautiful scenery at Cedar Falls (LEFT).

THOMAS WOLFE ONCE WROTE THAT, with autumn approaching, "the sun goes down in blood and pollen across the bronzed and mown fields."

Each year, when the hay's been stacked and the proverbial frost is on the pumpkin, Central Ohio itself goes from green to a splendid gold.

A HORSE IS A HORSE IS A HORSE, OF course, unless you're at Malabar Farm, located north of Columbus in Richland County (BOTTOM). Visitors can enjoy a horse-drawn carriage ride around the 914-acre estate, which was once home to Pulitzer Prize-winning author Louis Bromfield. It was also the site of Humphrey Bogart and Lauren Bacall's wedding.

THE FIELDS AT HARVESTTIME SHOW
their true colors, as do those who
work them. This fellow has a special
place in his heart for John Deere green.

THE KNOT AND BURL OF CENTRAL Ohio's weatherworn fences offer a peek at the area's rural history. The estate of former Governor Thomas Worthington in Chillicothe is home to the first burial mound in Ohio to be excavated (ABOVE). The culture that supposedly built the mound was given the name Adena, after Worthington's home.

One of only six left in the state, this round barn in Perry County provides a direct link to Ohio's agricultural past (OPPOSITE). Although the style was common around the turn of the 19th century, it soon died off in popularity.

▲ GEORGE C. ANDERSON

DISCOVER COLUMBUS

A MAINTENANCE MAN KEEPS THINGS neat and tidy around *Field of Corn*, a sprawling tribute to the Dublin area's agrarian heritage. Dedicated in 1994, the sculptural work features 108 ears of white concrete corn and was constructed as part of the community's Art in Public Places project.

AGRICULTURE IS EVERYWHERE IN Greater Columbus. Soybeans at their prime make for a carpet of green outside the urban sprawl (OPPOSITE), and some folks even measure the city's growth by how long it takes to get from downtown to the nearest cornfield (LEFT).

N ature has its own ideas about what constitutes art. Maybe it's Indian corn, purchased from one of the numerous markets freckling Route 23 south of the city (OPPOSITE TOP), or rows of colorful seeds (OPPOSITE BOTTOM) from which next year's crop will grow fat (TOP). But not all art is of the earth, as the handiwork of a student at the Fort Hayes Career Center attests (BOTTOM).

A t Madison County's Farm Science
Review, future growers can get up
close and personal with larger-than-life
farm equipment.

G OLDEN-HUED SUNFLOWERS SHOW OFF their petal bonnets in Pickaway County (PAGES 132 AND 133).

LARRY HAMILL

S PEAK TO ME OF THE FACE OF AGRICUL-
ture and horticulture in Central
Ohio. Is it the grin of a tractor grill? Or
the iris of a wheel that pulls the plow?

The crimson lips of Inniswood's blos-
soms? Or an actor who we hope is not
allergic to bees?

W HAT IS MERELY DIRT TO SOME
is cherished by others as the
lifeblood of Ohio's long agricultural
heritage (OPPOSITE). Educating visitors
about farming operations in the late 19th
century are the folks at Slate Run Living
Historical Farm in Pickaway County
(ABOVE).

136

Although at one time Fairfield County boasted more wooden truss bridges—most of which were covered—than any other county in Ohio, you'd be hard pressed to find many of them today. The Mink Hollow Covered Bridge over Arney Mill Run is one of only 12 such spans that remain (PAGES 138 AND 139).

A t Ohio Village, a team that calls itself the Muffins challenges visitors to imagine the era when baseball inspired poems about men named Casey and towns called Mudville.

DISCOVER COLUMBUS

A N EVENING CROWD GATHERS FOR A poetry reading at Thurber House (OPPOSITE LEFT), the boyhood residence of Columbus' most beloved literary persona, James Thurber. Although you won't find many cats at the home of this canine-obsessed writer and cartoonist, you *can* catch a glimpse of a unicorn in the garden (ABOVE). Thurber's humorous piece about a man who spies the mythical beast in his own yard has been read by folks the world over.

J AMES THURBER'S BOYHOOD BEDROOM (OPPOSITE) is the setting for his whimsical vignettes "The Night the Ghost Got In" and "The Night the Bed Fell." Although success took the renowned humorist (ABOVE) to New York City, he was fond of noting that the "clocks of Columbus" would ever chime in his memory. Thurber is buried in the city's Green Lawn Cemetery.

Although a number of fine old buildings were razed as Columbus reinvented itself, more than a few grand ones managed to dodge the wrecking ball (OPPOSITE). This is especially true in Victorian Village, which has made a stunning comeback over the past two decades (ABOVE). Only five minutes from downtown, the neighborhood boasts an impressive collection of vintage homes, several of which are listed on the National Register of Historic Places.

I N RECENT YEARS, AN EPIC, PRIVATELY funded resuscitation effort has saved German Village, now listed on the National Register of Historic Places. The 233-acre neighborhood south of down-town has become a showpiece for tourists and preservationists, not to mention families who like to walk their dogs along its brick promenades.

C OLUMBUS' DIVERSE NEIGHBORHOODS offer plenty of proof that residents like to turn their outdoor spaces into things of beauty.

▲ TOM HOGAN

DISCOVER COLUMBUS

A CROSS OUTSIDE THE KERNS RELIGIOUS
Life Center punctuates the autumn
landscape at Capital University, founded
in Bexley in 1830.

R ESCUED FROM COLUMBUS' now-
vanished Union Station, these
historic arches today frame the headquarters of Nationwide Insurance (ABOVE).
Not far from Nationwide, in the city's
rebounding Short North district, the
breathtaking Annunciation Greek Ortho-
dox Cathedral calls the faithful to services amid its striking iconography
(OPPOSITE).

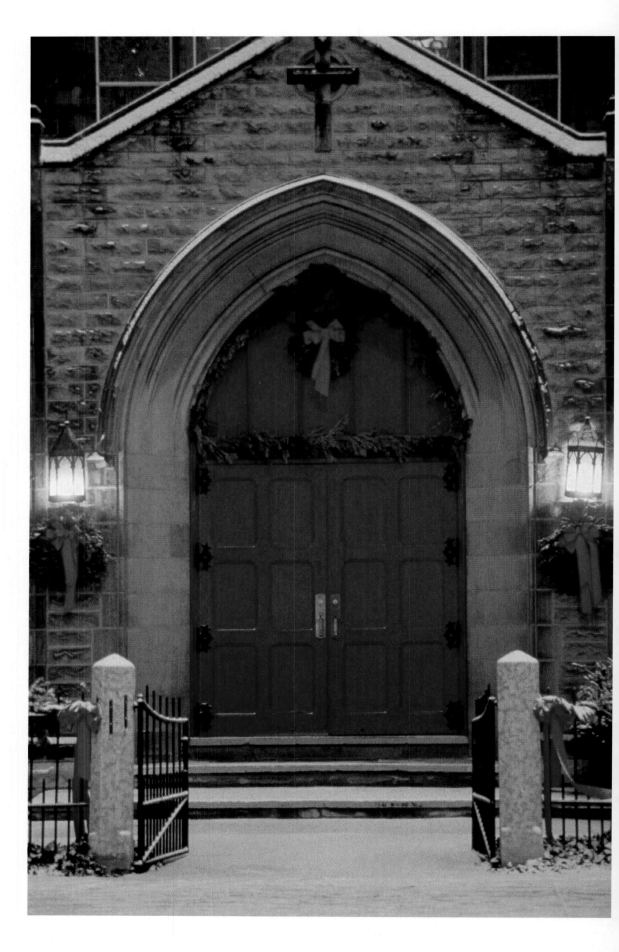

C OLUMBUS DRESSES UP FOR THE holidays, adding lights, garlands, and wreaths to local churches, homes, and parks. Even the Columbus City Center, a giant shopping mall downtown, decks its halls for Christmas (BOTTOM).

Discover Columbus

C OLUMBUS IS A CITY OF ONE-UPMANSHIP when it comes to stringing holiday lights, and locals often blow the utility budget vying to have their festive displays featured on the 11 o'clock news.

Even the replica of Christopher Columbus' *Santa Maria* wears lights in her rigging (OPPOSITE), though she holds no candle to the Columbus Zoo's Wildlight Wonderland (ABOVE).

Jack Hanna, longtime director and current director emeritus, plays a key role in making the Columbus Zoo one of the nation's finest (PAGES 166 AND 167), frequently taking his menagerie on *Late Night with David Letterman*. Home to creatures great and small, the zoo features more than 700 different species of animals.

COMMITTED TO THE PRESERVATION OF wildlife, the Columbus Zoo began its tradition of innovative breeding programs in 1956, when it became the first in the world to successfully breed gorillas. Today, the zoo boasts a wide range of animals, all of which are housed in naturalistic habitats.

LARRY HAMILL

I N COLUMBUS, THE REASON THE chicken crossed the road was to get to the Ohio State Fair. It's where we show off the feathered white meat, "the other white meat," a weigh-in winner by a "hare's breadth," and new dos all around for unshorn sheep.

▲ ED KREMINSKI ▲ RANDALL L. SCHIEBER

At the city's off-the-wall Doo Dah Parade on the Fourth of July, Spam is ahead by a nose. Meanwhile, at the Ohio State Fair, racing pigs churn and burn as though they know a Spam label awaits the losers.

A FEAST OF ABSOLUTE SUPERLATIVES,
the Ohio State Fair brings in the
largest, the greenest, and the fattest of
everything from gourds to melons. It all
comes together in a colorful display of
edible still lifes.

T HE EYES HAVE IT: THESE TATERS WIN
the prize at the State Fair.

F ROM JEANS TO RIBBONS, BLUE IS THE
favored color in the fair's agricultural and livestock barns.

Gɪᴠᴇ ᴀ ʙᴏʏ ᴀɴ ᴇɴɢɪɴᴇ ᴀɴᴅ ᴀ ꜰᴇᴡ wheels, and he'll find a way to race. Some cynics say the State Fair tractor pull demonstrates the wild ideas that can crop up in the minds of rural Ohioans when the cable goes out, but nothing draws a crowd like this heavyweight event.

From tooters and twirlers to tiara-topped beauties, folks in Columbus have plenty to smile about.

LOCALS TEST THEIR METTLE—AND their balance—at the State Fair logrolling competition. Held each year at the National Resources Park amphitheater, the event promises plenty of impromptu acrobatics.

F OR YOUNGSTERS WHO WANT TO put on a happy face, the folks at Clownfest will work their makeup magic, but the quickest route to a new look is the pie-eating contest at Ohio Village.

W AVE POOL COOL: WYANDOT LAKE, adjacent to the Columbus Zoo, lures area youth to take the summer plunge (PAGES 188 AND 189).

Since 1969, the Ohio State Fair's 125-car sky ride—the world's largest—has given folks a chance to enjoy the summer evening air and a bird's-eye view of the fair's colorful midway madness.

T HE SKY IS ABLAZE AS DUSK DESCENDS
upon the Scioto River (ABOVE) and
Franklin Park's 30,000-pound, stainless-
steel *NavStar '92*, which commemorates
the three ships used during Christopher
Columbus' voyage to the New World
(OPPOSITE).

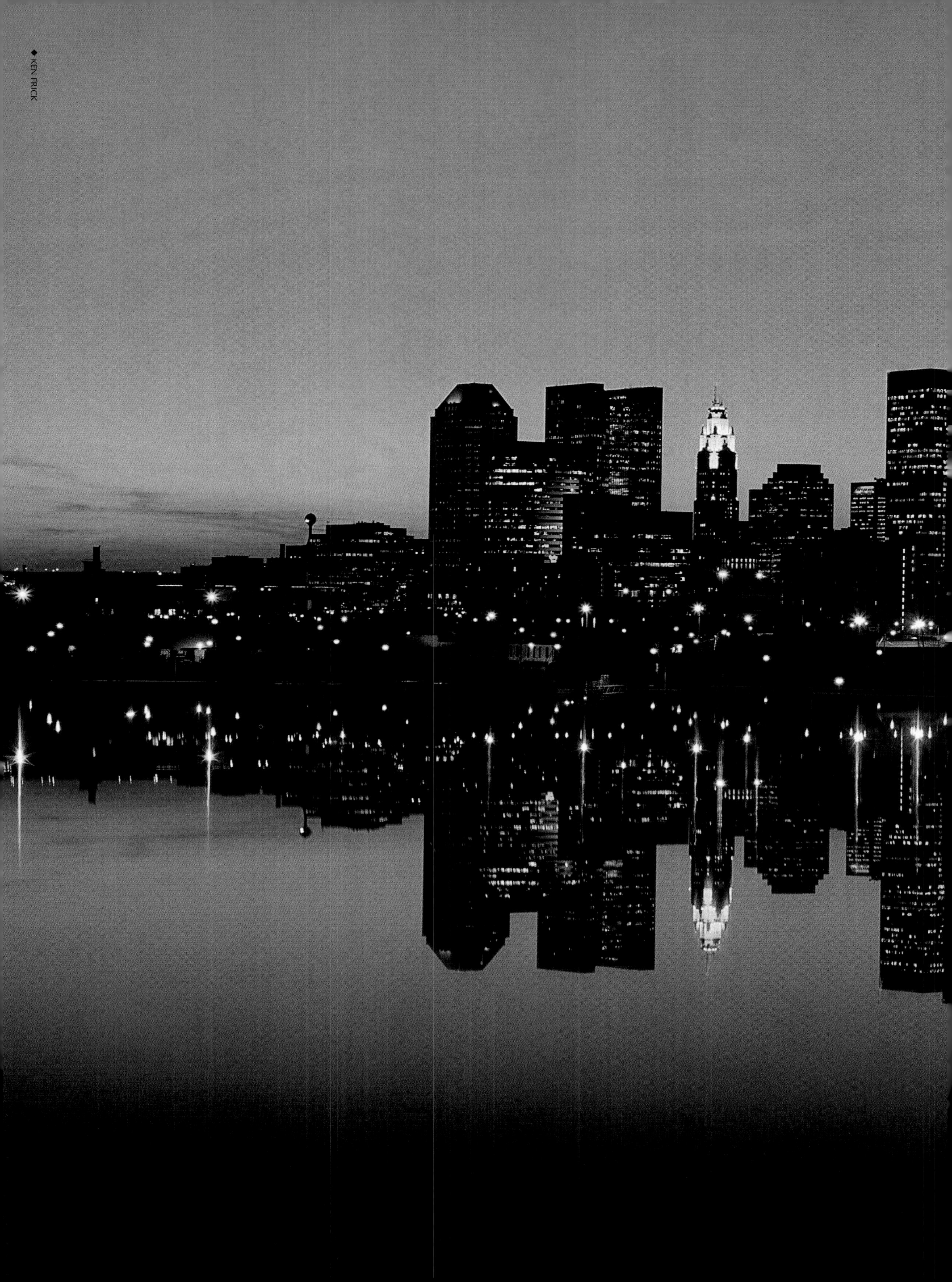

◆ KEN FRICK

C OLUMBUS' HYPNOTICALLY BEAUTIFUL skyline has lured many dreamers over the years. Locals will argue whether the best way to take in the inspiring vista is from across the Scioto River (PAGES 194 AND 195) or from an airplane flying high above the tall towers (ABOVE).

N o, it's not the parking lot at the Super Bowl—just one of the city's thriving new-car dealerships.

A YEAR AFTER WORLD WAR II ENDED, the 17-year-old Port Columbus Airport was a small-town operation, but today, it is one of the fastest-growing airfields in the nation. Located 10 minutes from downtown, the facility, which achieved international status in 1965, tallied more than 6 million passengers in 1996.

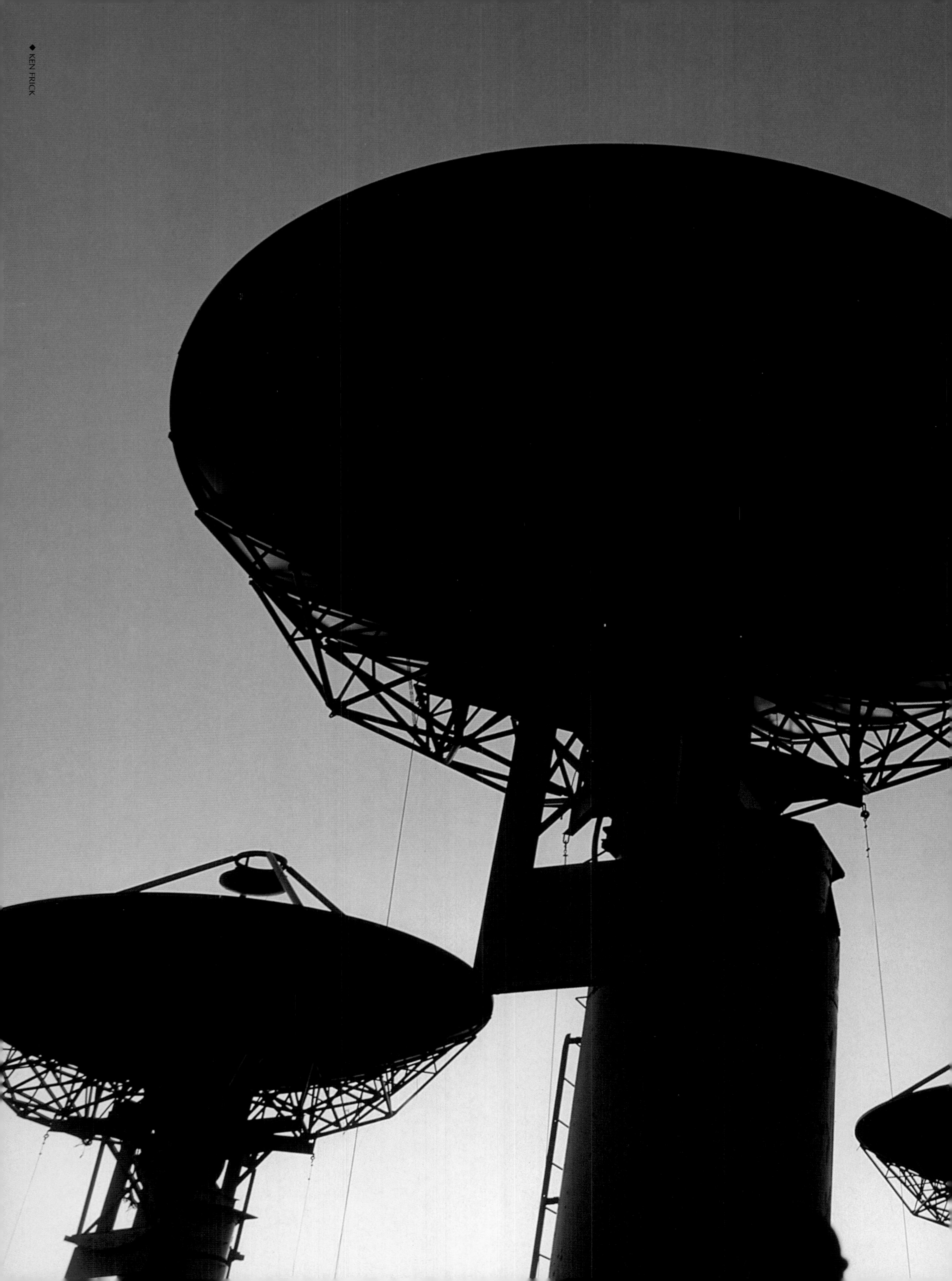

◆ KEN FRICK

S EVERAL LOCAL INSTITUTIONS DO THEIR part to further the study of science, including the Ohio State University, whose satellite dishes keep silent vigil (PAGES 200 AND 201), and the Center of Science and Industry, where a holograph wind sculpture enchants visitors (RIGHT).

Focusing on the cultural side of life in the city is the Columbus Arts Festival, a mainstay since 1961 (OPPOSITE). Held each June at Bicentennial Park on the riverfront, the event features the works of some 300 artists from around the nation, as well as poetry readings and craft booths.

SOMETIMES BEAUTY INSPIRES ART, AS evidenced by *Three Piece Reclining Figure: Draped,* a 2.5-ton Henry Moore sculpture fronting the Columbus Museum of Art (OPPOSITE). And sometimes, art inspires romance, as suggested by this moment at the Columbus Arts Festival (ABOVE).

A PLUME FROM THE FOUNTAIN AT Bicentennial Park reaches heavenward above the Scioto River (OPPOSITE). Similarly, *Brushstrokes in Flight*, created by artist Roy Lichtenstein, paints the sky at the Port Columbus International Airport (LEFT).

A DANCER FROM BALLETMET COLUMBUS strikes a spidery pose. The professional company has been thrilling audiences with its classical and contemporary performances for more than 20 years.

A TOUCH OF GOLD: A DANCER FOR BalletMet pushes herself to the limit (OPPOSITE), while a virtual peanut gallery of doll faces look on from their vantage point at the Mid-Ohio Historical Museum (ABOVE).

One of the most elegant jewels on downtown's Capitol Square, the restored and resplendent Ohio Theatre opened in 1928 and was saved from the wrecking ball in 1961. Since 1970, the Spanish-baroque venue has been home to the Columbus Symphony Orchestra, the 23rd-largest Philharmonic company in the United States.

LARRY HAMILL

216

THE SUZUKI METHOD OF MUSICAL instruction—a popular approach that helps young children develop their potential for performing high art—allows locals to cut their teeth on Mozart at a very early age.

Curious young minds find plenty of outlets around town. A couple of preschoolers dig up some new treasures at the School for Young Children (OPPOSITE LEFT), while a budding arts patron searches for a better view outside the Kingwood Center in Mansfield (RIGHT). At the Center of Science and Industry, children may have the world at their fingertips (LEFT), but they also have to learn the hard lesson that, while the sky may be the limit, a ladder has only so many rungs (OPPOSITE RIGHT).

CHILDREN LEAVE THEIR MAGIC MARK on Columbus in a number of ways, from pad and pencil to the fine art of finger painting.

I T HAS BEEN SAID THAT CHILDREN KEEP us at play all of our lives. In Columbus, pictures of racial harmony among the city's youth remind adults that we are all brothers and sisters under the skin.

RANDALL L. SCHIEBER

C OMBINING UNIQUE ARCHITECTURE AND beautiful landscapes with top-notch academics are the Ohio State University, whose College of Law (LEFT) annually adds some 200 attorneys to the ranks, and Kenyon College (RIGHT), whose celebrity alumni include Paul Newman and Jonathan Winters.

G REATER COLUMBUS OFFERS A NUMBER of options for higher education, and each year, these schools contribute thousands of learned graduates to the local workforce.

When the chimes of Orton Hall (opposite) ring out across the oval at Ohio State, the mood is set for another year of learning on one of the nation's largest college campuses. Columbus is also surrounded by a number of small liberal arts schools, including Wittenberg University in nearby Springfield (left).

▼ ED KREMINSKI ▲ ROGER BICKEL

Opened in 1857, the historic Ohio Statehouse is one of the best examples of Greek Revival architecture in the nation. Today nestled in a vale amid downtown's skyscraper mesas, the capitol's sprawling lawns make a favorite summer spot for brown-bagging office workers to gather and catch a few rays during lunch break.

THE OHIO GENERAL ASSEMBLY MEETS in the Statehouse, but it's within the bookend skyscrapers of the State Office Tower—on the right—and the Vern Riffe Center—on the left—that workers carry out the business of Ohio government (PAGES 232 AND 233).

THE OHIO STATEHOUSE RECENTLY underwent a $112.7 million renovation and remodeling that consumed some eight years. Today, with its refurbished grand stair hall, stunning rotunda, and brilliant marble floors, the structure is more than ever one of the city's architectural gems.

RANDALL L. SCHIEBER

Scattered about Columbus are sculptural reminders of the city's heritage. A likeness of Christopher Columbus stands sentinel before City Hall (LEFT), while at the Statehouse, replicas of Ohio's 19th-century political and mili- tary giants ring a pedestal whose crown- ing figure advertises to all: "These are my jewels" (RIGHT). Since 1928, this Peter Pan statue has graced the plaza of the Columbus Metropolitan Library's main branch (OPPOSITE).

B ECAUSE OF THE CITY'S RAZE-AND-
build-anew tendencies, Columbusites
have sometimes been accused of having an
"edifice complex," but the historic structures that still stand add immeasurable
charm to the local landscape. Visitors
to Columbus might pause to appreciate
all that remains of the elegant Union
Station in Arch Park (OPPOSITE) or to
observe City Hall (LEFT) and the Old
Post Office Building (RIGHT), captured
in moving shadows.

I n Columbus, the lines between work and play are not always so clearly drawn. A shower of sparks can mean that we're building and repairing, or that we're celebrating our independence at the annual Red, White & Boom!

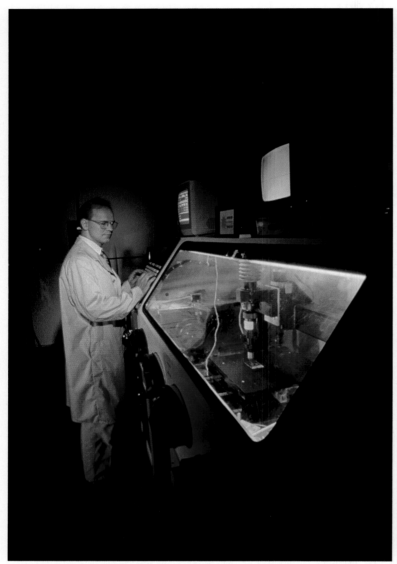

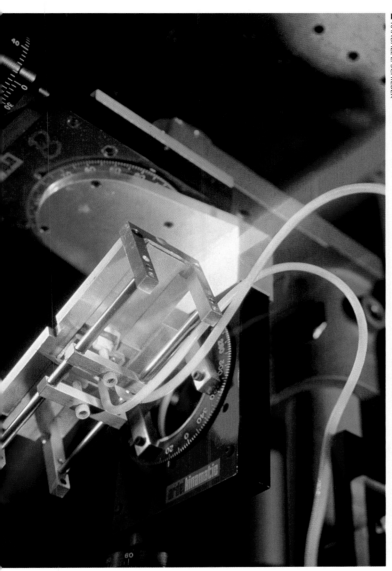

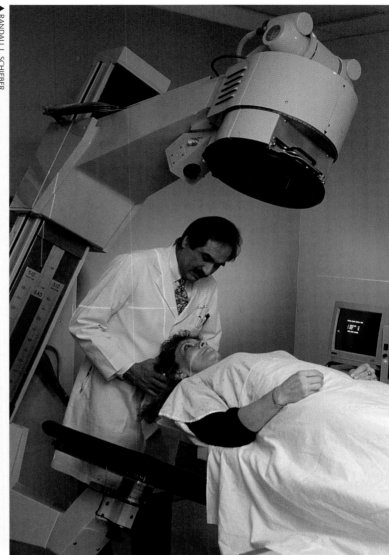

B OLSTERED BY ONE OF THE WORLD'S largest research and teaching institutes, the Ohio State University, it's no wonder that we are ever—as our namesake voyager—looking to discover brave new worlds.

Local sculptor Steven Canneto, creator of Franklin Park's unique *NavStar '92*, shows off his metallic life mask.

At the Center of Science and Industry, the final frontier is within reach at a number of the museum's fascinating exhibits.

246

RACE CAR DRIVERS BOBBY RAHAL (OPPOSITE LEFT) and Bryan Herta (OPPOSITE RIGHT)—both members of Team Rahal—call Columbus home.

The city welcomes other chariots of fire when the Street Rod Nationals brings thousands of Deuce Coupes and Stovebolts to town (ABOVE).

The Central Ohio Fire Museum and Learning Center likes to show off its hardware, especially the 1927 Seagrave model, manufactured in Columbus (BOTTOM).

THE FLAME-CROWNED FIREFIGHTERS Memorial downtown honors those who gave their lives battling the city's blazes, as well as the brave men and women who continue the heroic tradition (OPPOSITE LEFT). A modern-day firefighter rests an affectionate arm on his steel mount (OPPOSITE RIGHT), while mounts of a more traditional ilk help the Columbus Division of Police patrol the city (ABOVE).

FRESH VEGETABLES, HERE! AND CHEESES, poultry, pastas, and more. The North Market, now removed from its dowdy (but lovable) Quonset hut to more impressive digs, is still serving a city of discerning food shoppers.

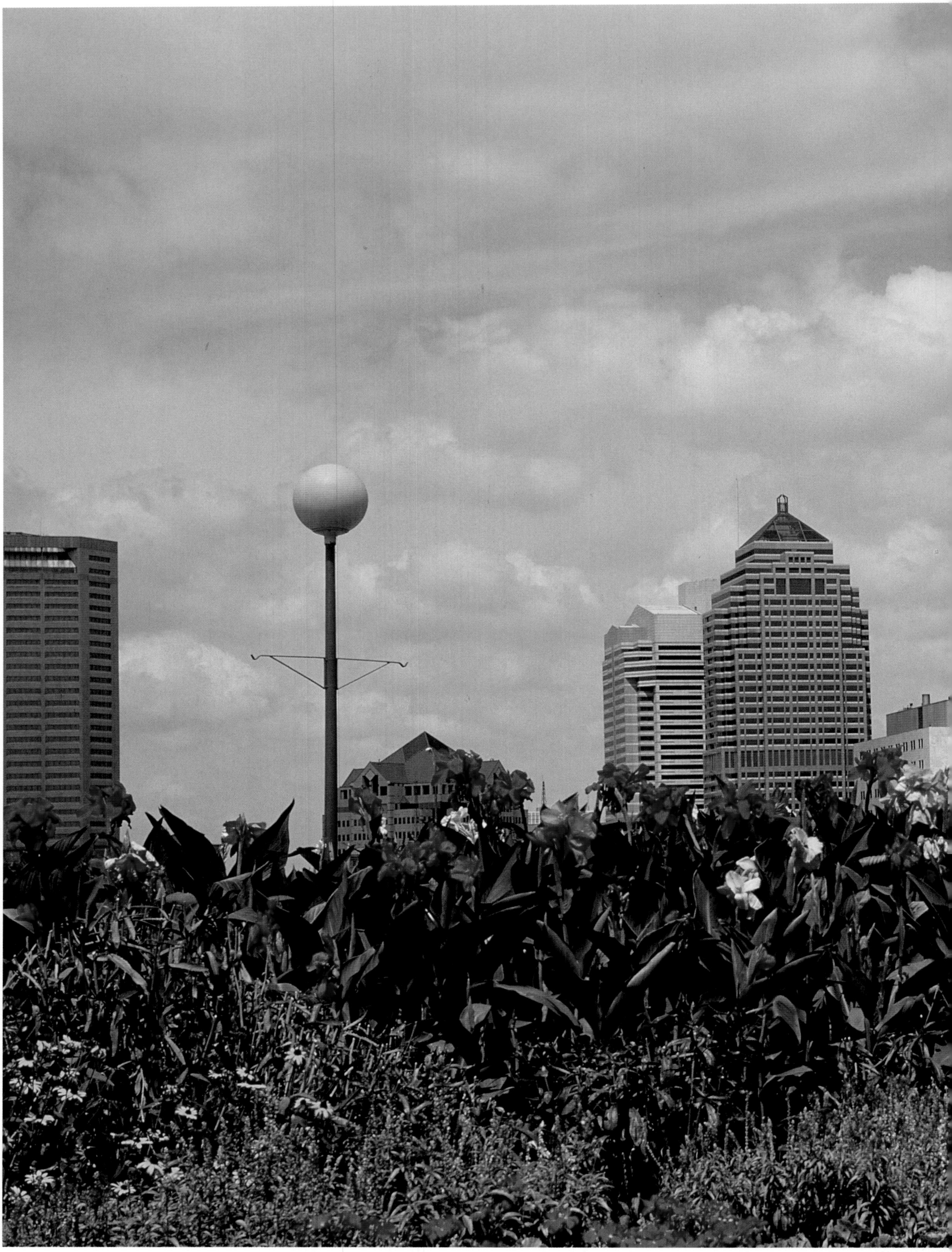

▲ WILLIAM A. HOLMES / THE IMAGE FINDERS

A LEGACY FROM COLUMBUS' CELEBRA-
tion of the 200th anniversary of
the American Revolution, Bicentennial
Park is home to a number of festivals
and other summertime activities, not to
mention outstanding views of downtown
Columbus (PAGES 254 AND 255).

A CELEBRANT AT THE JUNETEENTH Festival in Franklin Park slaps out a rhythmic tattoo (OPPOSITE), while local musical treasure Arnett Howard trumpets his way into the hearts of his fellow Columbusites (LEFT).

C OLUMBUS TRULY KNOWS HOW TO showcase its cultural and ethnic plurality, from the Latin-flavored Ballet Folklorico Mexico de los Hermanos Avila (OPPOSITE) to the Asian Festival at the Franklin Park Conservatory (LEFT) to a Rasta-spiced Music in the Air concert on the riverfront (RIGHT).

THE IRREPRESSIBLE ACCORDIONIST Esther Craw has been knocking out familiar tunes on her squeeze box since her USO touring days during World War II (OPPOSITE). Trumpeter, singer, and band leader Arnett Howard doubles as Columbus' chief chronicler of the vivid legacy of local African-American music (ABOVE).

N o, we don't do *Rocky Top*," Scrawl vocalist Marcy Mays might be saying (OPPOSITE). It's a sentiment echoed by rockers like the New Bomb Turks (TOP LEFT), Gaunt's Jerry Wick (TOP RIGHT), and the U2/Clash-inspired members of

The Toll (BOTTOM RIGHT). But if it's *Rocky Top* you want, Bela Koe-Krompecher at Used Kids Records (BOTTOM LEFT) can find it—even if it's an obscure Sex Pistols cover of the country favorite.

We've got Softails and Panheads and other hogs that never knew a farm. But even the most experienced rider might be stunned to find a motor-cycle powered by a Corvette V-8 at Columbus' A.D. Farrow Co. Harley-Davidson Museum, honoring the nation's oldest Harley dealership.

S URE, THIS GUY'S BIG FOR A CLAWING post, but so far no one has dared tell him that (OPPOSITE).

Ever pledging its allegiance, Columbus is really about mom, apple pie, the flag, and an old-fashioned parade to celebrate it all (ABOVE). Somewhere between "O say, can you see" and the "dawn's early light" of Independence Day, the city blows its top with Red, White & Boom! (PAGES 268 AND 269).

COLUMBUS: PROFILES IN EXCELLENCE

A LOOK AT THE CORPORATIONS, BUSINESSES, PROFESSIONAL GROUPS, AND COMMUNITY
SERVICE ORGANIZATIONS THAT HAVE MADE THIS BOOK POSSIBLE. THEIR STORIES—OFFERING
AN INFORMAL CHRONICLE OF THE LOCAL BUSINESS COMMUNITY—ARE ARRANGED
ACCORDING TO THE DATE THEY WERE ESTABLISHED IN COLUMBUS.

ACORDIA/MCELROY MINISTER ▪ AKZO NOBEL COATINGS INC. ▪ ALLIED MINERAL PRODUCTS, INC. ▪ AMERICAN ELECTRIC POWER ▪ ANCHOR HOCKING ▪ ANHEUSER-BUSCH, INC. ▪ APPLIED INNOVATION INC. ▪ ARC INDUSTRIES, INC. ▪ ARTHUR G. JAMES CANCER HOSPITAL AND RESEARCH INSTITUTE ▪ ATS OHIO, INC. ▪ BAKER & HOSTETLER LLP ▪ BATTELLE ▪ BIG BEAR STORES COMPANY ▪ BISYS FUND SERVICES ▪ BORDEN, INC. ▪ BRIDGESTREET ACCOMMODATIONS ▪ BURGESS & NIPLE, LIMITED ▪ CAPITAL UNIVERSITY ▪ CARDINAL HEALTH ▪ CATHOLIC DIOCESE OF COLUMBUS ▪ CENTRAL OHIO TRANSIT AUTHORITY ▪ CHARLES PENZONE, INC./GRAND SALONS AND DAY SPAS ▪ CHEMICAL ABSTRACTS SERVICES (CAS) ▪ CHILDREN'S HOSPITAL ▪ COCA-COLA USA ▪ COLUMBUS SCHOOL FOR GIRLS ▪ COLUMBUS SYMPHONY ORCHESTRA ▪ COMMERCIAL MOVERS, INC. ▪ COMMUNICOLOR ▪ CONSOLIDATED STORES CORPORATION ▪ CORE MATERIALS CORPORATION ▪ CRANE PLASTICS ▪ CUTLER-HAMMER ▪ CROSSMANN COMMUNITIES OF OHIO, INC./DELUXE HOMES ▪ DOCTORS HOSPITAL ▪ EXECUTIVE JET ▪ EXECUTIVE OFFICE PLACE ▪ EXXCEL CONTRACT MANAGEMENT ▪ G.E. SUPERABRASIVES ▪ HONDA OF AMERICA MFG. INC. ▪ ISP FINE CHEMICALS INC. ▪ THE KROGER CO. ▪ LAKE SHORE CRYOTRONICS, INC. ▪ LCI INTERNATIONAL ▪ LIEBERT CORPORATION ▪ THE LIMITED, INC. ▪ LS II ELECTRO-GALVANIZING CO. ▪ MADDOX-NBD, INC. ▪ MCDONALD'S CORPORATION ▪ METTLER-TOLEDO, INC. ▪ MOTORISTS MUTUAL INSURANCE CO. ▪ MOUNT CARMEL HEALTH SYSTEM ▪ MPW INDUSTRIAL SERVICES, INC. ▪ NATIONAL CITY BANK ▪ NATIONWIDE INSURANCE ENTERPRISE ▪ THE NEW ALBANY COMPANY ▪ NEWSRADIO 610 WTVN ▪ NORSE DAIRY SYSTEMS ▪ OCLC ONLINE COMPUTER LIBRARY CENTER, INC. ▪ THE OHIO STATE UNIVERSITY ▪ OHIO STATE UNIVERSITY HOSPITALS ▪ OHIO WESLEYAN UNIVERSITY ▪ OHIOHEALTH ▪ OLSTEN CENTRAL OHIO ▪ PIZZUTI DEVELOPMENT, INC. ▪ PORTER WRIGHT MORRIS & ARTHUR ▪ RANCO NORTH AMERICA ▪ RED ROOF INNS, INC. ▪ ROSS PRODUCTS DIVISION ABBOTT LABORATORIES ▪ ROXANE LABORATORIES, INC. ▪ SCHOTTENSTEIN STORES CORPORATION/VALUE CITY STORES ▪ SCHULER INC. ▪ THE SCOTTS CO. ▪ SHONAC CORPORATION ▪ SQUIRE, SANDERS & DEMPSEY L.L.P. ▪ STAR BANK ▪ STERLING COMMERCE ▪ TECHNEGLAS INC. ▪ T.G. BANKS SPECIAL PROJECTS DIVISION/BANKS CARBONE CONSTRUCTION COMPANY ▪ TIME WARNER COMMUNICATIONS ▪ TOMASCO MULCIBER INC. ▪ TOSOH SMD, INC. ▪ TRACEWELL SYSTEMS ▪ TS TECH NORTH AMERICA ▪ UNITED MCGILL CORPORATION ▪ VORYS, SATER, SEYMOUR AND PEASE ▪ WHITE CASTLE SYSTEM, INC. ▪ WILLIS CORROON CORP. OF OHIO ▪ WORTHINGTON INDUSTRIES ▪ WYN MOLDED PLASTICS INC. ▪

1830-1922

1830   CAPITAL UNIVERSITY

1842   OHIO WESLEYAN UNIVERSITY

1846   PORTER WRIGHT MORRIS & ARTHUR

1863   NATIONAL CITY BANK

1868   CATHOLIC DIOCESE OF COLUMBUS

1868   THE SCOTTS CO.

1870   THE OHIO STATE UNIVERSITY

1875   ACORDIA/MCELROY MINISTER

1885   ROXANE LABORATORIES, INC.

1886   MOUNT CARMEL HEALTH SYSTEM

1888   AKZO NOBEL COATINGS INC.

1892   CHILDREN'S HOSPITAL

1892   OHIOHEALTH

1898   COLUMBUS SCHOOL FOR GIRLS

1901   METTLER-TOLEDO, INC.

1903   ROSS PRODUCTS DIVISION ABBOTT LABORATORIES

1905   ANCHOR HOCKING

1906   AMERICAN ELECTRIC POWER

1907   CHEMICAL ABSTRACTS SERVICES (CAS)

1907   THE KROGER CO.

1909   SCHOTTENSTEIN STORES CORPORATION/VALUE CITY STORES

1909   VORYS, SATER, SEYMOUR AND PEASE

1912   BURGESS & NIPLE, LIMITED

1913   RANCO NORTH AMERICA

1914   OHIO STATE UNIVERSITY HOSPITALS
        ARTHUR G. JAMES CANCER HOSPITAL AND RESEARCH INSTITUTE

1922   NEWSRADIO 610 WTVN

1922   WILLIS CORROON CORP. OF OHIO

CAPITAL UNIVERSITY

FOUNDED BY THE LUTHERAN CHURCH IN 1830 AND CHARTERED AS A UNIVERsity in 1850, Capital University is dedicated to readying students for the future through a quality liberal arts education coupled with professional training. The ethical, moral, and religious values essential to leadership in society are integral to the Capital experience.

Capital is a full university, offering six graduate and six undergraduate degrees through its five colleges: College of Arts and Sciences, Conservatory of Music, School of Nursing, Graduate School of Administration, and Law School.

Increasingly, students seek the education Capital offers. Each year, more than 4,000 students attend classes at the university's main campus in Bexley, at the Law School in downtown Columbus, or at Adult Degree Program centers in Columbus, Cleveland, and Dayton. What draws students is the university's combination of academic strengths, professional training, leadership opportunities, and the focus on moral and ethical development.

And Capital's efforts to maintain affordable costs have earned the university the distinction of being included in each edition of *Barron's 300: Best Buys in College Education.*

ACADEMIC DIVERSITY

Capital is, among other things, home to one of the Midwest's largest collections of Inuit art; a 12-foot piece of the Berlin Wall; and the Capital Crusaders, the women's basketball team that captured the NCAA Division III championship in 1994 and 1995.

One of Capital's many program strengths is in dispute resolution, a process that uses a third-party mediator to facilitate negotiations between two disputing parties as an alternative to violence or litigation. Capital first gained prominence in this field in 1970, when professors from its Law School established the Columbus Night Prosecutor Program, the first court-affiliated mediation program in the nation.

In music, Capital's Conservatory is housed in one of the premier teaching and performance facilities in the Midwest. Capital was also the first Ohio university to offer a degree program in jazz. Capital is recognized as having one of the top 40 nursing pro-grams—from among more than 400 nationwide—by the U.S. Army ROTC.

Ohio's capital is a strong educational center, and Capital University is woven into the fabric of Columbus. Internships expose students to the richness and diversity of the city: Business students gain experience in major corporate settings; nursing students work in such areas as pediatric and geriatric care; education majors student-teach in both urban and rural classrooms; and other students work in government, with the arts, and in private industry.

To succeed, education must anticipate change; at the same time, the demands of change must be balanced against an institution's mission. That mission was well voiced in 1850 by Capital's first president, Dr. William M. Reynolds: "When we speak of educating our children, we mean not only their literary instruction in our schools, but also their preparation for the discharge of the duties of life by the formation and development in them of such character as they ought to have as intelligent and moral beings . . . both individually and in society, for time and for eternity."

Capital University strives to meet this challenge—and does so with great success.

CLOCKWISE FROM TOP:
EXPERIENCES IN PARALLEL COMPUTING—ONCE THE DOMAIN OF ONLY MAJOR RESEARCH UNIVERSITIES—NOW ARE AVAILABLE TO CAPITAL'S UNDERGRADUATE STUDENTS THROUGH THE NEW ADVANCED COMPUTATIONAL LABORATORY.

SMALL CLASSES WITH CLOSE WORKING RELATIONSHIPS BETWEEN PROFESSORS AND STUDENTS ARE HALLMARKS OF THE CAPITAL EXPERIENCE.

CAPITAL STUDENTS HAVE THE BEST OF BOTH WORLDS—THE ADVANTAGES OF A QUIET, RESIDENTIAL CAMPUS WITH ALL THE EDUCATIONAL, SOCIAL, AND CULTURAL ACTIVITIES OF OHIO'S LARGEST CITY JUST MINUTES AWAY.

MOUNT CARMEL HEALTH SYSTEM

"**M**OUNT CARMEL HEALTH SYSTEM IS A COMMUNITY OF COMMITTED PERSONS WORKing to extend God's ministry of health. We seek out and respond to the health needs of our communities. We serve and care for all people with fairness, respect, and compassion . . . . " ✴ So reads a portion of the mission statement at Mount Carmel Health System, which, by adhering to that philosophy, has become one of the leading health care providers in Central Ohio.

Through its core facilities and a network of additional primary care and community services, Mount Carmel Health System provides a full continuum of care—from preventive care before health care services are needed, through treatment and recovery. "In partnership with the medical staff, we provide accessible, high-quality, cost-effective health care services by delivering health care in the most appropriate setting, whether in the doctor's office, a hospital, a patient's community, or at home," says Dale St. Arnold, Mount Carmel Health System president and CEO.

Longevity is part of Mount Carmel Health System's history, which traces its roots in Columbus to 1886, when present-day Mount Carmel Medical Center was established as Hawkes Hospital of Mount Carmel. In 1995, the health system combined operations with St. Ann's, founded in Columbus in 1908. And today,

approximately 6,200 professionals provide integrated care across the Mount Carmel Health System, including Mount Carmel Medical Center, a 462-bed, tertiary teaching hospital located near downtown Columbus; St. Ann's Hospital, a 180-bed hospital located in Westerville; and Mount Carmel East Hospital, a 287-bed hospital located in east Columbus, that opened in 1972.

In addition to numerous community care and rehabilitation services, including Mount Carmel Hospice, Mount Carmel Home Care, Mount Carmel Connection, and Mount Carmel Home Medical Equipment, the system offers such specialty services as sports medicine, cardiology, orthopedics, women's health, palliative care, emergency, and oncology. Mount Carmel Health System also offers community health care facilities, such as Taylor Station Surgical Center on the east side of Columbus, River View Surgery Center in Lancaster, New Albany Wellness Center, and the Mount Carmel Health and Wellness Center at Wedegwood, featuring Wedgewood Surgery Center and

Wedgewood Urgent Care, in southern Delaware County.

Mount Carmel Health System also serves the Columbus community through the Bruce E. Siegel Center for Health Education, GOLDEN LifeStyles for seniors, and MediGold, a Medicare HMO.

Mount Carmel Health System is a member of the Holy Cross Health System, a not-for-profit organization sponsored by the Congregation of the Sisters of the Holy Cross, Notre Dame, Indiana. Because of its mission, Mount Carmel Health System is sensitive to the needs of the elderly and underserved members of the Central Ohio community, and provides health care services at more than 27 outreach sites. Each year, Mount Carmel Health System provides millions in charity care through nonbilled services and various outreach programs.

Such commitment continues to uphold the mission of Mount Carmel Health System, an organization that meets the needs of a changing health care industry while remaining focused on a long tradition of providing quality care.

MOUNT CARMEL HEALTH SYSTEM'S STATE-OF-THE-ART FACILITIES PROVIDE ACCESS TO THE HIGHEST-QUALITY HEALTH CARE SERVICES AVAILABLE THROUGHOUT CENTRAL OHIO (LEFT).

MOUNT CARMEL HEALTH SYSTEM HAS CELEBRATED LIFE FOR MORE THAN A CENTURY, PROVIDING FOUR GENERATIONS OF CARING TO WOMEN AND THEIR FAMILIES (RIGHT).

OHIO WESLEYAN UNIVERSITY

UCKED AWAY IN THE COMMUNITY OF DELAWARE, JUST NORTH OF COLUMBUS, Ohio Wesleyan University is among the nation's leading small liberal arts universities. Founded by the United Methodist Church in 1842, the university offers a superb education and top-quality faculty members, whose credentials and commitment to the learning process are second to none. In fact, 95 percent of the school's faculty members have attained the highest degree in their field.

Ohio Wesleyan faculty members earn praise as well for their mentoring relationships with students. To foster such relationships, classes are kept small, particularly in upper-level courses, and the student-faculty ratio is 13 to one. In addition, each summer a growing number of students remain on campus to conduct individual research with faculty members. These close relationships also extend beyond the college years, and alumni often return to the university many years after graduation to visit their professors.

High-quality interaction is fostered among the students. Drawing enrollees from 41 states and 50 countries, Ohio Wesleyan prides itself on its diverse student body, which comes from a wide range of socioeconomic backgrounds and represents a number of religious beliefs. Approximately 9 percent are international students and 8 percent are multicultural students from this country.

A UNIQUE EDUCATIONAL EXPERIENCE

The university has long maintained a reputation for encouraging students to combine academics with contributions to society. "There's an expression here that students try to leave the wood pile a little higher than when they found it," says Thomas B. Courtice, president of Ohio Wesleyan.

This approach distinguishes the university from competing institutions and ensures that students keep enrolling year after year. Courtice refers to this philosophy as educating the whole student. "There is clearly a balance in what a student can receive from the Ohio Wesleyan experience. It is intellectual challenge and academic accomplishment at a demanding, rigorous level, combined with social and personal development and spiritual growth."

Because philanthropic behavior is encouraged, it comes as no surprise that students make widespread contributions to the university and its surrounding communities. "Students have a sense of ownership about Ohio Wesleyan that's different from anything I've known before," Courtice explains. "They seem to find ways to

DOUG MARTIN

DOUG MARTIN

truly vest themselves in the life of the place and outside of the classroom, as well."

Approximately 90 percent of Ohio Wesleyan students are involved in on- and off-campus service projects. Students trek to low-income schools in Columbus to tutor. They are heavily involved in such organizations as Big Brothers/Big Sisters and Habitat for Humanity. There are also numerous personal projects through which students can work with neighborhood groups or churches.

Such a tradition has not gone unnoticed. Ohio Wesleyan was recently recognized by the *Princeton Review* as being one of three universities nationwide where community service is a top priority.

THE BEST OF BOTH WORLDS

Ohio Wesleyan's location in Delaware offers students what Courtice calls the best of both worlds. Delaware provides a small-town, small-campus environment where there is a sense of community and identity, as well as a real personality to the campus. At the same time, students have the advantage of being only 30 minutes away from a metropolitan community where cultural, educational, and recreational opportunities abound.

The university's proximity to Columbus also ensures numerous educational opportunities. While many students attend graduate school—80 percent of students plan to eventually pursue postgraduate studies,

according to a recent student survey—others wish to enter the working world. To that end, Ohio Wesleyan offers numerous internship opportunities with businesses in Columbus and other areas.

KEEPING PACE WITH TECHNOLOGY

Technological advancements, which are transforming all business sectors, are affecting academia as well. Many students come to campus armed with their own computers. And Ohio Wesleyan is keeping up: The university has its own home page on the World Wide Web, and residence halls are wired so that students can access the Internet from their rooms.

"While the impact of information technology on education should not—and I hope will not—change

the personal, mentoring quality we have, it nevertheless will have some significant impact on the educational process," says Courtice. As the learning environment changes, Ohio Wesleyan is embracing the changes, and responding by securing more resources, finding ways to address undergraduates' new learning styles, and creating faculty development programs to accommodate new teaching techniques. "The goal is to not lose sight of what we do for students on a personal level, but to use the technology as a helpful tool," Courtice adds.

With a firm handle on its rich heritage and a strong focus on where the school will go in the future, Ohio Wesleyan is poised to remain one of the nation's outstanding liberal arts universities for many years to come.

DOUG MARTIN

PORTER, WRIGHT, MORRIS & ARTHUR

WHETHER IT'S REPRESENTING BANKING, UTILITY, HEALTH CARE, INTERNATIONAL business, manufacturing, technology, environmental, governmental, entrepreneurial, or individual clients, Porter, Wright, Morris & Arthur has built a reputation as one of the premier corporate law firms in Ohio and the nation.

High-profile clients, involvement in landmark cases, and the breadth of its quality services are among the hallmarks of the firm, which has more than 250 attorneys practicing in offices throughout Ohio and in Naples, Florida, and Washington, D.C. The firm serves clients in more than 2,400 cities nationwide and 61 countries worldwide.

"We are a firm with a long tradition of providing very high-quality service to clients. We're focused on that and measure our success that way. What we have to offer is judgment, advice, and intellect. Companies rely on us to advise them on very difficult and important issues. That's the tradition here," says Robert W. "Buzz" Trafford, Porter Wright's managing partner.

LANDMARK CASES

Based on its legal experience and reputation, Porter Wright has been called on to handle numerous landmark cases. For instance, it represented the State of Ohio in connection with the collapse of Home State Savings Bank and 70 other savings and loans—the largest savings and loan financial crisis since the Great Depression. In another landmark case, the firm represented the Columbus-America Discovery Group in its efforts to win the rights to the treasure discovered aboard the sunken ship SS *Central America*.

The law firm has also helped entrepreneurial, high-tech companies grow, prosper, and become leaders in their fields, including Checkfree Corporation, now a public company and one of the leading electronic commerce firms nationwide.

Based on its tradition of quality, expertise, and size, Porter Wright is a leader among law firms offering a broad spectrum of legal services. Porter Wright created one of the first environmental law departments in Ohio nearly 20 years ago, and authors The Ohio Environmental Law Handbook, the only printed environmental law handbook in the state. Utilities were the first group of companies affected by environmental laws; because the firm traditionally represented utilities, including the country's largest utility holding company, it has

CLOCKWISE FROM TOP:
PORTER, WRIGHT, MORRIS & ARTHUR WAS FOUNDED IN 1846, AND HAS REPRESENTED SOME CLIENTS FOR MORE THAN 100 YEARS.

MEMBERS OF PORTER WRIGHT'S INTERNATIONAL PRACTICE GROUP SPEAK 16 DIFFERENT LANGUAGES AND REPRESENT CLIENTS IN 61 COUNTRIES.

PORTER WRIGHT IS COMMITTED TO DIVERSITY AND HAS MORE FEMALE ATTORNEYS THAN ANY OTHER COLUMBUS LAW FIRM.

been involved in environmental law since its infancy. Porter Wright was also the first large firm in Columbus to have an intellectual property group. In addition to these accomplishments, Porter Wright has an international law practice group, whose members speak more than 16 languages and represent the firm's worldwide base of clients.

Another distinguishing characteristic of Porter Wright is its lengthy history. The firm has existed for about as long as the city of Columbus, and boasts a client list that includes companies that have been associated with the firm for more than 100 years. They include some of the largest businesses in Central Ohio, such as The Huntington National Bank. Other clients include numerous private and public entities, such as the State of Ohio and many of its municipalities, professional partnerships and corporations, individuals, trusts, and various charitable and religious organizations.

Porter Wright has grown and prospered through several wars, stock market crashes, the Great Depression, recessions, and periods of social unrest. Richard Harrison, an emigrant from Thirsk, Yorkshire, England, founded the firm in 1846, several years after he and his family settled in Springfield, Ohio.

PROFESSIONAL, COMMUNITY CONTRIBUTIONS

In addition to providing quality services for its clients, Porter Wright's priorities include extensive involvement in the community and with professional organizations. Firm lawyers include a past president of the American Bar Association—the only Columbus firm to hold such a distinction—and numerous past presidents of the Ohio and local bar associations. Attorneys are actively involved in federal, state, and local bar associations and judicial organizations. The firm also has been an active participant in establishing professional standards and working for the betterment of the profession.

The United Way, the Columbus Museum of Art, the Center of Science and Industry, and Goodwill Rehabilitation Center are among the community organizations in Columbus that have benefited from Porter Wright's generosity. In 1997, when the firm celebrated its 150th anniversary, it made 150 gifts to community non-profit organizations.

Technology has played and continues to play a key role in the way Porter Wright conducts business as it moves into the 21st century. The firm has installed an advanced computer/communications network that links all offices, and all offices are connected by videoconferencing capabilities.

In the future, Porter, Wright, Morris & Arthur plans to remain at the forefront of its profession by taking advantage of technology to serve its clients more efficiently and effectively. "It's important to get the right result and to get it efficiently," Trafford says. "We spend a lot of time delivering legal services in ways that are affordable to clients."

CLOCKWISE FROM TOP LEFT:
AS COUNSEL IN MANY HIGH-PROFILE CASES, PORTER WRIGHT HAS EARNED A STERLING REPUTATION FOR ITS LITIGATION DEPARTMENT.

HEADQUARTERED IN COLUMBUS, PORTER WRIGHT REPRESENTS CLIENTS IN 2,400 CITIES THROUGHOUT THE UNITED STATES.

PORTER WRIGHT HAS A LONG TRADITION OF PHILANTHROPIC INVOLVEMENT. EACH YEAR, ATTORNEYS DONATE THOUSANDS OF HOURS THROUGH PRO BONO LEGAL WORK AND COMMUNITY INVOLVEMENT.

WITH MORE THAN 250 ATTORNEYS IN SIX OFFICES, PORTER WRIGHT PROVIDES FULL-SERVICE REPRESENTATION TO CORPORATE AND INDIVIDUAL CLIENTS.

NATIONAL CITY BANK

SINCE 1845, NATIONAL CITY HAS CONSISTENTLY PREPARED ITSELF FOR THE EVER CHANGING banking business by taking advantage of opportunities to continue to meet its customers' financial needs. In 1984, to prepare for the approaching opportunities of interstate banking, it was only natural for National City Corporation to acquire Ohio's first statewide bank, BancOhio Corporation.

Both banks enjoyed success through tumultuous times, building reputations of strength and stability that led them through recession and depression, paving a road of growth that included several acquisitions and introduction of new products and services.

By acquiring BancOhio, National City created the state's largest holding company, with $12.5 billion in assets and 350 branches. The acquisition set the stage for significant growth both locally and corporation-wide. With more than 3,000 employees in Columbus and 110 banking centers in Central Ohio, National City Bank is becoming a leading financial institution in Columbus. The strength of its Columbus base has enabled National City to build upon its success through a single statewide charter. In January 1998, National City's six Ohio charters unified to become National City Bank, a $23 billion bank with 9,000 employees, serving 2 million customers through more than 360 branches.

A focus on customer service, paired with steady growth, has made Cleveland-based National City Corporation what it is today—a $53 billion diversified financial services company that operates banks and other financial services subsidiaries principally in Ohio, Kentucky, Indiana, and Pennsylvania.

SERVICE BEYOND THE TRADITIONAL BANK

With customers as its primary focus, National City has committed itself to being more than the traditional bank. "We are in the business of bringing together a broad range of financial services to benefit our customers. By working with our customers, we identify and offer the best solutions that meet their financial needs at every stage of their business and personal lives," says Gary Glaser, chairman of National City Bank.

In order to be the gateway to a broad range of financial solutions, National City views itself as a partner, providing a variety of products and services to help customers follow their own lead.

National City Private Client Group is one resource to meet customers' complex financial needs. The Private Client Group relationship managers act as a single source of contact for their customers. Working with a team of specialists, they take a consultative approach to coordinate and facilitate meeting the financial planning and management needs of affluent and emerging affluent clients.

A commitment to its customers also means more convenience. The single Ohio charter has made banking easier and more convenient. Customers are able to access their accounts and any National City product in any National City branch in Ohio. Installation of additional branches

CLOCKWISE FROM TOP LEFT: GARY A. GLASER HAS SERVED AS PRESIDENT AND CEO OF NATIONAL CITY BANK OF COLUMBUS SINCE APRIL 1988.

NATIONAL CITY, FOUNDED IN 1845, IS LOCATED AT 155 EAST BROAD STREET IN DOWNTOWN COLUMBUS.

NATCITY INVESTMENTS DIVISION OFFERS CUSTOMERS A WIDE VARIETY OF INVESTMENT OPTIONS TO MEET THEIR FINANCIAL GOALS. REGIONAL MANAGER AND VICE PRESIDENT RUSS GOCHNEAUR DEMONSTRATES THE ON-LINE COMPUTER FOR CUSTOMERS WHO WANT THE CONVENIENCE OF ACCESSING THEIR STOCK INFORMATION IN A SELF-SERVE FORMAT.

in grocery stores, additional ATMs, 24-hour banking by telephone, and its World Wide Web site at www. national-city.com have increased convenience as well.

Businesses also find banking with National City easier. Through National City's Information Technology products, corporate treasurers are able to access account and transaction information, as well as initiate a variety of banking transactions from their personal computers.

Other products and services such as treasury management and international banking are available for middle-market businesses through the corporate banking division. The recently implemented Corporate Select Rate Management Loan Program allows businesses to choose from a menu of options to customize rates and terms so borrowers can design a loan tailored to their specific needs.

By using on-line information from the recently implemented data warehouse, National City employees are able to access accurate profiles of their customers. This information enables employees to recommend products and services specific to customers' financial needs.

COMMITMENT TO THE COMMUNITY

To National City, customer focused means much more than quality service and premier products. Rather, this focus includes serving the bank's

communities through contributions. National City's commitment to the communities in which it operates can be easily observed in the Columbus area. During 1997, National City contributed to many worthy causes and events such as Christmas in April, the Columbus Museum of Art, Communities in Schools, Operation Feed, UNCF Walk-A-Thon, and United Way.

Monetary contributions are not the only gifts National City gives. Its employees also volunteer their time to various causes, including many

hours spent at Ohio Avenue Elementary, National City's Columbus City Schools Adopt-a-School partner.

"Public service is just another aspect of our organization. Not only is it our duty, but also it is necessary for our growth as we seek approval from the citizens of the communities that give so much to our institution," Glaser says.

A LOOK AHEAD

"We want to be the premier financial services company in the Midwest by providing our customers with advice, information, and services to meet their financial needs," Glaser says.

In order to meet those needs, National City has utilized database marketing and has implemented new products such as image-based technology, purchasing cards, PC banking, and retail sweep accounts.

Though products and services meet customers' needs, one simple principle enables National City to continue to excel. "Our customers are our primary focus," Glaser says. "As long as we continue to make them the top priority and invest in our communities, our goal of becoming the premier financial services company in the Midwest will be easily attained."

CATHOLIC DIOCESE OF COLUMBUS

THE FIRST CATHOLIC CHAPEL IN OHIO, A LOG STRUCTURE, WAS ERECTED AT ST. Joseph's, near Somerset in Perry County, December 6, 1818. The congregation consisted of 10 families, and a humble convent was built nearby. In 1838, the first Catholic church in Columbus, St. Remigius, was built. It was replaced

in 1853 by a larger church, called Holy Cross, on South Fifth Street; that same year, Columbus' second Catholic church, St. Patrick, on East Naghten Street, also opened for services.

In June 1866, some 6,000 people were present for the laying of the cornerstone of St. Joseph Cathedral, located on Broad Street. A Columbus landmark, the French Gothic Revival church is built of boasted ashlar. The stone, three feet thick at the base, came mostly from Licking and Fairfield counties, which are in the diocese.

Today, through the St. Vincent de Paul Society, the cathedral provides emergency assistance to homeless persons. The undercroft, its unique underground area, is used by community and diocesan groups for adult education, faith formation classes, and other activities. The St. Joseph Cathedral Concert Series, a full season

of sacred and classical music, brings nationally acclaimed artists to join the cathedral's own chamber singers and orchestra, symphony string quartet, choir, and organist.

THE COLUMBUS DIOCESE

The Columbus diocese was canonically established by Pope Pius IX on March 3, 1868, with the Right Rev. S.H. Rosecrans, the auxiliary bishop of Cincinnati, appointed as first bishop. Bishop Rosecrans celebrated the first Pontifical High Mass at St. Joseph on Christmas Day in 1872. The cathedral was consecrated October 20, 1878, in a four-hour ceremony that began at 5 a.m. Bishop Rosecrans died the following day, and his remains lie in a crypt beneath the sanctuary.

Since 1983, Bishop James Griffin has led the diocese, which consists of 23 Central Ohio counties and in-

cludes 108 parish churches, eight missions, two colleges, 45 elementary schools, and 11 secondary schools. More than 220,000 registered Catholics are members of the Columbus diocese. In 1996, more than 4,000 children and 400 adults were baptized in the faith. In 1997, some 800 people in the diocese participated in the Rite of Election, a step in the conversion to being Catholic.

In 1985, Bishop Griffin established the Catholic Foundation of the Diocese of Columbus to support its many diverse activities by allowing donors to make endowed contributions.

Information about diocesan activities can be found in the *Catholic Times*, which reaches more than 29,000 Catholic households each week with news and feature stories about the church and the faithful.

The activities supported by the diocese include the Joint Organization for Inner-city Needs (JOIN), which provides direct service to about 2,000 households a month in the form of food, clothing, utility help, infant formula, and other assistance. The Family Life Office identifies and ministers to the needs of families within the diocese in every area of

BISHOP JAMES GRIFFIN IS THE LEADER OF THE CATHOLIC DIOCESE OF COLUMBUS AND PROVIDES GUIDANCE THROUGH MANY MEANS, INCLUDING THE CELEBRATION OF THE SACRAMENT OF CONFIRMATION AT DOZENS OF PARISHES EACH YEAR AND THE DEDICATION OF NEW PARISH BUILDINGS, SUCH AS THE ADDITION TO THE SCHOOL AT ST. BRENDAN IN HILLIARD (LEFT).

ST. JOSEPH CATHEDRAL AT 212 EAST BROAD STREET IN COLUMBUS SERVES AS THE MOTHER CHURCH OF THE 23 COUNTIES IN THE CATHOLIC DIOCESE OF COLUMBUS. THE UNDERCROFT OF THE CATHEDRAL IS USED BY THE COMMUNITY AND DIOCESAN GROUPS FOR A VARIETY OF ACTIVITIES, AND THE CATHEDRAL IS ALSO HOME TO A CONCERT SERIES OF SACRED AND CLASSICAL MUSIC (RIGHT).

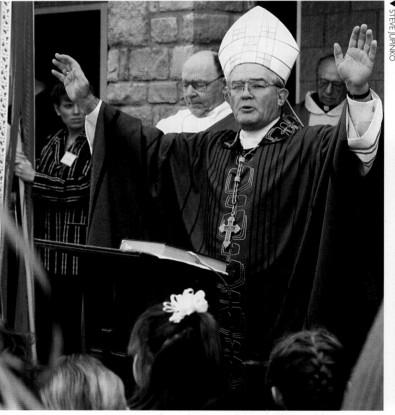

STEVE JUPINKO

STEVE JUPINKO

STEVE JUPINKO

family ministry, from marriage preparation and parenting skills to support for the widowed.

The Department of Social Concerns undertakes the Campaign for Human Development, Catholic Relief Services, Respect Life, and Rural Life programs, as well as produces programs for the elderly. The Diaconate Office coordinates the ministry of men who serve the church as deacons.

The Department of Religious Education offers religious education preparation for Catholic school teachers and parish catechists of all ages. In addition, the department holds a Religious Education Institute each fall for 500 parish catechists, leaders, and Catholic school teachers and principals.

The diocese is also home to several religious orders and educational institutions. The Pontifical College Josephinum is a fully accredited, four-year, liberal arts college and graduate school in theology. The Josephinum was established as a pontifical institution in 1892 and is the only pontifical seminary outside of Italy. The school, which focuses on educating students in financial need, has prepared 1,500 young men for the priesthood. Its current 130 students come from 44 dioceses and from countries as diverse as Uganda, Latvia, and China.

Ohio Dominican College is an undergraduate, coeducational facility founded in 1911 by the Dominican Sisters. Today, the college offers more than 30 majors to its 1,900 students.

Ohio Dominican is noted for the strength of its education school, business and science programs, and sociology and psychology departments. The well-landscaped, wooded campus is located 10 minutes from downtown Columbus.

The Dominican Sisters of St. Mary of the Springs are also headquartered at Ohio Dominican College. Seventy sisters live in the congregational center, where they teach, maintain a literacy center in Corpus Christi parish, and manage the Nazareth Towers housing project for low-income persons.

The Seton Squares Homes combine the pastoral concern of the church with federal government construction loans to create nondenominational housing for retired persons who qualify for government financial assistance. In the past 20 years, 13 Seton Squares living complexes have been constructed

in Central Ohio, with more than 1,000 units in all.

The Salesian Fathers came to Columbus 30 years ago so that their students could study theology at the Josephinum. In keeping with their traditional concern for the young, the Salesians in 1967 began developing a diocesan building on Sixth Street into a club for inner-city boys. Today, the facility is coeducational, with about 100 children using the club each day. Additionally, the Salesians operate a 10-week summer camp serving 350 children a year.

For more than 125 years, the Catholic Diocese of Columbus has been an integral, active part of the community. The tradition continues today, with the many educational, ministerial, and outreach programs sponsored by the diocese, and the tradition of service by the diocese promises to continue for many years to come.

CLOCKWISE FROM TOP LEFT:
THE CATHOLIC DIOCESE OF COLUMBUS PRODUCES THE TELEVISED MASS FOR THOSE UNABLE TO ATTEND MASS ON SUNDAY. THE MASS IS CELEBRATED BY PARISHES FROM THROUGHOUT THE 23-COUNTY DIOCESE AT THE CHAPEL IN THE PONTIFICAL COLLEGE JOSEPHINUM.

A YOUNG PARISHIONER OF ST. PIUS PARISH IN REYNOLDSBURG CROWNS OUR LADY QUEEN OF THE ROSARY, AT AN ANNUAL CELEBRATION OF FAMILY ROSARY DAY.

SISTER ANNUNCIATA CHEN O.P. (LEFT) AND SISTER CATHERINE MALYA CHEN O.P. ARE DOMINICAN SISTERS OF ST. MARY OF THE SPRINGS LIVING AT THE CONGREGATIONAL CENTER AT OHIO DOMINICAN COLLEGE.

AMONG THE ACTIVITIES IN PARISH AND DIOCESAN SCHOOLS DURING THE ANNUAL CATHOLIC SCHOOLS WEEK IS GRANDPARENTS DAY AT BISHOP WATTERSON HIGH SCHOOL.

THE SCOTTS COMPANY

THE SCOTTS COMPANY IS THE WORLD'S LEADING PRODUCER AND MARKETER OF products for consumer do-it-yourself lawn care and gardening, professional turf care, and horticulture, but don't look for Scotts, whose brands include Scotts®, Miracle-Gro®, Hyponex®, and Osmocote®, to rest on its laurels.

Scotts plans to continue exploring new domestic and international marketing opportunities, building on the strength of the company's brands. Says Scotts Chairman Charles M. Berger, "We're poised for growth and profitability as we develop a more focused company . . . based on the strong foundation of our brands."

Founded by O.M. Scott in Marysville in 1868 as a seed company, Scotts later expanded its offerings with the addition of lawn fertilizers. When the company celebrated its centennial, Scotts' sales were just under $25 million; by comparison, 1997 sales were about $900 million. Helping to secure Scotts' industry leadership position was the May 1995 merger with Stern's Miracle-Gro Products Inc., the leading garden fertilizer company begun in 1950 by Horace Hagedorn and Otto Stern.

LEADERSHIP COMMITMENT

Scotts plans to retain its number one spot in the United States and the world—its major products currently have more than 50 percent market share in the United States—

by continuing to invest in advertising, market research, and R&D. In fiscal 1997, for example, the company invested more than $30 million to enhance and develop products, improve packaging, ensure product superiority, and update its facilities. Another $30 million was invested in advertising the Scotts and Miracle-Gro brands. It's all part of being a leader, according to Berger.

BUILDING RELATIONSHIPS

Since its founding more than a century ago, Scotts has nurtured a reputation for quality, and for helping

consumers and professionals obtain the best results possible. Studies show that customers acknowledge the company's commitment: In a 1996 survey of discount store shoppers, its Scotts, Miracle-Gro, and Hyponex brands were rated the top three most preferred lawn and garden brands.

Market research indicates an extremely high awareness level for the Scotts and Miracle-Gro brands, placing them on a par with the most famous brands in the world in any product category. Scotts is focusing its research efforts on learning more about which lawn and garden prod-

CHARLES M. BERGER, CHAIRMAN, PRESIDENT, AND CHIEF EXECUTIVE OFFICER OF THE SCOTTS COMPANY (LEFT)

SINCE ITS FOUNDING MORE THAN A CENTURY AGO, SCOTTS HAS NURTURED A REPUTATION FOR QUALITY, AND FOR HELPING CONSUMERS AND PROFESSIONALS OBTAIN THE BEST RESULTS POSSIBLE (RIGHT).

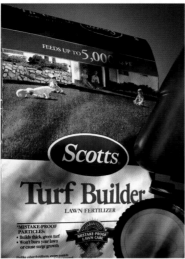

ucts consumers use and how frequently. "The consumer can give us a road map to the future of this company," Berger says. "We have to listen carefully."

The company does listen. The Scotts Consumer Helpline receives about 400,000 calls each year, and Scotts' No-Quibble Guarantee provides consumers with reassurance that they are, in fact, making the right purchasing decision.

BUSINESS GROUPS

Scotts' business is structured into five groups: Consumer Lawns, Consumer Gardens, Organics, Professional, and International. A sixth group, Operations, supports each of these business groups.

In the Consumer Lawns Group, for example, the Scotts Turf Builder® brand leads the way, along with Scotts grass seed and Scotts spreaders. In the Consumer Gardens Group, the Miracle-Gro brand dominates. Miracle-Gro Plant Food is considered one of the world's best-known brands.

In the Organics Group, Scotts' Hyponex brand leads the category. Organics products include potting and planting soils, barks and mulches, and related lines.

Scotts' Professional Group includes the company's professional turf care and horticultural product lines. Scotts products are used on more than 7,000 golf courses and by the majority of professional growers.

Scotts' International Group, which has grown strongly in recent years, has primarily served professional markets in the past. However, aggressive launches of Scotts and Miracle-Gro consumer products in Europe and Australia, coupled with the 1997 acquisition of Miracle Garden Care, Ltd., suggest strong future growth for Scotts' offshore consumer products business, too. Miracle Garden Care, a wholly owned affiliate, is the United Kingdom's leading lawn care and garden products manufacturer.

The company's sixth group, Operations, manages Scotts' manufacturing, distribution, and purchasing. Scotts' patented product technologies provide competitive strengths in the market, and Operations assures product quality and timely delivery.

As it looks to the future, The Scotts Company's goal is to secure

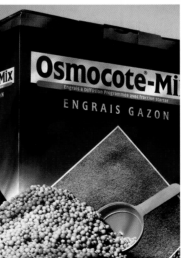

THE SCOTTS COMPANY'S BRANDS ARE ALL LEADERS IN THEIR FIELDS; IN FACT, MIRACLE-GRO PLANT FOOD IS CONSIDERED ONE OF THE WORLD'S BEST-KNOWN BRANDS.

its leadership position by continuing to produce quality, environmentally sound products that meet consumers' needs. As Miracle-Gro founder and current vice chairman of the Scotts board, Horace Hagedorn, says, "We don't have customers—we have fans!"

ONE OF COLUMBUS' GREATEST ASSETS, THE OHIO STATE UNIVERSITY IS THE leading comprehensive teaching and research institution in the state. Combining a responsibility for the advancement and dissemination of knowledge with a heritage of public service, Ohio State offers an extensive

array of academic programs to its student body.

Ohio State was founded in 1870, when the Ohio General Assembly established the Ohio Agricultural and Mechanical College. The institution was made possible through the provisions of the Land Grant Act, which was signed by President Lincoln on July 2, 1862. This legislation revolutionized the nation's approach to higher education and helped to bring a college degree within reach of every high school graduate.

Classes began at the new college on September 17, 1873, with 24 students meeting at the old Neil farm, just two miles north of Columbus. In 1878, the college's name was changed to The Ohio State University. That same year, the first class of six men graduated, and in 1879, the university graduated its first woman.

With more than 330,000 alumni all over the world, Ohio State has attained international distinction in education, scholarship, and public

service. Closer to home, the university provides a sense of history and identity to the Columbus community and to the state as Ohio's flagship university.

World-Class Education

Ohio State offers a magnificent environment for learning at one of the largest universities in the United States. The Oval, the heart of the Columbus campus, is beautifully landscaped and surrounded by such stately buildings as historic Orton Hall, the Main Library, and University Hall. Within their walls, Ohio State's rich history sits in harmony with state-of-the-art classrooms and laboratories.

Consistently ranked among the top national public universities for undergraduate, graduate, and professional programs, Ohio State is a student-centered research university that provides a well-rounded experience both inside and outside the classroom. Ohio State's range of academic offerings is exceedingly broad; combined with

related interdisciplinary opportunities, it includes hundreds of undergraduate majors, instructional areas, graduate fields of study, and professional programs. All of Ohio State's academic programs are designed to challenge students, prepare them for the future, and position them for success.

Students come to Ohio State from every county in Ohio, every state in the nation, and nearly every nation in the world. The faculty at Ohio State is among the finest in the world; the professors and instructors are internationally known for their academic credentials, real-world experience, and cutting-edge research in areas as diverse as supercomputing, human behavior, and transportation. They include a Nobel laureate, Sloan Foundation Fellows, National Science Foundation Presidential/National Young Investigators, Fulbright and Rhodes scholars, and Pulitzer nominees. Their work extends well beyond Columbus: Ohio State faculty members are involved in scholarship and

UNIVERSITY HALL IS A REPLICA OF THE OHIO STATE UNIVERSITY'S FIRST BUILDING, OPENED AS A CLASSROOM AND STUDENT DORMITORY IN 1873 (LEFT).

OHIO STATE'S CAMPUS WAS BUILT AROUND A NATURAL SPRING, WHICH TODAY IS THE SITE OF MIRROR LAKE, A POPULAR SPOT FOR IMPROMPTU CLASS MEETINGS ON SPRING AFTERNOONS (RIGHT).

UNIVERSITY COMMUNICATIONS, THE OHIO STATE UNIVERSITY

CLOCKWISE FROM TOP LEFT: A SOURCE OF PRIDE FOR BUCKEYE FANS OLD AND YOUNG IS THE INTERCOLLEGIATE ATHLETIC PROGRAM AND THE EXCITEMENT OF BIG TEN SPORTS, INCLUDING TBDBITL—THE BEST DAMN BAND IN THE LAND—THE UNIVERSITY'S NATIONALLY RESPECTED MARCHING BAND.

THE UNIVERSITY'S MAIN LIBRARY SITS MAJESTICALLY AT THE HEAD OF THE OVAL, THE CENTRAL GATHERING PLACE FOR CAMPUS LIFE—PERFECT FOR STUDYING, FRISBEE THROWING, AND PEOPLE WATCHING.

OHIO STATE OFFERS MYRIAD CULTURAL OPPORTUNITIES FOR THE PUBLIC EVERY YEAR. THE WEXNER CENTER FOR THE ARTS, AN AWARD-WINNING ARCHITECTURAL ACHIEVEMENT ITSELF, HAS DRAWN VISUAL AND PERFORMING ARTISTS FROM AROUND THE WORLD.

service in more than 100 countries around the world.

Much of the basic and applied research in the United States is carried out by some 50 national universities, and Ohio State is one of the most comprehensive. University researchers are making important discoveries in fields as diverse as engineering, biology, human behavior, and the arts. Striving to understand the unknown, explore the uncharted, and discover new knowledge, they enjoy access to state-of-the-art technology and a library system with one of the largest research and academic collections in North America. At Ohio State, students have singular opportunities to study with leading scholars and scientists and to develop the creativity, independence, and problem-solving skills necessary for success in life.

SERVICE TO THE COMMUNITY AND THE NATION

Public service has always been central to Ohio State's mission, and the university is engaged in a multitude of contributions to the quality of the city's life. Touching virtually everyone in Columbus, faculty and staff bring knowledge and methods from the classroom and the laboratory to the community. University hospitals and clinics bring care and healing to hundreds of thousands every year. The

university's radio and television stations provide news, information, and culture. Ohio State also brings its people and facilities to the public through continuing education and noncredit programs.

Ohio State is an arena for exchange. It is a major conference center, offering professionals and executives from any field the opportunity to meet with one another and with specialists on the faculty. The university's College of Food, Agricultural, and Environmental Sciences is a place where

all people—from farmers and landscapers to environmentalists and businesspeople—can come for unbiased, research-based educational programs and information on subjects of interest.

For more than 125 years, Ohio State has taken the lead in furthering education and research, not only for the citizens of Columbus and Ohio, but for the nation as well. Today, its faculty, staff, and students continue the same quest for knowledge and skills envisioned by its founders so many years ago.

ACORDIA/McElroy-Minister

FOR NEARLY 125 YEARS, ACORDIA/McELROY-MINISTER HAS BEEN MEETING THE insurance needs of the citizens of Columbus. When the agency was established in 1875, insurance was a simple matter of providing fire insurance for vulnerable wooden homes. Later, horse-drawn carriages were added to insurance policies,

and with the early 1900s came automobile coverage. As each new need arose, Acordia/McElroy-Minister responded by providing protection and security for its clients. By 1995, the insurance firm that was founded not long after the end of the Civil War had grown to become the largest independent insurance agency in Ohio.

At the end of 1995, McElroy-Minister became part of the Acordia network of insurance agencies. The seventh-largest insurance brokerage in the world, Acordia consists of a national and international network of brokerage, managed care, and consulting companies. Under this arrangement, Acordia/McElroy-Minister can maintain local control of its business operations, while strengthening those operations through access to the services and financial resources of Acordia.

Whatever the area of insurance—property and casualty risk management, employee benefits, home and automobile coverage, or life protection—Acordia/McElroy-Minister can make sense out of all of it. With professional efficiency, the company answers insurance questions and replaces confusion with effective and cost-efficient programs.

As President Bill Gillam points out, "Our founders stressed the building of relationships, not just numbers. This management philosophy has guided our firm across more than a century and is the primary reason for our growth. Relationships with our clients are still one-on-one, and service is paramount." The watchwords at Acordia/McElroy-Minister are accessibility, responsiveness, and professionalism.

INSURING THE RISKS

The risks faced by people at the end of the 20th century are much more complex than in years past. Acordia/McElroy-Minister provides protection and security for a wide variety of enterprises, including employee

benefit plans, bond underwriting for construction projects, and property and casualty risk management programs.

The size and varied strengths of Acordia/McElroy-Minister are reflected in its client list, which shows the diversity of the highly developed Ohio economy. The company's customers include small, family-owned businesses; multistate organizations; start-up commercial enterprises; large corporations; manufacturing plants; and professional associations.

Acordia's in-house staff includes the mix of professionals needed to make sense of complicated insurance requirements, including account executives, engineers, underwriters, and claims adjusters. Their efforts are coordinated by management and fa-

FROM ITS HEADQUARTERS IN DOWN-TOWN COLUMBUS, ACORDIA/McELROY-MINISTER SERVES CLIENTS ACROSS OHIO AND THE MIDWEST. IT IS A FULL-SERVICE AGENCY—INSURANCE BROKERS WITH ANSWERS (LEFT AND RIGHT).

cilitated by the latest in computer technology.

BROADENING THE PROTECTION

Acordia/McElroy-Minister's offerings cover the range of human endeavor and concern. Through its College Department, for example, the company provides student health and NCAA-approved college athletics insurance programs. Through its Life Department, Acordia/McElroy-Minister offers individual life and health policies, and designs executive benefit programs.

Today, Americans are greatly concerned about health care, a field that is constantly changing. Acordia/McElroy-Minister addresses that concern and stays current with the changes providing a single source for a full spectrum of health care plans and administration. The benefit plans are designed to match the employer's specific needs and financial requirements in today's rapidly changing managed care environment. The client list for these services includes large corporations, small businesses, and colleges and universities.

A specialized small business unit works closely with the Greater Columbus Chamber of Commerce to provide cost effective health insurance for businesses with up to 150 employees. Acordia/McElroy-Minister administers this plan for the Chamber and also offers dental, vision, and disability insurance options.

The personal lines department provides protection for homes and

To celebrate its 120th anniversary year, Acordia/McElroy-Minister gave $120,000 to children's organizations—$10,000 grants each month with the theme, Today's Children . . . Tomorrow's Hope.

rental properties, with complete appraisals and rapid claims handling. Automobiles, boats, jewelry, and fine art are also insured.

A GOOD NEIGHBOR

Acordia/McElroy-Minister actively contributes to the communities in which it does business. In 1995, for example, the company celebrated its 120th birthday by donating $120,000 to community organizations that serve the needs of children, and five members of the company's senior management staff currently serve on the boards of local charitable organizations. "We have always been distinguished by our concern for the community," says Gillam.

Today's world presents a variety of risks that must be expertly assessed and covered. Acordia/McElroy-Minister works to answer those questions and solve those problems. For insurance, risk management, consulting, and financial planning, Acordia/McElroy-Minister is the experienced, full-service agency that can handle them all—true to the company's theme, Insurance Brokers with Answers.

ROXANE LABORATORIES, INC.

L EADERS, INNOVATORS, AND PIONEERS ARE ALL TERMS THAT APTLY DESCRIBE THE management and staff at Roxane Laboratories. Founded in 1885 as Columbus Pharmacal, the company has made a commitment to fulfilling patient needs through new health care initiatives, concepts, products, packaging, research, and

ARTOG/D.G. OLSHAVSKY

therapies. And in achieving that commitment, Roxane has distinguished itself as a dominant player in the health care industry.

Not content to sit on the sidelines and follow the lead of others, Roxane Laboratories' dedication to innovation has led to a series of firsts in health care—all driven by the discovery of a market niche and the development of products to address the particular market's needs. For example, the company enhanced its reputation as a pioneer in the 1960s by offering and advocating the use of unit doses of medicine for patients. The concept offered health care providers convenience, and reduced dosage errors as well. In addition, the company introduced the first oral solutions of major drugs like morphine, codeine, potassium chloride, and propranolol, which were previously available only in tablet, capsule, or intravenous form. And Roxane was the first enterprise to use form, fill, and seal technology for sterile, prediluted inhalation solutions for respiratory therapy.

INDUSTRY PIONEER
Roxane Laboratories launched the concept of palliative care—where

the utmost concern is control of symptoms and quality of life—after working with the National Cancer Institute in the 1970s and 1980s. The company discovered that not much progress had been made in the treatment and development of effective therapies for cancer patients, who were suffering from severe pain and whose illnesses were incurable. "Unfortunately, severe pain was not being treated as aggressively as it should have been," says Kirk Shepard, senior vice president of marketing, medical affairs, and product development at Roxane Laboratories.

In response, the company worked to develop new drugs and therapies. When company officials discovered that no uniform preparation of morphine existed, they developed the first standardized morphine solution. Building on that success, the company developed additional drugs to address other cancer symptoms, including the nausea and vomiting associated with chemotherapy. Along with drug development, Roxane initiated a Palliative Care Program, consisting of the publication of the *Palliative Care Letter*, distribution of educational literature, and creation

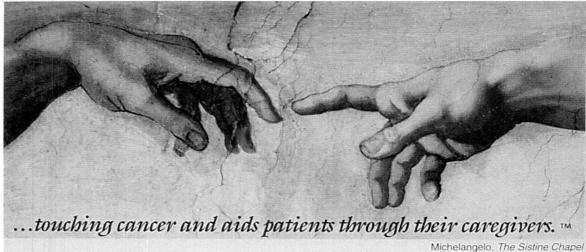

...touching cancer and aids patients through their caregivers. ™

Michelangelo, *The Sistine Chapel*

and sponsorship of Palliative Care Scholar Programs. These Scholar Programs, now at the Cleveland Clinic Foundation, Johns Hopkins, Ohio State University, Northwestern University, and the University of California-Davis, train practicing health professionals about palliative medicine for one to two weeks at the institution. Further initiatives are anticipated. "The work has only begun in this area," Shepard says, "but the ramifications have far-reaching effects. Helping patients maintain their dignity and cope with their pain reduces the need for euthanasia as an alternative for relief."

In the early 1990s, Roxane began addressing the palliative care needs of patients living with AIDS by developing the first pain management treatment guidelines and other programs, and by obtaining approval for Marinol™ as the first appetite stimulant for AIDS patients with weight loss.

Because studies estimated that only half of the patients suffering from advanced cancer received effective pain treatment, Roxane Laboratories created the Roxane Pain Institute, designed to educate the medical com-

munity about palliative care and the development of products in the area.

To spark interest in the field, the company also developed a number of educational programs, including materials that are reviewed by an editorial board composed of leading health care professionals from all over the continent. In addition, Roxane maintains a toll-free telephone information service, where callers can learn about the latest breakthroughs in treating severe pain or talk to a pain

management expert. There is also a home page on the World Wide Web where users can review the latest scientific papers. More than 100,000 users access the Web site each month.

INNOVATIVE PRODUCTS

In addition to helping severely ill patients find relief through leading-edge formulations, potencies, and dosage forms, Roxane Laboratories has developed a number of drugs and related products to rehabilitate

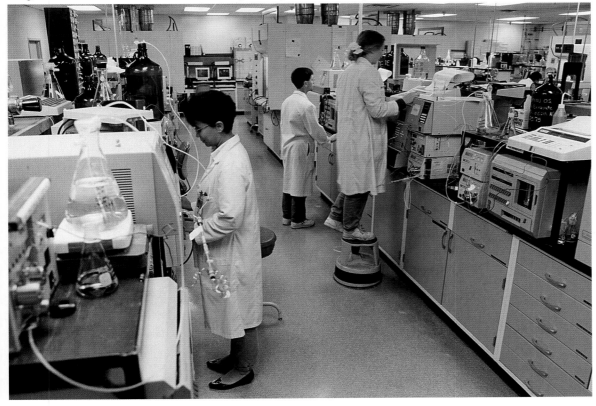

heroin addicts. Other product areas include developing oral cancer chemotherapeutics—several new drugs are currently involved in clinical trials—and researching new applications for existing products. For example, Marinol™, originally approved for patients undergoing cancer chemotherapy, was also found to be effective in stimulating AIDS patients' appetites and was eventually approved for that use.

The company's innovation and expertise also include packaging improvements. Roxane Laboratories developed the first unit dose glass for oral liquids. Today, the container is made of aluminum and referred to as the Patient Cup™.

Helping to secure Roxane Laboratories' leading-edge health care position is its ownership by Connecticut-based Boehringer Ingelheim Corporation Inc., a leading researcher, manufacturer, and marketer of pharmaceuticals, animal-health products, and specialty chemicals. Roxane Laboratories, Boehringer Ingelheim's most profitable subsidiary, receives encouragement and support for its unmatched health care efforts.

Affiliation with Boehringer Ingelheim, which purchased Roxane Laboratories in 1978, also contributes to the company's position as a leading marketer of generic products. Having played a major role in passing legislation that permitted generic substitutions for drugs in the 1960s, Roxane launches generic versions of a sister company's specialty drugs when the patent life or exclusivity period ends.

ENTREPRENEURIAL SPIRIT
Also contributing to Roxane Laboratories' reputation as an innovative company is an entrepreneurial group of approximately 1,000 engineers, scientists, technicians, and support staff, who are dedicated to enhancing the lives of severely ill patients through the discovery of new drugs, new uses for existing drugs, and new products. It's all summed up in the company's credo: "The characteristics of our success are an entrepreneurial spirit,

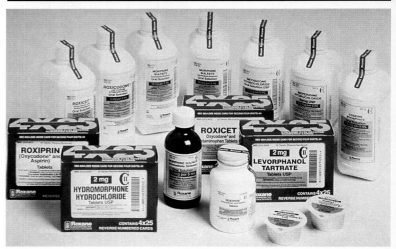

intuitive decision making, an effective intelligence-gathering network, planning for the future using analogies from the past, and a penchant for keeping options open."

From its headquarters on North Wilson Road and a plant on Oak Street, Roxane Laboratories manufactures, packages, and markets more than 400 different oral liquids, tablets, capsules, and sterile respiratory therapy solutions. Among them are one of the world's best-known lines of oral Schedule II narcotic analgesics, including Oramorph SR™ and Roxanol, two of the leading morphine formulation brands; Viramune™, used in the treatment of AIDS; and Orlaam™, a methadone analog used to treat drug addicts. The company's products are sold to a variety of health care providers, including large and small hospitals, pharmacies, nursing homes, and hospices.

To ensure its leading position in the field, Roxane Laboratories recently completed an expansion at its 300,000-square-foot North Wilson Road headquarters, bringing the total square footage to 500,000. Included was additional space for distribution, quality control, research, marketing, and manufacturing.

Roxane Laboratories' leadership and pioneering role, as well as its dedication to innovation in pain-control drugs, palliative patient care, and addiction therapies, will continue in the future. The company recently launched a new pain-relief drug called Duraclon™, which is designed to provide relief for types of cancer-related pain that traditionally have been difficult to treat, and is researching products to treat other types of addictions and exploring new packaging techniques that will take it and the health care industry well into the 21st century.

ALONG WITH DRUG DEVELOPMENT, ROXANE INITIATED A PALLIATIVE CARE PROGRAM, CONSISTING OF THE PUBLICATION OF THE *Palliative Care Letter*, DISTRIBUTION OF EDUCATIONAL LITERATURE, AND CREATION AND SPONSORSHIP OF PALLIATIVE CARE SCHOLAR PROGRAMS.

FROM ITS HEADQUARTERS ON NORTH WILSON ROAD AND A PLANT ON OAK STREET, ROXANE LABORATORIES MANUFACTURES, PACKAGES, AND MARKETS MORE THAN 400 DIFFERENT ORAL LIQUIDS, TABLETS, CAPSULES, AND STERILE RESPIRATORY THERAPY SOLUTIONS.

COLUMBUS SCHOOL FOR GIRLS

ENTER ANY CLASSROOM AT COLUMBUS SCHOOL FOR GIRLS (CSG) AND IT QUICKLY becomes obvious that a different approach to learning is under way. One class may be studying Latino and African-American women in history and literature, using the Internet to conduct research and computer applications for pre-

sentations. Or a bioethics class may be debating genetic cloning or completing an insurance project, where groups of students form their own health insurance company.

Such interdisciplinary approaches encourage students to think and learn, and are an everyday occurrence at Columbus School for Girls. CSG's faculty seek to instill intellectual curiosity, a commitment to social responsibility, and the lifelong pursuit of learning in the students who have passed through the school's doors since it was founded in 1898.

As CSG celebrates its 100th anniversary, the liberal arts-oriented, college-preparatory day school proudly reflects on its heritage and history as a place where some of the brightest young minds from Central Ohio have been challenged for years.

School officials compare the ambience at CSG to that of a small college, where students are guided by faculty and staff who cultivate intellectual curiosity and help students strive for academic excellence. Other hallmarks include freedom of expression and a feeling of safety in sharing thoughts and ideas.

UNIQUE EDUCATIONAL ENVIRONMENT

CSG creates its unique educational environment in a variety of ways. First and foremost is a thematic approach to learning, where core disciplines, such as math, science, history, and English, are combined under one topic. "What we know about children and their learning is that they will retain information longer and understand it at a deeper level if it is connected to something that is very real to them," says Dr. Patricia T. Hayot, head of the school.

Also integral to its environment are the school's single-gender status, its diverse student population, and its commitment to helping students

recognize their responsibility to society and the community. CSG has numerous community partnerships that help to foster this mode of thinking in its students, whether it's tutoring students from nearby neighborhoods or serving meals to the homeless.

Helping to fulfill the school's mission are dedicated and highly qualified faculty members—approximately 65 percent hold advanced degrees—who are committed to their disciplines and the development of students.

The results are impressive. CSG boasts a 100 percent four-year college admission rate for its students throughout its 100-year history. In addition to high scores on college entrance

exams such as the SAT and the ACT, numerous CSG students have been named presidential scholars. Countless CSG graduates today are well-known medical researchers, musicians, and business executives.

Ever forward thinkers, school officials today are asking themselves what skills students will need to be prepared for the next century. This involves not only evaluating the curriculum, but also determining how to maintain an environment that encourages sharing and learning to the highest degree possible. In these and many other ways, Columbus School for Girls continues its long tradition of excellence in education.

CLOCKWISE FROM TOP LEFT: COLUMBUS SCHOOL FOR GIRLS (CSG) WAS FOUNDED IN 1898.

SPORTS AND EXTRACURRICULAR ACTIVITIES PROVIDE CSG STUDENTS WITH WELL-ROUNDED OPPORTUNITIES FOR LEADERSHIP.

AT CSG, GIRLS EXCEL IN ALL SUBJECTS, INCLUDING MATH AND SCIENCE.

SERVING THREE-YEAR-OLDS THROUGH 12TH-GRADE STUDENTS, CSG HAS A 100 PERCENT FOUR-YEAR COLLEGE ADMISSION RATE.

AKZO NOBEL COATINGS INC.

KZO NOBEL COATINGS INC. IS THE WORLD'S LEADING SUPPLIER OF COIL COATings. Coil coating is a highly specialized painting process that provides both decoration and protection for a variety of products. Now owned by the international firm of Akzo Nobel, the Columbus location can trace

its local roots for more than a century.

Akzo Nobel's history in Ohio's capital began in 1888, when the Orr, Hanna and Abbott Company incorporated "for the purpose of manufacturing and selling paints, colors, varnishes, and painters' sundries, and dealing with the same." By the turn of the century, the company, renamed Hanna Paint, was selling its interior and exterior paints throughout seven midwestern states. In 1930, Hanna acquired Columbus Varnish, a maker of industrial finishes for automobiles, appliances, and metal containers.

A major breakthrough for Hanna Paint came during the Second World War. The war had ended importation of essential paint ingredients, and Hanna, making a virtue of necessity, undertook development of synthetic substitutes. Following the war, Hanna used its discoveries to become a major supplier of industrial coatings in the Midwest.

In 1989, the company—by then a subsidiary of Reliance Universal,

Inc.—was purchased by Akzo Nobel, a $13 billion company with headquarters in Arnhem, Netherlands. Akzo Nobel operates in more than 50 countries, producing chemicals, pharmaceuticals, and fibers, as well as coatings.

A BETTER IDEA

Coil coating—first developed in the 1930s as a means of applying a finish to venetian blinds—is a specialized, continuous process whereby highly automated finishing lines coat coils of steel, aluminum, or other metallic substrates with paint. These coated metal coils are then shaped by specialty fabricators into components for such end products as appliances; heating, ventilating, and air-conditioning equipment; metal office furniture; and vehicles.

The largest market for high-quality coil coatings is in construction—panel and roof components for the architectural, pre-engineered, agricultural, and residential sectors. In these applications, such high-end Akzo Nobel coatings as Trinar ® combine

protection with decoration to achieve striking results. Trinar was used, for example, on the roofs of the architecturally stunning Swan and Dolphin hotels at Disney World.

Beyond appearance and protection, coil coatings offer the advantages of lower cost and reduced impact on the environment. By purchasing coils of metals already coated to their specifications, manufacturers eliminate the need—and the cost—of painting their products after they are fabricated. Further, the process that coats coils is environmentally more friendly than that used in standard painting operations.

Coil coatings are environmentally preferred because their production process captures solvents and reuses them as a fuel, thus eliminating emission of volatile organic compounds. Says Michael Quinn, company vice president, "This will prompt more and more paint operations—like those handling metal office furniture, HVAC systems, and other products—to convert to coil coating."

A NEW AKZO NOBEL COIL COATINGS PRODUCTION FACILITY RECENTLY OPENED IN COLUMBUS.

The development of coatings, Quinn adds, takes the knowledge and experimentation of highly skilled and educated formulators. As one result of that skill, Akzo Nobel recently introduced TRI-escent II. This coating produces a brilliant metallic appearance that does not depend on the orientation of the metallic flakes. This feature solves a problem that had long caused applicator difficulties and color flopping on large surface areas such as curtain wall.

EXPANSION ADDS CAPABILITY

Akzo Nobel's recent Columbus expansion—a $32 million project—added 90,000 square feet to its operations. The project expanded manufacturing space by 50 percent, created a new finished goods warehouse to speed product delivery, doubled the space available to the technical department, and converted older manufacturing space to office operations.

The market for coil coatings is one demanding higher quality and quicker cycle times. Akzo Nobel's expansion brought technical advances that will help it respond to these demands. The new production facility includes totally enclosed tanks made of electropolished stainless steel to minimize contamination and emissions to the atmosphere; process equipment driven by electronic variable frequency drives to provide precise control of dispersion and process; and a new resin and solvent dispensing system that features mass flow meters and a computer-controlled dosing system that provides accuracy of greater than 99 percent.

In expanding, Akzo Nobel reinforced its ties to its Columbus location. The facility's immediate neighborhood is undergoing rehabilitation. "We made the investment here, rather than relocating to another site," says Quinn, "to contribute to that rehabilitation." The expansion was designed to be complementary to the neighborhood, Quinn adds, with landscaping planned to help the plant blend in.

From a small company producing paints and "painters' sundries" for a local market, Akzo Nobel has grown to supply its products nationally and internationally. Through its continuing research, technological advances, and expanded presence in Columbus, Akzo Nobel will continue its tradition of success for many years to come.

CHILDREN'S HOSPITAL

INSTITUTIONS ESTABLISH COVENANTS WITH THOSE THEY SERVE. AT COLUMBUS' CHILDREN'S Hospital, that commitment has been sustained for more than 105 years: to provide the community with the finest care available, regardless of ability to pay. In turn, the community helps to sustain the hospital's capacity to do so. ✷ This contract

COLUMBUS CHILDREN'S HOSPITAL IS THE MAIN PEDIATRIC HOSPITAL FOR 37 COUNTIES, WITH MORE THAN 300,000 PATIENT VISITS EACH YEAR.

CHILDREN'S IS ONE OF THE NATION'S TOP 10 FACILITIES FOR RESEARCH INTO THE DISEASES OF CHILDHOOD (LEFT).

IN KEEPING WITH ITS COMMITMENT TO CHILDREN, THE HOSPITAL DELIVERS $12 MILLION IN UNCOMPENSATED CARE A YEAR, ADDRESSING THE NEEDS OF CHILDREN WITH CARE—CARING, ADVOCACY, RESEARCH, AND EDUCATION (RIGHT).

was formed in 1892, when a group of young women, members of the King's Daughters of St. Paul's Episcopal Church, met to discuss ways and means of funding a children's hospital for Columbus. The group secured $18,000 for a 15-bed institution that opened December 30, 1893.

In the century since, Children's has grown, emerging as a nationally recognized, comprehensive pediatric health care system. Today, Children's is the main pediatric hospital for 37 counties, with more than 300,000 patient visits each year. In fact, one out of every three children in Franklin County is served in some way by Children's each year. In keeping with its commitment to children, the hospital delivers $12 million in uncompensated care a year, addressing the needs of children with CARE—caring, advocacy, research, and education.

CARING

Children's Hospital maintains 313 inpatient beds, extensive outpatient facilities, and more than 650 medical staff members—all regarded as excellent. Its trauma center, for example, was the first children's hospital in

Ohio to receive Level I certification, the highest level awarded.

There's something else that makes Children's a leader in pediatric health care, and that's the special brand of caring that focuses on the emotional, as well as the physical, needs of patients. Doctors, nurses, technicians, volunteers—everyone at Children's seems to have a gift for knowing when and how to give children the tenderness, comfort, and encouragement they need.

Children's has taken its special kind of care beyond the walls of the main hospital into the community through its Close to Home™ Network of more than 12 off-site locations, offering primary care and diagnostic

and therapeutic services including counseling services for children, adolescents, and their families.

Children's Homecare Services (CHS) provides exclusively pediatric health care to children from birth to 21 years of age, and to select adults.

ADVOCACY

Advocacy for children begins with the knowledge that children are not miniature adults—they have their own diseases, their own emotional realities, and their own responses to treatment.

Many diseases common to childhood are preventable by timely vaccination. Children's Hospital is an original partner in Project LOVE

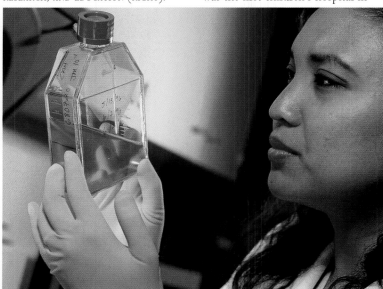

(Love Our Kids, Vaccinate Early), and works with numerous community groups to address shared areas of concern, including violence, smoking, and teen pregnancy.

On another front, Children's has been named by the National Committee to Prevent Child Abuse as the state clearinghouse for child abuse prevention information.

RESEARCH

Children's is one of the nation's top 10 facilities for research into the diseases of childhood. At the Children's Hospital Research Foundation (CHRF), nearly 100 principal investigators and more than 100 research staff work on hundreds of research projects.

One researcher's work allows for the more complete removal of cancerous cells by using a radioactive molecule which, when administered during surgery, "sticks" to tumor cells. Once the surgeon has removed all of the tumor visible to the unaided eye, a handheld instrument that detects radioactivity identifies the remaining tumor cells so they, too, can be removed.

Not all diseases yield readily to science. Today, half the children diagnosed with cystic fibrosis (CF) do not survive past age 16. Children's is tackling CF through new technologies, improved treatments, and, most promising, a gene transfer procedure that researchers hope will eliminate CF within the next decade.

Children's has received a five-year, $1.8 million award from the National Institutes of Health to participate in an effort to increase the number and variety of drugs approved by the FDA for use with children. In addition, CHRF staff are researching mental illness, and developing vaccines that work against various bacteria and viruses, including HIV.

EDUCATION

Children's goal is to have the public make wise decisions for their children. Education enables patients and their families to better manage their own health. Informed patients are more likely to follow recommended treatments and seek care more appropriately, and are more satisfied with the care they receive. Education is a cornerstone of health promotion and wellness. Between 70 and 90 percent of health problems are self-diagnosed and self-treated.

Education is also evident in the fact that Children's is the sole clinical setting for education in pediatric medicine delivered to students of the Ohio State University (OSU) School of Medicine. Education assures a continuous stream of highly qualified pediatric providers. Annually, Children's Hospital trains more than 2,000 students in medicine, nursing, and all of the allied health areas. In addition, Children's provides specialty training to more than 100 medical and surgi-

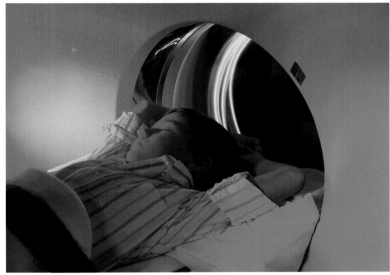

cal residents each year, many of whom will remain in the community after completion of their training. Since health care information doubles every two years, care would quickly become antiquated without continuing education.

The community that has benefited from Children's continues to support it. The annual community support of organizations such as the Children's Hospital Women's Auxiliaries, Children's Development Board, and Miracle Network Telethon helps to support Children's mission of caring for children regardless of their family's ability to pay. Community support also helps fund important programs, research, education, and patient care.

CLOCKWISE FROM TOP: CHILDREN'S HOSPITAL OFFERS COMMUNITY-BASED PRIMARY CARE AS WELL AS DIAGNOSTIC AND THERAPEUTIC SERVICES TO CHILDREN, ADOLESCENTS, AND THEIR FAMILIES THROUGH THE CLOSE TO HOME™ NETWORK OF OFF-SITE LOCATIONS.

CHILDREN'S IS A LEADER IN PEDIATRIC HEALTH CARE, EMPHASIZING A SPECIAL BRAND OF CARING THAT FOCUSES ON THE EMOTIONAL, AS WELL AS THE PHYSICAL, NEEDS OF PATIENTS.

DOCTORS, NURSES, TECHNICIANS, VOLUNTEERS—EVERYONE AT CHILDREN'S SEEMS TO HAVE A GIFT FOR KNOWING WHEN AND HOW TO GIVE CHILDREN THE TENDERNESS, COMFORT, AND ENCOURAGEMENT THEY NEED.

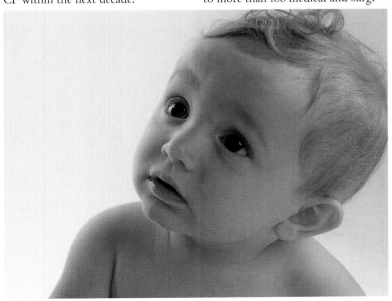

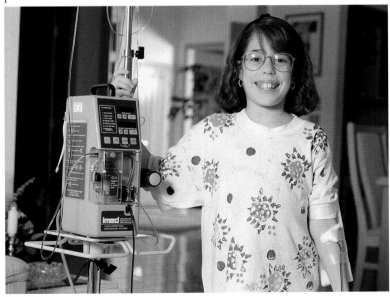

OhioHealth

HEALTH CARE IN AMERICA IS BECOMING INCREASINGLY COMPLEX. MEDICAL KNOWLedge is expanding, technologies are being refined, and systems of reimbursement are becoming more complicated. An individual's health, however, can depend on the ability to manage that complexity, so that individuals get

what they need, when they need it. Such a philosophy is the driving force behind the mission of OhioHealth, a single, integrated system that can trace its roots in Central Ohio to 1892.

In the reorganization that created OhioHealth, two things were paramount. First, the organization reaffirmed that its reason for being was to improve the health of the people it serves. Second, the organi-

zation committed itself to creating and maintaining a system that made possible the delivery of that care.

UTILIZING ENORMOUS RESOURCES

OhioHealth brings enormous resources to this task. As Central Ohio's single largest provider of health care, it maintains a presence in 46 counties and owns or manages nine hospitals, in-

cluding Grant Medical Center and Riverside Methodist Hospital in Columbus. OhioHealth also has a medical staff of 2,500 physicians, a partnership with more than 1,000 members of the Medical Group of Ohio integrated provider association, 10,000 employees, 3,700 volunteers, a growing selection of managed care health benefit plans, and a myriad of outpatient, education, and home health services.

Building a regionally integrated health care system is a huge task. In creating OhioHealth, every aspect of corporate operations was scrutinized and refined. Staffing was adjusted; a systemwide planning process was implemented; a consensus was reached on the mission, vision, and values; and a new corporate management structure was developed.

Gaining increased market attention are such managed care products as HealthPledge HMO; HealthReach PPO, covering nearly 150,000 people; and Medicare Extra, an HMO for those eligible for Medicare. Medicare Extra is a joint venture between Ohio-Health, Ohio State University, and the physicians of Grant, Riverside, and University hospitals, and offers improvements over traditional Medicare coverage by saving participants money, paperwork, and the unwelcome stress of navigating the health care system on their own.

RESOURCES DIRECTED BY CONCERN

OhioHealth continuously shows its concern for people while protecting the financial viability of the organization. In Columbus, for example, Grant and Riverside hospitals provide more than $20 million in uncompensated medical care a year. In addition, when Grant Medical Center recognized the relationship between infant mortality and low-birth-weight babies, it took

OHIOHEALTH IS MOST VISIBLY RECOGNIZED IN COLUMBUS AS GRANT MEDICAL CENTER (TOP) AND RIVERSIDE METHODIST HOSPITAL. TOGETHER, THESE HOSPITALS CARE FOR MORE PATIENTS THAN ANY OTHER HEALTH CARE PROVIDER IN CENTRAL OHIO.

◄ MICHAEL HOUGHTON

◄ MICHAEL HOUGHTON

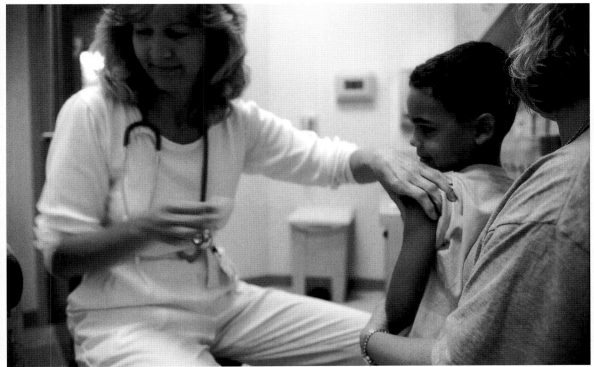

TONY ARMOUR

TONY ARMOUR

action by instituting a partnership with the Columbus Public Schools. Through this partnership, Grant offered prenatal care to pregnant high schoolers via a large mobile unit equipped with two exam rooms and an office for nutrition and social work counsel. Grant and Riverside hospitals have also provided more than $2.1 million to such initiatives as the Project to Reduce Infant Mortality, Women's Health Day, Columbus Area Rape Treatment Program, and other community health and wellness programs.

OhioHealth is focusing attention where it is needed. Approximately half the heart attack patients in Columbus are admitted to Grant and Riverside. Riverside was one of the first hospitals in the country to open a chest pain center to quickly diagnose and treat patients who come to the emergency room with heart attack symptoms.

OhioHealth is taking cost-effective health care to Columbus neighborhoods, opening two suburban health centers in 1997. These centers provide outpatient surgery, primary medical care, women's health, imaging, lab services, physical therapy, occupational medicine, and an array of wellness and health education courses.

And OhioHealth is taking steps to head off emergencies before they occur. The 105,000-square-foot McConnell Heart Health Center, near the Riverside campus, promotes heart disease prevention, risk factor management, and wellness.

Ties to the Community

OhioHealth's ties to the community are numerous and strong. Since it opened in 1985, the Elizabeth Blackwell Center at Riverside and Grant has established a national reputation for its programs of consultation, education, and support, serving more than 300,000 men, women, and children with its wellness, parenting, and women's health programs. In addition, each year, hospice care is provided to 1,200 terminally ill people, including those in 25 Franklin County nursing homes. More than 70,000 home care visits are also made annually.

Grant and Riverside train nearly 200 resident physicians and fellows a year, preparing them for careers in family medicine, internal medicine, obstetrics/gynecology, orthopedics, surgery, and other specialties. This training places emphasis on recognizing the physical and psychological issues in health care, considering the

special needs of all patients, and practicing medicine in a managed care environment.

OhioHealth's regional integrated health care system is rooted in the code and values of the Methodist tradition of respect for the dignity and well-being of all. As a regional integrated health care system, it offers all levels of care to ensure that people receive the care they need, at locations convenient to them and in a cost-effective manner. By doing so, OhioHealth continues to fulfill its mission of managing the complexities of the health care system to best serve the citizens of Central Ohio.

CLOCKWISE FROM TOP LEFT: PATIENT/FAMILY-FOCUSED CARE HAS LONG BEEN AN OHIOHEALTH HALLMARK. THE ORGANIZATION'S MISSION, "TO IMPROVE THE HEALTH OF THOSE WE SERVE," IS CARRIED OUT DAILY BY MORE THAN 2,500 PHYSICIANS, 10,000 EMPLOYEES, AND 3,700 VOLUNTEERS.

WITH THE OPENING OF THE MCCONNELL HEART HEALTH CENTER IN NORTHWEST COLUMBUS, OHIOHEALTH IS AT THE FOREFRONT OF PREVENTIVE AND REHABILITATIVE HEART CARE. THE 105,000-SQUARE-FOOT FACILITY COMBINES MEDICINE, FITNESS, AND EDUCATION TO HELP PEOPLE PRONE TO HEART DISEASE ACTUALLY REDUCE THEIR RISK.

GRANT MEDICAL CENTER AND RIVERSIDE METHODIST HOSPITAL RANK AMONG THE BEST COMMUNITY TEACHING HOSPITALS IN THE UNITED STATES. THE COMBINED RESOURCES, EQUIPMENT, STAFF, AND PATHOLOGY MAKE THE PROGRAM COMPARABLE TO MANY ACADEMIC TEACHING CENTERS. EACH YEAR, GRANT AND RIVERSIDE PROGRAMS TRAIN NEARLY 200 RESIDENT PHYSICIANS AND FELLOWS.

METTLER-TOLEDO, INC.

THE PRODUCTS MANUFACTURED BY METTLER-TOLEDO, INC. TOUCH PEOPLE'S LIVES every day. This includes shopping trips to the grocery store and other commercial establishments, industrial manufacturing, scientific research, and even the weighing of a newborn baby. And, many sporting events, such as horse

racing and boxing, are enhanced by the accuracy of the scales Mettler Toledo manufactures.

The company's involvement in sanctioned athletics continues to this day. Mettler Toledo has been the official supplier of scales to the Olympic Games almost constantly since the 1932 winter games in Lake Placid. This has been especially true since electronic scales were introduced at the 1976 Olympic Games in Montreal, continuing through the 1996 Centennial Olympic games in Atlanta. In fact, one gold medal in a weight-lifting event was actually determined by a Mettler Toledo scale.

The independent company was founded as Toledo Scale Company at the turn of the century, when a new retail weighing concept that measured weight against weight, instead of with springs, was developed. Sold under the slogan No Springs—Honest Weight, the product was the first invention in a long line of innovative developments that would eventually make Mettler Toledo the world's largest manufacturer of scales

and weighing systems. Columbus is the headquarters for Mettler Toledo Industrial Retail/Americas, serving the United States, Canada, Mexico, Latin America, and Australia.

Since its founding, the company has manufactured virtually all scale components, including weight sensors, instrumentation, and printed circuit boards. Many of its scales connect directly into customers' centralized database and process control systems. Today, Mettler Toledo offers the broadest range of scales and scale systems on the market.

RESOURCE LEADER

The company's products range in weighing capacity from more than 1 million kilograms to 1 ten-millionth of a gram. In addition, the company sees itself as more than just a manufacturer. "We can only succeed by helping people solve problems," says John Robechek, division head, Industrial/Americas Division.

Much of the company's growth over the years has been due to a commitment to total quality management.

Every facility operates under ISO (International Organization for Standardization) standards for manufacturing quality and product development. Also key is cost consciousness. The company's ability to control costs and operate efficiently allows it to respond quickly to customer demands and changing industry trends.

Mettler Toledo services generations of its equipment. If a scale from 1920 loses a part that is no longer available, the company will go to its archives for the original plans and make a new part. "We have a tradition of standing behind our equipment for as long as it stays in service," says Robechek.

WIDE ARRAY OF PRODUCTS

Mettler Toledo markets its laboratory balances, analytical instruments, industrial and retail scales, and a wide variety of scientific measurement devices to customers around the globe. Mettler Toledo's products are used to control mixing and batching processes in the pharmaceutical, food, and chemical industries, as well as in

TRUCKS ARE WEIGHED IN EMPTY AND WEIGHED OUT FULLY LOADED WITH VARIOUS GASES ON LEGAL-FOR-TRADE METTLER TOLEDO DIGITOL® TRUCKMATE® TRUCK SCALES. A METTLER TOLEDO HIGH-PERFORMANCE DATA TERMINAL KEEPS TRACK OF ALL TRANSACTIONS (LEFT).

PRECISION COUNTING SCALES PROVIDE A FASTER AND SIMPLER METHOD FOR INDUSTRY TO COUNT AND DOCUMENT LARGE QUANTITIES OF PARTS. METTLER TOLEDO'S EXCLUSIVE ULTRARES TECHNOLOGY PERMITS PARTS TO BE COUNTED WITH A HIGHER DEGREE OF ACCURACY THAN ALTERNATIVE COUNTING METHODS (RIGHT).

the manufacture of rubber tires and glass. They also are used to determine price by the pound or the truckload, track bulk inventories in tanks, and count small parts.

In addition to its headquarters, the company operates three other facilities in Columbus. One manufactures heavy-capacity truck and railroad track scales. Another houses a training center for customers and manufactures printed circuit boards and industrial and retail scales. The third provides after-sales support, including spare parts, a repair center, and a rental department. There are 650 employees in Columbus and more than 6,400 worldwide.

In recognition of its commitment to quality manufacturing, *Industry Week* named the company's plant in the Columbus suburb of Worthington as one of the 12 best plants in America. The company was also one of the first two industrial companies ever to apply Intel microprocessors in their equipment.

Mettler Toledo has always been a leader in technology. With its broad range of products and global market position, it plans to continue to develop the new technology to meet its customers' changing demands. Developing countries provide potential for growth, so the company plans more global expansion, as well.

Mettler Toledo recently developed a home page on the Internet (www.mt.com) and is using electronic media applications, including catalogs on CD-ROM, for distribution of product specifications and application information. The company believes that customers spur innovation. "The more you understand your customers and their needs, the better you are able to serve them," Robechek explains.

Backed by agility, aggressiveness, cost consciousness, initiative, innovation, and quality, Mettler Toledo is well positioned to meet ambitious product and expansion goals.

CLOCKWISE FROM TOP LEFT: THE JAGUAR® TERMINAL IS A POWERFUL, EASY-TO-USE SCALE INSTRUMENT THAT IS DESIGNED TO BE INTEGRATED INTO A CUSTOMER'S FACTORY AUTOMATION SYSTEM. JAGUAR MAKES IT EASY FOR THE CUSTOMER TO DESIGN, BUILD, INSTALL, START UP, OPERATE, AND MAINTAIN RELIABLE PROCESS SYSTEMS WHERE ACCURATE WEIGHTS ARE A MUST.

FILLING SYSTEMS ARE USED TO ACCURATELY FILL DRUMS, PAILS, TOTES, AND OTHER CONTAINERS SEMIAUTOMATICALLY IN ANY ENVIRONMENT—SAFE OR HAZARDOUS. THEY ARE CAPABLE OF FILLING A SINGLE CONTAINER OR MULTIPLE CONTAINERS ON A PALLET—AS STAND ALONES OR IN A CONVEYOR LINE.

A MERCHANT WEIGHS AND PRICES GOURMET COFFEE FOR A CUSTOMER ON A METTLER TOLEDO PRICE COMPUTING SCALE. THE SCALE DISPLAYS THE WEIGHT, PRICE PER POUND, AND TOTAL PRICE ON LARGE, EASY-TO-READ DIGITS FOR BOTH THE CUSTOMER AND THE VENDOR.

THE ESTIMATING SCALE WITH ITS LARGE, EASY READING DIAL ALLOWS THE CUSTOMER TO QUICKLY ESTIMATE THE WEIGHT AND PRICE OF THE APPLES HE WANTS BEFORE REACHING THE CHECKOUT COUNTER, WHERE THEY ARE OFFICIALLY WEIGHED AND PRICED.

FOR NEARLY A CENTURY, ROSS PRODUCTS DIVISION HAS BEEN PROVIDING A WIDE RANGE of nutritional products for infants, children, and adults. The company traces its beginnings to 1903, when Harry C. Moores and Stanley M. Ross founded the Moores & Ross Milk Company in Columbus. ✳ Establishing what would

become a tradition of customer service, the young entrepreneurs sought new ways to fulfill customer needs. To distinguish themselves from the competition, they began using the first stand-and-drive milk truck, and were the first to use glass bottles for home delivery.

Over the next 20 years, their business prospered. In 1924, the partners took the daring step of producing and marketing a new concept, milk-based infant formula. As the product grew in popularity, Moores & Ross sold its dairy, ice-cream, and milk processing operations to another prominent Columbus firm, the Borden Company, to focus on producing infant formula.

In 1928, the company was renamed the M&R Dietetic Laboratories. Free to concentrate fully on the emerging field of pediatric nutrition, the company became known for one of the most respected and successful infant formulas ever—Similac®. Similac was first available in powder, and then in 1951, after extensive research, a concentrated liquid. In 1959, the company introduced Similac With Iron to help prevent iron deficiencies in infants.

In 1964, the company was renamed Ross Laboratories after merging with one of the world's largest health care corporations, the North Chicago-based Abbott Laboratories. Abbott is a diversified health care company devoted to the discovery,

development, manufacture, and marketing of innovative products that improve diagnostic, therapeutic, and nutritional practices.

In 1973, Ross entered the adult medical nutritional market with the introduction of the Ensure® line of nutritional supplements. Increased awareness of proper nutrition's role in maintaining good health has been the key to this rapidly expanding market. Today, Ross offers the broadest portfolio of medical nutritional products in the industry.

INNOVATION LEADERS

Under the leadership of President Thomas M. McNally, the range of Ross products has expanded significantly, yet the company's longstanding commitment to listening to the customer and championing quality products remains the hallmark of its business. Says McNally, "Our successes have always been based on a passion for excellence and innovation in everything that we do. The highly dedicated people who work here continually care about improving the quality of life."

Survanta® is one of many Ross products that have saved lives. This pharmaceutical product is a bovine-derived lung surfactant that has had a significant impact on the prevention and treatment of infant respiratory distress syndrome (RDS), the number one cause of death of premature infants.

Ross introduced an improved version of Similac With Iron in 1997. The new product, backed by extensive clinical research, is so advanced that it is the subject of six new patents. Improved Similac With Iron is based on nutrient levels found naturally in breast milk, and contains an improved fat blend that supports visual, cognitive, and psychomotor development.

AN ONGOING COMMITMENT TO RESEARCH IS A KEY FACTOR IN THE FORMULA FOR SUCCESS OF THE ROSS PRODUCTS DIVISION OF ABBOTT LABORATORIES.

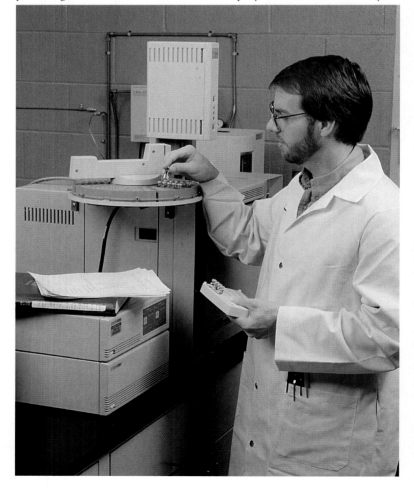

Ross recently entered into an alliance whereby it will market a line of proprietary vaccines produced by North American Vaccine. On the medical nutritional side, the company is introducing new flavors of Ensure, an Ensure Bar, and Ensure in quart plastic bottles for high-volume users.

These innovative efforts in quality research, cutting-edge science, and technological know-how have earned Ross an unsurpassed reputation among pediatricians and health care professionals, who consistently award the company's sales forces the top ranking. "The relationship we have cultivated with health care professionals is second to none," McNally says, "and it's one of the first things that differentiates us from the competition."

AN EXCITING FUTURE

As Ross looks toward the challenges of its second century of market leadership, more innovations are on the horizon. Building on its existing strength in the nutritional field, Ross is expanding into nonnutritional markets, such as pharmaceuticals. Research in pharmaceutical development is focused on finding solutions to serious problems, such as respiratory distress syndrome and neonatal jaundice.

Always on the lookout to identify key partners, products, and technologies to fill strategic gaps, Ross plans to make strides in the pediatric pharmaceutical industry. "There is significant untapped potential in the pediatric pharmaceutical business," says McNally. "Traditionally, companies have not paid as close attention to pediatric pharmaceuticals as they have to adult pharmaceuticals because of their relative sizes."

Ross will also continue to research and develop disease-specific products for its adult medical nutrition business, and will continue researching other ingredients to enhance its infant formulas.

A GOOD FIT
WITH COLUMBUS

Community support is a company goal in all of the cities in which Ross has plant operations—Columbus; Sturgis, Michigan; Altavista, Virginia; and Casa Grande, Arizona. More than half of Ross' 2,500 Columbus-based employees volunteer their talents and time to various community organizations ranging from Special Olympics to Adopt-a-School, and the company matches its employees' financial donations dollar-for-dollar.

Ross assists employees through a wellness program that includes no-cost, on-site cholesterol and prostate screenings, mammography exams, flu shots, and more. "We're a health care company, so it fits for us to offer these services. It's the right thing to do," McNally notes.

"We offer community support through our people and contributions to certain programs," McNally adds. "Many of us are very fortunate, and we realize this. We represent an excellent organization and mean a lot to so many people. Our service to the community is one way of giving thanks and giving back by giving some of ourselves."

THE COVER FOR THE CHOCOLATE CAKE, THE BOWL FOR THE BANANA SPLIT, THE glass that holds the orange juice, and casseroles, canisters, and kitchen jars: these and hundreds of other items are created by Anchor Hocking. ✴ With more than 90 years' experience, the Lancaster, Ohio, company is a

major manufacturer of glass beverage ware, bake ware, serving ware, storage ware, and food-service glassware. As this list suggests, Anchor Hocking's product line is a broad one. This, company President Mark Eichhorn explains, is key to its success: "We are a market leader in a number of glass tabletop categories. Our competitors generally concentrate on one category; we are the only domestic glass manufacturer that is diversified enough to offer so many different product categories to the customer."

The company markets to such major retailers as Wal-Mart, Kmart, and Target; supplies glassware through food-service distributors to large restaurant chains, hotels, and caterers; and, more recently, has been focusing on growing its international sales in Canada, Central and Latin America, Europe, Australia, and the Philippines.

COMPETITIVE ADVANTAGE

The tabletop glass business, Eichhorn says, is "driven by fashion. The challenge for us is to be trend-right, and to be first in the market with some of those trends—whether it's a design, color, or innovative product feature."

In a very competitive marketplace, Eichhorn adds, Anchor Hocking brings three advantages. Most glassmakers can draw upon a specific process expertise, but Anchor Hocking has expertise in a variety of processes. "The fact that we can manage as many different processes at the level of expertise we do is a competitive advantage," Eichhorn notes. The second advantage is experienced personnel; the average plant seniority among production associates is 25 years. The third advantage is the company's customer-oriented approach to business. This includes being sen-

sitive to a retailer's need to differentiate its products from those of other retailers, being timely with responses, and offering basic, everyday values and solid promotions.

Anchor Hocking is grounded in the tradition of glassmaking, a craft to which it has made notable contributions. The company was founded in 1905 when Isaac J. Collins—the head of the decorating department at a small, local glassmaking company—joined with friends to raise the $25,000 needed to acquire the failing Lancaster Carbon Company. Collins renamed the enterprise Hocking Glass. In its first year, the company sold $20,000 worth of glassware; by 1919, it had grown to 300 employees.

In a sense, what made Hocking Glass was its response to disaster. In 1924, its plant, known as the Black

WITH MORE THAN 90 YEARS EXPERIENCE, ANCHOR HOCKING IS A MAJOR MANUFACTURER OF GLASS BEVERAGE WARE, BAKE WARE, SERVING WARE, STORAGE WARE, AND FOOD-SERVICE GLASSWARE.

Cat, was reduced to five acres of ashes and rubble by a fire of such magnitude that its light was visible 25 miles away. At Hocking Glass, however, the fire spurred advance rather than retreat. A new factory was built on the ashes of the old; that same year, the company expanded by acquiring the Lancaster Glass Company and the Standard Glass Manufacturing Company.

A TECHNOLOGICAL BREAKTHROUGH

Technological advances followed. In the mid-1920s, Hocking revolutionized tableware production by creating a machine that pressed glass automatically. Production soared—first from one item a minute to 20, and later to 35 items per minute. When the stock market crash drove down consumer spending, Hocking Glass sought a way to produce glassware at a price even depression budgets could afford. The breakthrough was a 15-mold machine that turned out 90 pieces of blown glass per minute, allowing the company to sell two tumblers for a nickel—less than half the former price.

The Anchor Hocking Glass Company came into existence on December 31, 1937, with the merger of Hocking Glass Company with Anchor Cap and Closure and its subsidiaries. By 1940, the company was operating nationally; in 1963, it created an international division to serve customers outside the United States. Tremendous growth followed, and in 1969, the Tableware Division completed a 900,000-square-foot, state-of-the-art distribution center in Lancaster.

In 1987, Anchor Hocking Glass was acquired by the Newell Company, a decentralized group of 18 companies that manufactures and markets high-volume staple consumer products: housewares, hardware, home furnishings, and office products. Since the acquisition, Anchor Hocking has invested more than $100 million in capital improvements to the manufacturing operations. That investment brought greater efficiency and flexibility, allow-

The tabletop glass business, Anchor Hocking President Mark Eichhorn says, is "driven by fashion. The challenge for us is to be trend-right, and to be first in the market with some of those trends—whether it's a design, color, or innovative product feature."

The cover for the chocolate cake, the bowl for the banana split, the glass that holds the orange juice, and casseroles, canisters, and kitchen jars: these and hundreds of other items are created by Anchor Hocking.

ing Anchor Hocking to produce a greater range of higher-quality products, with the fashion, color, and features to break into new market segments. Investment also provided the computer and materials management tools that let Anchor Hocking provide its customers with tremendous expertise in logistics, electronic data interchange, and vendor-managed inventory.

With 1,500 associates, Anchor Hocking is the leading employer in

Lancaster and, as such, plays a lead role in the well-being of the community. It supports an extensive range of school programs and is active with United Way, American Cancer Society, Chamber of Commerce, YMCA, Habitat for Humanity, Salvation Army, Soap Box Derby, Lancaster festival, and other activities. As Anchor Hocking nears its 100th anniversary, the company continues its tradition of innovation and success in practicing one of the oldest of crafts, glassmaking.

AMERICAN ELECTRIC POWER

 ROM AIR CONDITIONERS TO ASSEMBLY LINES, TELEVISIONS TO TOASTERS, ELECTRICITY powers the world. In Columbus, that electricity flows from American Electric Power (AEP). Columbus has been AEP's headquarters city since 1983, when the company moved its offices from New York City to 1 Riverside Plaza.

That move followed AEP's 1980 acquisition of the Columbus and Southern Ohio Electric Company.

American Electric Power is the second-largest investor-owned utility in the United States, generating more than 120 billion kilowatt-hours annually and delivering that energy to almost 7 million people in Ohio, Michigan, Indiana, Kentucky, West Virginia, Virginia, and Tennessee. To create this energy, AEP operates 21 major generating plants, 19 of them coal-fired. To transmit this energy, AEP maintains 125,000 miles of transmission and distribution lines, including a 2,022-mile "backbone" of 765,000 volt lines extending across six states.

A TIME OF RAPID CHANGE

America's electric utility industry is in the midst of what may be the most far-reaching change in its history. Customers—business, commercial, and residential—will soon be free to shop for their electricity provider, somewhat like telephone customers may now select the long-distance carrier they prefer.

For consumers, this change will bring new options and, for many, lower costs. For the utility industry, it will mean a more fluid marketplace with increased competitive pressures. For American Electric Power, that new marketplace is one it has welcomed and one for which it is prepared.

E. Linn Draper Jr., chairman, CEO, and president of American Electric Power, observes, "When retail customers have an opportunity to choose their energy supplier, we want the obvious choice to be AEP. But that won't happen out of habit. The choice has to be earned."

To earn that choice, AEP has completed a corporate reorganization designed to make it more responsive to changing requirements, and is offering new energy solutions to its customers. As a sign of the change, in 1996 the utility replaced the names of the various operating companies under which it had done business with the name American Electric Power. With the restructuring and name change, AEP can compete as one system, one company, with one look and one voice.

A HISTORY OF DOING THE JOB

The history of AEP recapitulates much of the history of investor-owned utilities in America. Originally known as American Gas and Electric (AG&E), the company incorporated in 1906 with the belief that a profitable operation could be established by combining small, independent utilities into a unified whole. Characteristically, these small companies had inadequate and unreliable generating facilities, poorly constructed and maintained power lines, and no way to share electric current as demand fluctuated or in an emergency. Further, their rates were high: often 16 to 18 cents per kilowatt-hour. In 1958, after numerous acquisitions, the company adopted its current name of American Electric Power.

The 1980 acquisition of Columbus and Southern Ohio Electric brought into the AEP fold a company that had been generating electricity for Columbus for more than a century.

AEP, ONE OF THE NATION'S LARGEST INVESTOR-OWNED UTILITIES, PROVIDES ELECTRIC ENERGY TO ALMOST 7 MILLION PEOPLE IN OHIO, INDIANA, MICHIGAN, WEST VIRGINIA, VIRGINIA, TENNESSEE, AND KENTUCKY. IN ADDITION, WHOLLY OWNED SUBSIDIARIES PROVIDE POWER ENGINEERING, CONSULTING, AND MANAGEMENT SERVICES THROUGHOUT THE WORLD.

DAVID H. JENTGEN ◀

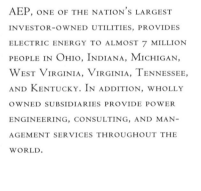

Columbus' first generating company, the Columbus Electric Light and Power Company, was incorporated in 1883, just 13 months after Thomas Edison's Pearl Street Station in New York demonstrated the feasibility of large-scale municipal lighting. Other utilities were acquired over time. These included the Nelsonville (Ohio) Electric Light Company, which operated the first alternating current generating station west of the Alleghenies.

Consolidating many small utilities presents major technical tasks, which AEP mastered. Among other accomplishments, in 1923, AEP built in southeastern Ohio the world's first plant to use reheated steam to generate electricity. In 1962, AEP completed the hemisphere's first natural-draft

cooling tower in Kentucky: This closed-loop, water-recirculation system eliminates thermal discharges that can affect aquatic life. At one time, AEP operated all of the nation's five most efficient generating stations.

Power generation takes great resources, and AEP focuses on the need to conserve and restore such resources. The company, for example, plans to plant 15 million trees by the year 2000. In 1986, AEP donated 9,154 acres near Zanesville to the International Center for the Preservation of Wild Animals, as a sanctuary for threatened or endangered species. Today, this land is home to such non-Ohio natives as camels, rhino, giraffes, and hartebeests. Nearby, AEP's Recreation Land, established

in 1962 on reclaimed mining land, has welcomed an estimated 3.2 million visitors since it was opened to the public.

Much changes in the utility field; much remains the same. These words from an early AG&E general manager, George Tidd, remain true today: "Our job is generating electricity and getting it to where it's used, efficiently and with respect for the environment. We're in this business because it is concerned with the supply of a fundamental requirement of modern living, because it's an honorable one, because we like it, and because we want to earn a living at it. Such is our job as we see it. We are trying to do it well and to do it better all the time."

CLOCKWISE FROM TOP LEFT: AS PART OF ITS COMMITMENT TO ENVIRONMENTAL LEADERSHIP, AEP HAS PLANTED THOUSANDS OF TREE SEEDLINGS ON RECLAIMED MINING LANDS IN EASTERN OHIO. COAL WAS ONCE SURFACE-MINED THERE TO FUEL AN AEP GENERATING PLANT.

AEP PROVIDES RELIABLE, AFFORDABLE ELECTRIC SERVICE TO NEARLY 500,000 CUSTOMERS IN ITS COLUMBUS REGION, WHICH ENCOMPASSES FRANKLIN COUNTY AND PORTIONS OF EIGHT SURROUNDING COUNTIES.

AEP HAS ONE OF THE STRONGEST TRANSMISSION AND DISTRIBUTION SYSTEMS IN THE WORLD, WITH ALMOST 22,000 CIRCUIT MILES OF TRANSMISSION AND 104,000 MILES OF DISTRIBUTION LINES CONNECTING CUSTOMERS WITH 38 POWER PLANTS.

AEP'S POWER GENERATION GROUP STRIVES TO PRODUCE ELECTRICITY SAFELY AND RELIABLY AND AT THE LOWEST COST. POWER PLANTS, SUCH AS THE 2,600-MEGAWATT GEN. JAMES M. GAVIN PLANT IN SOUTHEASTERN OHIO, FORM THE BACKBONE OF AEP'S POWER GENERATION CAPABILITIES.

Chemical Abstracts Service (CAS)

Access to information, especially on patents and scientific discoveries, has become an increasingly important competitive advantage worldwide. And Chemical Abstracts Service (CAS), a division of the American Chemical Society, is recognized as the world's most important source of chemistry-related information. In fact, most serious chemical research begins with Columbus-based CAS' databases. Today, CAS' electronic databases contain references to more than 14 million scientific articles and patents and catalog more than 17 million unique chemical substances.

Tracing its roots to 1907, CAS has met the challenges of the information explosion by providing easy access to international chemistry-related literature and patents published in 50 languages at the rate of more than 2,000 documents per day. Functioning much like a library's card catalog, CAS products, in printed and electronic form, index and summarize this overwhelming quantity of chemical research, thus permitting researchers to quickly find the information they need. Just as scientists consider chemistry the central science—vital to the study of many technical disciplines, from biomedicine to physics—CAS is known as the central source of chemical information.

CAS Chemical Registry System

New substances are identified every day in the chemist's lab, and chemical substance identification is a special strength of CAS. The organization is widely known for the CAS Chemical Registry System, which is the largest substance identification system in existence. When a chemical substance is newly encountered in the literature processed by CAS, its molecular structure diagram, systematic chemical name, molecular formula, and other identifying information are recorded in the registry and assigned a unique CAS Registry Number®.

In 1995, for the first time, CAS registered more than 1 million substances in a single year. In total, the registry contains records for some 17 million chemical substances. The numbers are used in reference works, databases, and regulatory compliance documents.

Comprehensive Searching by Computer

The Chemical Abstracts (CA) database and its associated databases provide indexes and abstracts of patents; articles from approximately 8,000 scientific journals; conference proceedings; and other documents pertinent to chemistry. CA evolved from a printed publication of the same name, which is still being published after more than 90 years. The volume of scientific information dictated a need for CAS to computerize its operations long before computers became commonplace in businesses. CAS began to develop computer-based publication technologies in the 1960s. Today, the CAS document analysis and publishing operation is a highly integrated system of human intellectual effort

More than 1,200 staff members, most with scientific degrees, now work at Chemical Abstracts Service.

assisted by advanced information technology.

Quality is as important as quantity in a scientific database and is a major focus at CAS. More than half of CAS' 1,200 employees are scientists, many of whom are adept in one or more foreign languages, as well as in a scientific specialty. They ensure the abstracts and indexing in CAS databases will lead researchers to the literature relevant to their queries.

CAS information produced after 1967 is available for on-line searching through the STN International network, widely acknowledged as the world's leading network of scientific and technical databases. STN International is operated by CAS in cooperation with Germany's FIZ Karlsruhe and the Japan Science and Technology Corporation. In addition, CAS produces a line of CD-ROM titles and Internet services, among other information products.

Abstracting and indexing the information is only part of the mission. CAS strives to harness the best new technologies to create products and services that deliver CAS information in ways that are most convenient for its customers. One of the latest CAS products, STN Easy, gives anyone interested in science and technology World Wide Web access to CAS information.

CHANGING THE WAY SCIENTISTS CONDUCT RESEARCH

CAS was a pioneer in providing electronic information, but as its database continued to grow, information-searching techniques became more complex. Today, while many scientists rely on information experts to retrieve information from CAS databases, CAS has introduced search tools that make it easy for scientists to find information for themselves as well.

The vision of providing easy access to chemical information at the desktop inspired the creation of SciFinder®, an award-winning client-server application that is changing the way scientists conduct research. Released in March 1995, this tool combines CAS' extensive databases with an intelligent, easy-to-use desktop interface. Without any training in information retrieval, scientists can answer most of their routine questions simply by entering a few key words and clicking an on-screen button.

In the future, CAS will continue combining its expertise in chemistry and information technology to develop more innovative products and services. The organization is also striving to play the central pathfinder role in the new Internet and intranet world of information management, and plans to open up vistas for new services that will greatly facilitate future scientific research.

"Although CAS is not a household name, the work we do indirectly affects everyone's life," says Director Bob Massie. "Scientists use CAS information to do everything from discover new medications to create stronger plastics for our automobiles. CAS is a critical partner for scientists around the world."

CLOCKWISE FROM TOP:
CHEMICAL ABSTRACTS' FILES IN ELECTRONIC FORM OCCUPY TRILLIONS OF BYTES.

IN 1907, CHEMICAL ABSTRACTS SERVICE BEGAN KEEPING CHEMISTS UP TO DATE.

INFORMATION TOOLS LIKE SCIFINDER® HAVE REVOLUTIONIZED CHEMICAL RESEARCH.

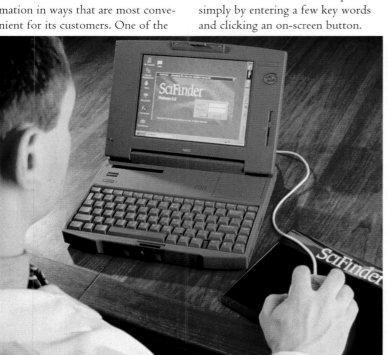

CHEMICAL ABSTRACTS

| Vol. 1. | JANUARY 1, 1907 | No. 1 |

APPARATUS
W. H. WALKER.

New Apparatus for the Determination of Sulphur and Carbon. A. KLEINE. Z. angew. Chem., 19, 1711.—The flask which serves as generator in the determination of sulphur by the evolution method, is, in this apparatus, blown with a long neck, the diameter of the upper three-fourths of which is considerably larger than the neck of the flask proper. Into the narrowest part of this neck is ground a delivery-tube which carries a small groove or slit to within a short distance of the lower end. By turning the delivery-tube this groove may be made to connect with a small groove cut in the neck of the flask, thus forming a channel from the funnel to the interior of the flask. The acid for the reaction is placed in this funnel-shaped neck, with the delivery-tube so placed with respect to the two grooves as to offer a tight stopper. When the flask is connected with the absorbing system the acid is allowed to enter the flask by turning the delivery-tube so that the two channels connect. The opening is again closed and the funnel is filled with water, which serves as a cooler for the escaping gases and also as a water seal for the flask. W. H. WALKER.

KROGER FOOD STORES

RICK LINDNER HAS WORKED AT THE KROGER BAKERY ON CLEVELAND AVENUE FOR 30 years. During that time he has seen many changes, from the automation of the ovens to the introduction of fat-free food substitutes, but the most important things have remained the same. Frosting sweet goods, rolling fruit-filled

Danish pastries, and boxing premium chocolate chip cookies—these are tasks which, to ensure quality, must still be done by hand.

With 36 stores in Franklin County and a total of 104 in the Columbus marketing area, Kroger Food Stores is committed to the enduring quality of its products and its people. A national company that uses state-of-the-art technology to better serve its customers, Kroger has never lost sight of the importance of providing fresh, quality food and excellent customer service.

TODAY, THE KROGER LIMITED PARTNERSHIP I HAS A TOTAL OF 104 STORES IN THE COLUMBUS MARKETING AREA, AND IS ONE OF THE AREA'S 10 LARGEST PRIVATE EMPLOYERS.

SYMBOLS OF COMMITMENT

People are a symbol of Kroger's success—such as Helen Myers, a cashier with 50 years' experience; Len Madama, a risk manager who has been with the company for 40 years; and the numerous other longtime employees of the Columbus operation. They represent the customer service and community involvement that is rooted in the long association between Kroger and Columbus. The key to customer loyalty, Kroger knows, is the reciprocal loyalty that exists between Kroger and its employees.

Says Bruce Lucia, president of Kroger Food Stores' Columbus operations, "Our founder, Barney Kroger, always said he sold those things he would want to have for himself and his family. He took that one step further by treating people the way he wanted to be treated, and we follow that philosophy today."

Bernard Henry Kroger entered the grocery business in 1883 at the age of 23. With a partner and $722 in shared capital, he opened his first grocery in a small frontage on Cincinnati's Pearl Street. Two years

later, he had four stores. By 1902, he had 40.

Kroger's philosophy was simple: First, buy quality goods in volume to permit low prices. Second, advertise those prices. Indeed, Kroger may have been the country's first grocer to make regular use of newspaper display advertising.

DEBUT IN COLUMBUS

The first Columbus Kroger store opened in March 1907 at 494 North High Street, across from what was then the city's main train terminal. The day before opening, the Kroger store introduced itself to the community in an advertisement in the *Columbus Dispatch*: "The Kroger Grocery and Baking Co. will pursue the same methods in Columbus that have made Kroger stores in Cincinnati, Dayton, and Hamilton the most popular and successful stores. It has been our rule to handle nothing but the highest grades of food products that money can buy and sell them in quantities to suit at reduced prices to the consumer."

The store advertised prices that were unheard of at the time, including Peerless Coffee for 20 cents a pound—sold elsewhere for 40 cents a pound; select early June peas at nine cents a

THIS HISTORIC PHOTO OF DOWNTOWN COLUMBUS SHOWS THE LOCATION OF THE VERY FIRST KROGER STORE THAT OPENED IN CENTRAL OHIO. THE STORE OPENED ON MARCH 14, 1907, AND WAS LOCATED AT THE CORNER OF SPRUCE AND HIGH STREETS.

can; mackerel, a "nice fat fish," for five cents each; and, of course, Kroger's own home baked bread, selling then for two-and-a-half cents a loaf.

The advertisement went on to announce that Kroger had leased a large warehouse to supply the additional stores it intended to open in the future. By 1909, Kroger's Columbus division had nine stores. By 1917, there were a total of 59 Kroger Food Stores and a bakery in the Columbus area.

Kroger has always been committed to being a full-service grocery. Early on, the company initiated the practice of selling meat in grocery stores, so customers need not make a separate trip to a butcher shop. In 1947, Kroger pioneered the idea of selling farm-fresh eggs in its stores, establishing its own egg processing plants in growing areas. In 1978, it

established Tamarack Farms Dairy, in Newark, Ohio, as a processing site for local milk and milk products.

Since its inception, the Kroger name has been synonymous with quality. Kroger was the first grocer to establish quality assurance laboratories for product testing. In those labs, Kroger food scientists, for example, used the "shortometer" to ensure that Kroger crackers and cookies contained enough shortening to crumble at the point most customers preferred, yet would be strong enough to hold up in the package, and a "consistometer" to make sure jams and preserves had the correct consistency.

INVOLVED IN THE COMMUNITY

Kroger Food Stores makes it a priority to listen and respond to custom-

ers, establishing the first consumer research department in the industry. The company uses the results to develop new concepts, such as supervised play areas and video rental departments, for its stores nationwide.

As one of the Columbus area's 10 largest private employers, Kroger Food Stores has had a major impact on the area's economy. The company has more than 17,000 employees in the Columbus marketing area, with a payroll of $130 million a year. Each store is a significant business venture in its community, with each Kroger adding 200 to 300 jobs to the local economy.

But Kroger adds more to the community than employment and tax revenue. In 1996, the company helped area nonprofit organizations raise more than $9.5 million. It is one more way in which Columbus' largest grocer adds to the community it serves.

CLOCKWISE FROM TOP LEFT: SINCE ITS INCEPTION, THE NAME KROGER HAS BEEN SYNONYMOUS WITH QUALITY.

PEPE'S PLAYHOUSE, NAMED FOR THE KROGER COLUMBUS MASCOT PEPE THE PENGUIN, WAS INITIATED IN 1995. THE PLAYHOUSE IS A FREE, SUPERVISED CENTER WITHIN THE STORE WHERE CHILDREN AGES THREE THROUGH NINE CAN PLAY WITH TOYS, COMPUTER GAMES, VIDEOS, AND EDUCATIONAL ACTIVITIES, WHILE THEIR PARENTS SHOP WORRY-FREE.

THE KROGER HOT-AIR BALLOON IS A POPULAR ATTRACTION.

A NATIONAL COMPANY THAT EMPLOYS STATE-OF-THE-ART TECHNOLOGY TO BETTER SERVE ITS CUSTOMERS, KROGER HAS NEVER LOST SIGHT OF THE IMPORTANCE OF PROVIDING FRESH, QUALITY FOOD AND EXCELLENT CUSTOMER SERVICE.

Schottenstein Stores Corporation/ Value City Stores

Schottenstein's/Value City Department Stores and Value City Furniture were founded on one basic tenet: excellent quality at the guaranteed lowest prices. It is this belief that has turned one store, which opened in 1914, into the retail empire that it is today. ✦ While Schottenstein's/Value City Department

Schottenstein's/Value City Department Stores stocks famous store brands and designer label clothing in its many unique departments (top).

The company was founded on one basic tenet: excellent quality at the guaranteed lowest prices (bottom).

Stores and Value City Furniture may differ in the merchandise they sell, their basic philosophy is the same: Getting the deal and passing it on to the customer. Schottenstein's/ Value City Department Stores has three major ideas that form the foundation for this off-price giant: buying, manufacturing, and unique merchandising.

Buying

There are many off-price retailers in the country, but none can match the buyouts that are found at Schottenstein's/Value City Department Stores. This is true because Schottenstein's/Value City Department Stores has the strongest buying staff in the retail business and is constantly on the lookout for the hottest items.

It is the strong relationships that buyers have built with other businesses, such as Barney's and Bergdorf Goodman, that have allowed Schottenstein's/ Value City Department Stores to stock famous department store brands in its many unique departments at

prices up to 70 percent off comparable retail prices.

On any given day, customers will find these departments stocked with products bearing the labels of famous name designers. In the ladies' department, customers can find Donna Karan, Byblos, Anne Klein, and more. The men's department is overflowing with designer collection suits, including Armani, Zegna, Louis Roth, Hugo Boss, Brioni, Ralph Lauren, and others.

Clothing is only the beginning of the Schottenstein's/Value City experience. The shoe department spans 9,000 square feet, and is filled with shoppers' favorite labels, including Cole Haan, Charles David, Nine West, and all the famous athletic shoe labels.

In the jewelry department, there are Tourneau and Gucci watches, Limoges Collectibles, and Waterford Crystal. Schottenstein's/Value City Department Stores has even had buyouts on Lladro.

Every time a customer walks into a Schottenstein's/Value City Department Store, it is a different experience. The inventory is constantly changing, with new and exciting buyouts. However, one thing always remains consistent: These buyouts are always priced lower than anywhere else.

Manufacturing and Merchandising

Schottenstein's/Value City Department Stores has also started creating new lines of its own. This merchandise is similar in quality to that in specialty stores, but is sold at much

lower prices. Public Supply Company is a durable line of children's clothes in all the latest styles. U.S.A. Classics offers traditional outdoor lifestyle clothing for men and women. I.O.U. carries the latest in urban chic for teenage and young men. Montana Blue provides denim jeans for the entire family in fashionable styles.

In addition to buying and manufacturing, Schottenstein's/Value City Department Stores has recently introduced a new marketing concept: creating eye-catching areas that display home furnishings, housewares, giftware, gourmet food, sporting goods, and seasonal items. An example of this is the gourmet food department, where customers can find such items as Silver Palette dressings and sauces, coffees from around the world, Famous Biscotti, and even risotto from Italy.

VALUE CITY FURNITURE

One of the divisions that emerged from Schottenstein's/Value City Department Stores was furniture, which grew out of an increasing demand for quality furniture at a low price. Eventually, Value City Furniture was born and became its own chain of stores. Value City Furniture is the largest independently owned furniture store in the country, and currently ranks fourth on *Furniture Today*'s list of the top 100 U.S. furniture retailers.

This size creates tremendous buying power, which comes to the customer in the form of low prices and high quality. This buying power also accounts for the tremendous selection. Contributing factors to this selection are worldwide sourcing, factory direct selling, and central distribution.

Value City Furniture's buying staff combs the world for some of the most unique and exquisite accessories for the home. Customers can find hand-carved jewelry boxes from Italy, authentic collector nutcrackers from Germany, African walking sticks, and Czechoslovakian cut glass, among other items.

Value City Furniture can offer such unparalleled low prices because it manufactures many of the items

it sells, thereby cutting out the middle-man and the markups. It manufactures such items as Englander Bedding, the seventh-largest manufacturer of bedding in the United States; Kroehler Furniture, a fine line of upholstered furniture offered at many furniture retailers from coast to coast; and Roanoke, a leader in all-wood furniture.

Value City Furniture has the largest single distribution center devoted entirely to furniture in America. This means the quickest delivery and the widest selection for the customer.

Worldwide sourcing, factory direct selling, and central distribution combine to offer the Value City Furniture customer unique collections exclusive to its stores. Among these collections are the Valenza Collection®, handcrafted, 100 percent Italian leather furniture; the Passport Treasure Collection®, an exclusive line of imported gift items and collectibles; and American Signature Collection®, a selection of premium sofas, love seats, and chairs by Kroehler.

Schottenstein's/Value City Department Stores and Value City Furniture started as one entity, and now they are approaching a combined 200 stores. Historically, the growth is due to consistently providing the customer with the best-quality merchandise at the guaranteed lowest prices. This has been achieved by getting and giving the best deals. It is this history that will fuel Schottenstein's/Value City's growth into the future.

VORYS, SATER, SEYMOUR AND PEASE

GUIDED BY TRADITIONS ESTABLISHED SINCE ITS FOUNDING IN 1909, VORYS, Sater, Seymour and Pease has become the largest full-service law firm in Columbus. With 300 attorneys, Vorys was recently ranked by the *National Law Journal* as one of the largest law firms in the United States,

ranking among the top 100.

The firm's lengthy history, its deep roots in Columbus, and its place of prominence in the legal profession are evident throughout its offices at 52 East Gay Street, which has been home to the firm since 1912. Hallways and nooks located throughout the firm's offices are filled with photographs of its founders and American historical figures. In the lobby sits a bust of former President William Howard Taft, which was presented

by the sculptor Robert Ingersoll Aitken as a gift to Arthur I. Vorys, one of the firm's founders. Vorys was the eastern campaign manager for Taft's 1908 presidential campaign.

The firm's offices are located in four buildings—one of which was originally a livery stable—that were joined together by the firm over the years. While the firm traces its name and founding to 1909, its roots actually go back to the late 1800s, when John E. Sater opened a law office

in Columbus. Lowry Sater, Edward Pease, and Augustus Seymour eventually joined him. In 1909, John Sater, who was appointed as the first federal judge in Central Ohio, left the firm and was replaced by Vorys. Following in Judge Sater's footsteps, two former partners today serve on the federal bench. Judge R. Guy Cole sits on the Sixth Circuit Court of Appeals, and Judge Algernon L. Marbley is a federal district court judge in Columbus.

Many partners of the firm have left their political marks. John M. Vorys, Arthur's son, was a U.S. congressman for 20 years and later a delegate to the United Nations. Arthur I. Vorys and Arthur, his grandson, both served as superintendents of insurance for the State of Ohio. Herbert R. Brown served as an associate justice of the Ohio Supreme Court.

STRONG TRADITIONS

Reflecting on the growth and success enjoyed by Vorys, Sater, Seymour and Pease during the past nearly 90 years, the firm's leaders—which include fourth-generation family members of cofounder Vorys—cite a strong sense of continuing traditions, many of which were instituted when the founding partners established the firm.

Among its key traditions is a team approach to serving clients and mentoring lawyers. Such an approach ensures that the right lawyer is selected for the right job, and fosters stability, collegiality, and loyalty. Senior lawyers work side by side to mentor younger lawyers. Also key is the practice of treating the staff as important members of the team. When successes are achieved, it is a team victory. Clients are regarded as clients of the firm, not of individual lawyers.

VORYS, SATER, SEYMOUR AND PEASE'S EARLY LAW OFFICES WERE LOCATED ON THE THIRD FLOOR OF 52 EAST GAY STREET. THIS PHOTOGRAPH SHOWS GAY STREET CIRCA 1917.

As a result, Vorys experiences less turnover in staff and attorneys when compared with other law firms. "Keeping turnover low promotes consistent service to our clients and consistent application of the traditions and principles of the firm," notes Managing Partner Bob Werth. As proof of the positive working environment, summer law clerks and midlevel associates in recent years have rated the firm as one of the top five in the country, based on such criteria as work environment, treatment by partners, and training and guidance, according to a survey by *American Lawyer* magazine.

Vorys strives for diversity in the workplace. For example, in 1971, it was the first large firm in Central Ohio to hire a female attorney, who later became the first female partner in the area and one of the first female partners in the state. A 1995 survey showed Vorys with the second-highest number of African-American partners of the major law firms in the country.

Yet another tradition has to do with Vorys' policy of hiring partners from other firms. These lawyers initially join Vorys as counsel, not partners, to ensure that they are a good fit with the culture of the firm. "We want to look at that person and let them look at us for a while," Werth says.

A cultural tradition was established in the 1970s by James O. Seymour, son of one of the original founders and an experienced world traveler. Concerned that the firm's lawyers worked too much and traveled too little, he created the Seymour Plan to encourage them to see more of the world. The fund pays for travel abroad for associates, partners, and staff.

COMPETITIVE STRENGTHS

"The firm believes our number one strength is our outstanding lawyers," Werth states. "But we have other strengths that we are proud of. One is that the firm owns its own buildings, as opposed to residing in nearby

high-rises. This enviable position allows the firm to convert savings on rent to competitive prices and value for its clients. It also helps to foster a family environment, because the firm is the only business situated in the buildings. When you come in, you only see people you work with, as opposed to a high-rise, which is full of unassociated people," explains Werth.

Another strength for the firm is a large, diversified client base. This ensures that Vorys doesn't depend on a single client, unlike some other firms, which may have a significant percentage of their business with a single client.

When it comes to technology, Vorys is at the forefront, installing the most up-to-date communications systems designed for law firms. All offices are networked and are continually being upgraded to meet clients' needs.

The firm also places a high priority on internal growth. It is common

(FROM LEFT) ROBERT W. WERTH, MANAGING PARTNER AND CHAIRMAN OF THE EXECUTIVE COMMITTEE; SANDRA J. ANDERSON, FELLOW, AMERICAN COLLEGE OF TRIAL LAWYERS, AND FIRST WOMAN PRESIDENT OF THE COLUMBUS BAR ASSOCIATION; AND THOMAS M. TAGGART, A SENIOR LITIGATOR AND PRESIDENT OF THE OHIO STATE BAR ASSOCIATION

ARTHUR I. VORYS WAS WILLIAM HOWARD TAFT'S EASTERN CAMPAIGN MANAGER DURING THE 1908 PRESIDENTIAL CAMPAIGN.

in the legal profession for firms to grow through mergers and acquisitions, but at Vorys, all growth has been internal. This strategy helps preserve the firm's values.

Vorys maintains an emphasis on training first-year associates. In order to reinforce the team concept, first-year associates are involved in a program that exposes them to a variety of different practice areas and the firm's approach to that particular area.

Due to Vorys' quality of service; reputation for honesty, integrity, competence, and hard work; and client satisfaction, demand for the firm's service is growing rapidly. In response, the firm's four offices, located in Columbus, Cleveland, Cincinnati, and Washington, D.C., are all expanding. Werth notes that as Columbus has grown, the firm's

client base has grown, enabling the firm to grow also.

COMMITTED TO COMMUNITY AND PROFESSIONALISM

Vorys, Sater, Seymour and Pease—which has more than 600 employees, including its 300 attorneys—has contributed significantly to its hometown. Werth recalls the comment made by Webb I. Vorys, a former managing partner: "The community has been awfully good to us; we need to be good to the community." Lawyers and staff are encouraged to participate in community activities, organizations, and professional associations. The firm is a leading supporter of the local United Way, arts organizations, and a wide variety of other important civic, cultural, and charitable groups.

At one point in 1997, the presidents of both the Ohio State Bar

Association and the Columbus Bar Association (CBA) were Vorys lawyers. Partner Sandra Anderson, the first woman president of the CBA, also was the 10th Vorys partner to have served as president of the CBA.

Other professional highlights for the firm include having the first female members from Ohio elected to the American College of Trial Lawyers (ACTL) and more overall ACTL memberships than any other firm in Ohio.

Vorys is the first Ohio firm to participate in the American Bar Association's Pro Bono Challenge program. As a participant, the firm commits to pro-viding pro bono services each year equal to at least 3 percent of its billable hours. The firm also has been the recipient of the Legal Assistance Foundation award for the firm's dedication to pro bono work in Ohio.

DIVERSE CLIENTS

Clients at Vorys, Sater, Seymour and Pease are located around the world and represent a wide base of business sectors and sizes; a number are publicly traded and a number are start-up companies and individuals. The firm's clients include manufacturers, financial institutions, insurance companies and retailers.

The firm has a growing international presence, led by such clients as Boehringer Ingelheim Pharmaceuticals, Inc.; The Limited, Inc. and its subsidiaries; Honda of America Mfg., Inc.; and a number of the Japanese supply companies that moved operations to Ohio in order to serve Honda. Other recent international clients include a consortium of U.S. companies that are in the process of making a loan of equipment and materials to the Ukraine.

The firm's reputation has helped it expand its client base. "Client satisfaction is the number one factor that has enabled us to keep and attract clients," Werth says. "We do a good job for our clients, and they keep coming back. The firm has a tradition of en-

THE ORIGINAL ANNOUNCEMENT OF THE FORMING OF THE LAW FIRM READ: "JOHN E. SATER, HAVING RETIRED FROM THE FIRM OF SATER, SEYMOUR AND SATER TO BECOME UNITED STATES DISTRICT JUDGE, IS SUCCEEDED BY ARTHUR I. VORYS, FORMERLY SUPERINTENDENT OF INSURANCE OF OHIO, WHO WITH LOWRY F. SATER AND AUGUSTUS T. SEYMOUR AND EDWARD L. PEASE, HERETOFORE ASSOCIATED WITH THE FIRM, WILL CONTINUE THE PRACTICE OF LAW UNDER THE NAME OF VORYS, SATER, SEYMOUR AND PEASE, MARCH 1, 1909."

317

DISCOVER COLUMBUS

suring top quality service, and adapting to clients' needs and changes. The firm's long history is also appealing. People are comfortable with a firm that has longevity."

THE FUTURE

In the future, Vorys, Sater, Seymour and Pease plans to continue building its business by adhering to the traditions, principles, and values that have guided it throughout its successful past. On the other hand, the firm understands that it has to adapt to a continually changing environment caused by such changes as the technological revolution. By maintaining a state-of-the-art computer system, Vorys is able to rapidly communicate and exchange information with its clients through E-mail, direct networking, and customized databases.

"While we are proud of our history, we realize that technology and competitive pricing are essential to delivering the level of legal representation that our clients expect," says Werth. "We listen to our clients and are sensitive to business trends that will have an impact on them. Our formula for success has been, and will continue to be, to represent our clients and community by anticipating and addressing their concerns, and serving their best interests by providing excellent legal services at a reasonable cost."

IN ADDITION TO THE MANAGING PARTNER, MEMBERS OF THE FIRM'S EXECUTIVE COMMITTEE INCLUDE (FROM LEFT) RUSSELL M. GERTMENIAN, A SENIOR BUSINESS LAWYER; THOMAS B. RIDGLEY, FELLOW, AMERICAN COLLEGE OF TRIAL LAWYERS; AND DUKE W. THOMAS, FELLOW, AMERICAN COLLEGE OF TRIAL LAWYERS, AND RECIPIENT OF THE OHIO STATE BAR ASSOCIATION'S OHIO BAR MEDAL FOR MERITORIOUS SERVICE TO THE LEGAL COMMUNITY.

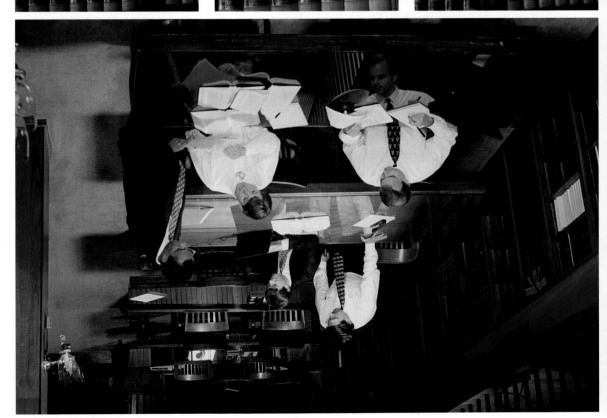

MIXING TRADITION WITH TECHNOLOGY, VORYS ATTORNEYS USE LAPTOP COMPUTERS FOR LEGAL RESEARCH, IN ADDITION TO TEXTBOOKS. THE FIRM'S LAW LIBRARY USED TO BE A HARDWARE STORE IN THE EARLY 1900S.

BURGESS & NIPLE, LIMITED

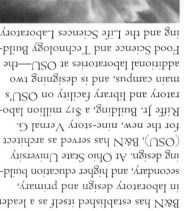

WHEN PHILIP BURGESS AND CHESTER NIPLE WENT INTO BUSINESS IN 1912, THEY each brought something to the partnership that far exceeded their education and technical expertise. Inherent in each man's character were attributes like honesty, integrity, service to the client and the community, high ethical standards, and professional excellence.

Now, more than 85 years later, the firm's architects, engineers, planners, scientists, technicians, and support staff still retain these values as fundamental to every project. Today's Burgess & Niple, Limited (B&N) takes pride in its reputation for integrity, professionalism, and quality of service for all clients, large and small.

With headquarters on Reed Road, in northwest Columbus, the firm operates offices in Ohio, Indiana, Kentucky, Arizona, and West Virginia, and employs more than 370 people, 215 of whom live and work in the Columbus area. B&N's core services include architectural, environmental, transportation, and utility infrastructure consulting. These areas will continue to be the focus for the firm during the next century.

A DIVERSE ARRAY OF CLIENTS

More than 25 architects provide a diverse range of design services for both private and public sector clients. B&N has established itself as a leader in laboratory design and primary, secondary, and higher education building design. At Ohio State University (OSU), B&N has served as architect for the new, nine-story Vernal G. Riffe Jr. Building, a $17 million laboratory and library facility on OSU's main campus, and is designing two additional laboratories at OSU—the Food Science and Technology Building and the Life Sciences Laboratory.

Many industrial and commercial clients, including Highlights for Children, Newman Technologies, Ohio Education Association, Honda of America, and Longaberger, have received design services from B&N.

Excellent bridge design, inspection, and plan review have established B&N as a leader in the field of bridge engineering. Extensive experience in bridge plan review, acquired through more than 10 years of service for the Ohio Department of Transportation, recently led to the firm's review of plans for a 2,960-foot bridge in Pusan, South Korea.

Other design projects include new primary and secondary schools in Perry and Solon, Ohio, and school renovations in Strongsville, Painesville, and Marietta, Ohio; the renovation of Hoyt Hall at Miami University; the School of Nursing, Allied Health building, and Library/Learning Center at Hocking College; and a new business school for the University of Rio Grande. Health facility projects include a major renovation project at Children's Hospital in downtown Columbus; a new medical facility in Lake County, Ohio; and a senior center in Preston County, West Virginia.

CLOCKWISE FROM LEFT: THE VERNAL G. RIFFE JR. BUILDING AT THE OHIO STATE UNIVERSITY FEATURES RESEARCH AND LIBRARY SPACE.

LAKE HOSPITAL AMBULATORY CARE CENTER IS SERVING THE NEEDS OF NORTHEAST OHIO RESIDENTS.

BURGESS & NIPLE PROVIDED ROADWAY AND BRIDGE DESIGN SERVICES FOR I-670, COLUMBUS' INNER-BELT SYSTEM.

B&N's nationally recognized bridge inspection engineers and technicians pioneered the use of rock-climbing techniques to access large bridges, buildings, and sports stadiums. Since 1980, some 240 inspections of more than 2,200 bridges in Ohio, Kentucky, West Virginia, Arizona, Oregon, Idaho, and New York, have incorporated this state-of-the-art technique.

In the area of bridge design, B&N has been involved in more than 100 prominent projects, including designs for two bridges crossing the Ohio River and the Broad Street Bridge over the Scioto River in downtown Columbus. The firm has also been heavily involved in designing the Emerald Parkway, a new roadway including two bridges through the city of Dublin in northwest Franklin County. In addition, B&N is designing the widening of twin bridges crossing the Scioto River on I-270.

Highway projects in Ohio have included major portions of the I-670 inner belt and the I-270 outer belt, as well as the I-280/Maumee River Crossing project in Toledo and I-271/I-480 improvements in Cleveland. The firm also designed $13 million in improvements to a one-mile-long corridor of High Street in downtown Columbus. Improvements included upgrades to bus lanes, vehicle lanes, sidewalks, curbs, lighting, and transit shelters.

B&N served as lead consultant for the Rickenbacker Parkway Corridor Study, which examined the poten-

tial for economic development resulting from construction of a 17-mile roadway in southern Franklin County. The firm also was the lead consultant for the Cincinnati–Northern Kentucky Northeast Corridor Major Investment Study, which examined impact assessments, environmental studies, and economic impacts of construction of a multimodal transportation corridor.

Providing environmental services and creating quality utility infrastructure systems have been hallmarks for B&N since its beginning. Signature projects include design of the Hoover Dam and Reservoir—Columbus' main water supply—and improvements to the Jackson Pike and Columbus Southerly wastewater treatment plants. B&N has provided environmental and related services to the Solid Waste Authority of Central Ohio for the closure of the model landfill. Additional clients include LTV Steel, Browning-Ferris Industries, and Ford Motor Company.

Development of the Columbus Floodwall Local Protection Project

century.

STRONG COMMUNITY TIES

While B&N maintains a strong commitment to Columbus through the projects that it designs, it also supports the community in other ways. B&N serves as host for the Columbus-area Boy Scouts of America Engineering Explorer Post, and many local art organizations display their works at B&N's headquarters. B&N has been a dedicated supporter of the Columbus Museum of Art, through the sponsorship of major exhibits and the donation of a sculpture to the museum's permanent collection. Backed by an 85-year history, a commitment to Columbus, and a strategic plan for success in the future, B&N is well poised for success in the 21st

will provide flood protection for the downtown Columbus peninsula and Franklinton areas. In addition to flood protection, benefits include attention to the aesthetics of the flood wall and recreational opportunities.

Clockwise from top left:

THE MILL RUN DEVELOPMENT NEAR HILLIARD PROVIDES COMMERCIAL AND RESIDENTIAL SPACE IN THIS FAST-GROWING AREA.

COLUMBUS' BROAD STREET BRIDGE HAS WON LOCAL, STATE, AND NATIONAL DESIGN AWARDS.

THE NEW, NINE-STORY RIFFE BUILDING IS A $17 MILLION LABORATORY AND LIBRARY FACILITY.

COLUMBUS SOUTHERLY COMPOST FACILITY SERVES THE ENVIRONMENTAL NEEDS OF FRANKLIN COUNTY.

THE OHIO STATE UNIVERSITY HOSPITALS

IN 1996, THE OHIO STATE UNIVERSITY HOSPITALS WAS RECOGNIZED AS ONE OF THE nation's top 100 hospitals by *U.S. News & World Report* for the fifth consecutive year. The pursuit of its central mission—to improve the lives and health of the people of Central and southeastern Ohio—is the guiding force in achieving this

RECOGNITION OF EXCELLENCE

The Ohio State University (OSU) Hospitals is firmly established as a world-renowned institution: it is among the elite 4 percent of hospitals in the United States to receive Accreditation with Commendation from the national accrediting agency for health care. The Hospitals' Department of Emergency Medicine was named a National Center of Excellence by the American College of Emergency Physicians in 1996. It is a designated National Center of Excellence in Women's Health as well. OSU Hospitals operates the only adult burn center in Central Ohio, and the nation's fourth-largest organ transplant program. According to *U.S. News & World Report*, it is also one of the top 10 comprehensive rehabilitation centers in the country. It was one of only three hospitals to receive the 1996 national Quality HealthCare Award by health care leaders from across America.

and numerous other recognitions of excellence.

Key to this mission is "intensive caring." Intensive caring begins with leadership, and is delivered by skilled teams of physicians, nurses, and other health professionals, who collaborate on patient care.

The extremely high quality, personalized care provided by the Hospitals' staff belies the organization's great size. In 1995-1996, it maintained 619 staffed beds, admitted 26,422 patients, was the site of 3,282 births, treated 45,429 emergency room visits, and saw more than 227,000 outpatients in nearly a dozen community locations. In all, it employs more than 4,200 persons, and serves more than 800 physicians on its medical staff.

A partner in improving the health of the community, OSU Hospitals offers such collaborative programs as Health for Life, community classes, Senior Health Services, Heart Partners health risk assessment screening, and Consumer and Corporate Health Education and Wellness Services.

Speaking on the institution's future, R. Reed Fraley, executive director of University Hospitals, says, "I am confident in promising . . . that we will continue to ask ourselves the tough questions, we will continue our commitment to our mission, and we will continue to serve as a resource for our community. That's what intensive caring at The Ohio State University Hospitals is all about."

THE OHIO STATE UNIVERSITY MEDICAL CENTER INCLUDES UNIVERSITY HOSPITALS, THE JAMES CANCER HOSPITAL, AND THE OSU COLLEGE OF MEDICINE (LEFT).

THE PHYSICIANS AND STAFF OF UNIVERSITY HOSPITALS EXTEND THEIR EXPERTISE TO FAMILIES THROUGHOUT CENTRAL OHIO WITHIN A GROWING NETWORK OF SPECIALTY CLINICS AND AFFILIATED PRIMARY CARE PHYSICIAN OFFICES NOW IN MORE THAN 30 LOCATIONS (RIGHT).

Arthur G. James Cancer Hospital and Research Institute

T HE OHIO STATE UNIVERSITY'S COMPREHENSIVE CANCER CENTER—ARTHUR G. James Cancer Hospital and Research Institute—has achieved a national and international reputation. The James is one of only nine freestanding cancer hospitals in the United States, and the only one located in the Midwest. In addition, it is one of just 31 National Cancer Institute-designated Comprehensive Cancer Centers in the nation, and the only one in Ohio. This recognition allows The James to offer advanced diagnostic programs and the latest treatment options, clinical trials, and drug therapies to its patients.

Patient Care at The James

The James achieves an important balance between compassionate and personal care at the bedside, and the latest medical treatments and technologies.

The James' comprehensive approach to care is conducted by skilled professionals in multidisciplinary health care teams. This team approach allows patients to benefit from the experience and knowledge of a diverse group of specialists—physicians, nurses, researchers, rehabilitation therapists, dietitians, psychologists, and social workers. Patients, families, and referring physicians are vital links in this circle of care.

The staff and physicians at The James strive to balance the physical aspects of cancer care with an appreciation for the psychological, social, and emotional dynamics of health and wellness. By combining pioneering research, aggressive treatment, and a compassionate perspective, its health care teams ensure that patients receive the most advanced care available.

Research Initiatives at The James

Research is a fundamental part of the mission and heritage of The James. Through research, the latest advances in cancer prevention, detection, and treatment have dramatically improved survival rates, as well as the quality of life, for cancer patients at The James and for people everywhere.

Researchers are a vital part of The James' team of caregivers. At The James, the close collaboration between research and patient care brings the study of cancer directly to the bedside. In that way, research findings can be rapidly translated into high-quality patient care.

In basic, clinical, and applied research, The James' reputation for quality and its status as a part of The Ohio State University have attracted some of the country's leading oncology researchers. Today, the Comprehensive Cancer Center's interdisciplinary programs in clinical and basic research involve more than 200 researchers within 11 colleges at Ohio State.

Cancer Education at The James

The cancer prevention and education programs at The James are evidence of its commitment to changing high-risk behaviors and promoting early detection of cancer. In the United States alone, 400,000 individuals die each year of tobacco-related cancers. And, one out of every eight women will develop breast cancer. In Ohio, there are approximately 62,000 new cancer cases each year.

Since its founding in 1990, The James has conducted a high-profile, ambitious program aimed at reducing

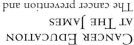

the incidence of cancer in Ohio and beyond. Its efforts to reach health care consumers range from cancer screenings and a toll-free telephone information service to seminars, lectures, and videotape information programs.

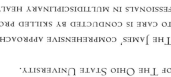

Clockwise from top:

Research is a fundamental part of the mission and heritage of the Arthur G. James Cancer Hospital and Research Institute.

The James is located on the campus of The Ohio State University.

The James' comprehensive approach to care is conducted by skilled professionals in multidisciplinary health care teams.

WILLIS CORROON CORPORATION OF OHIO

A LL BUSINESSES, LARGE AND SMALL, ARE EXPOSED TO A CERTAIN AMOUNT OF RISK inherent in their day-to-day operations. To remain successful, organizations must effectively manage and reduce the risks they face. Willis Corroon Corporation of Ohio, one of the largest commercial insurance brokers in Columbus, helps organizations limit their exposure to risk through customized risk management solutions, insurance expertise, and specialized consulting services.

"In today's highly competitive, increasingly demanding marketplace, the last thing a company wants to worry about is liability," CEO Gary L. Friedhoff says. "We at Willis Corroon take on that burden, so our clients in Central Ohio can remain focused on the business of doing business."

LONGTIME NEIGHBOR WITH GLOBAL TIES

Willis Corroon Corporation of Ohio has been doing business in Columbus for 75 years, dating back to 1922 with the founding of the Atkinson Dauksch Agency. In 1977, Corroon and Black, a large New York insurance firm, merged with Atkinson Dauksch. Thirteen years later in 1990, Willis Corroon, plc, was formed through the merger of Willis Faber Dumas, a London-based provider of insurance, reinsurance, and human resource consultative services worldwide, and

Corroon & Black, which offered similar services primarily in the United States. Today, Willis Corroon is the fourth-largest insurance services firm in the world, has revenues in excess of $1 billion, and employs 9,500 insurance professionals in 75 countries.

Willis Corroon Corporation of Ohio is a wholly owned subsidiary of Willis Corroon, plc. As such, the local office combines its strong tradition in Columbus with ties to its global parent to serve clients both with the resources of a giant and the sensitivity of a concerned neighbor.

SUCCESSFUL COMBINATION

Risk management and education are crucial tasks for the modern corporation. Loss of property, loss of life, extensive legal liability—these and other consequences can follow upon inadequate provision for risk. Through its Columbus office, Willis Corroon works with each client to develop the management tools that minimize loss, thus making invest-ment in risk management a profit-making activity, not an expense.

Willis Corroon takes a unique approach to this challenge. Unusual in the insurance industry, it combines experts in loss control and experts in claims management into a single team of quality risk management specialists. This combination is known as Integrated Management Services.

"Our Integrated Management Services allows professionals from both ends of the spectrum to work together, sharing information and ideas, to provide clients a clear view of their exposures and the effective-ness of their management programs," says Friedhoff. "The end result is exceptional, comprehensive service for our clients."

WILLIS CORROON EXPERTISE

Willis Corroon of Ohio uses the Integrated Management Services approach and its professional staff's specialized knowledge and expertise to serve clients in four areas of concentration: construction/environmen-tal, risk management/commercial, institutions, and employee benefits.

Willis Corroon leads the indus-try in construction insurance and surety bonding. With a thorough understanding of the construction industry, Willis Corroon's construc-tion team offers contractors creative risk management and surety programs designed to grow their revenues and/or reduce costs.

CEO GARY L. FRIEDHOFF

MEMBERS OF WILLIS CORROON'S EXECU-TIVE STAFF WORK TOGETHER TO ENSURE THAT THEIR CLIENTS RECEIVE THE HIGH-EST-QUALITY SERVICE IN THE INDUSTRY.

▶ JOHN P. TUPPER

▶ JOHN P. TUPPER

Willis Corroon's experts in environmental risk and regulation work hand in hand with construction specialists. Most construction sites carry the potential for hazardous wastes; Willis Corroon provides specific coverages to handle any removal or remediation needs.

The risk management/commercial unit offers risk management services to medium- and large-sized businesses that require more than standard insurance plans. Willis Corroon's risk consultants identify and analyze exposures, help minimize risks, design and arrange necessary insurance protection, and provide financial and actuarial consultation on a continuing basis.

Colleges and universities historically have been subject to the fluctuations and inconsistencies of the property and casualty insurance marketplace. Willis Corroon of Ohio offers a purchasing plan providing a stable insurance marketplace from which educational institutions can shop for their needs. Members are grouped together to provide greater buying power in negotiating broader coverages and competitive premiums. Similarly, Willis Corroon offers government agencies cost-effective risk management and insurance programs tailored to their needs.

Willis Corroon has a long, successful record in its employee benefits operation. Its team of experienced professionals has the sophistication to design employee benefit programs that balance employee welfare with a company's own financial health. Willis Corroon analyzes every aspect of a company's benefits programs, evaluates available alternatives, and designs appropriate incentives to maximize efficiencies within the program.

Client Focused, Quality Driven

In all its work, Willis Corroon takes a client-centered approach to quality. In doing so, it draws upon a professional staff experienced in providing

companies with quality programs and services that minimize their particular risk exposures while controlling their costs.

Willis Corroon's success lies in its commitment to providing its clients with exceptional value and innovative, customized solutions to their risk management and insurance problems. With Willis Corroon, businesses are confident their assets are protected and their exposures are understood. Providing this kind of peace of mind is what has made Willis Corroon one of the leading brokers in Columbus.

Columbus Community Hospital is one of the many local companies that rely on the expertise of Willis Corroon's Employee Benefits staff (right).

Many colleges and universities enjoy Willis Corroon's consolidated insurance programs for educational institutions (left).

Willis Corroon leads the industry in construction insurance and surety bonding for projects such as the construction of the Rock and Roll Hall of Fame in Cleveland (shown at left).

NewsRadio 610 WTVN

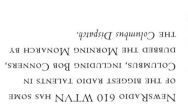

WHEN CENTRAL OHIOANS WANT THE MOST RECENT UPDATES ON A BREAKING news story, they don't have to wait for a television newscast or their morning newspaper to get the latest details. They simply tune into NewsRadio 610 WTVN-AM, the only station in the area committed to news and information.

THE BEST OF NEWS AND TALK RADIO

In addition to news, WTVN represents the voice of Central Ohio, where talk show programs give listeners an open forum to speak their views and opinions on a variety of topics. The station also carries the nation's leading syndicated talk shows, including such icons as Dr. Laura Schlesinger, Rush Limbaugh, Dr. Dean Edell, and Paul Harvey, the nation's number one newscast commentator.

What listeners don't tune in for is music. The station gradually eliminated music from its broadcast over a period of years. In 1977, the station dropped music from evenings, switching to an all-talk format during those midday hours. In 1993, midday music was replaced with Limbaugh's show. By early 1997, the station had dropped music entirely.

"WTVN really hasn't changed over the years, it's evolved," says John Potter, vice president and general manager of the station, which is owned by Jacor Communications Inc. Other Jacor stations in Columbus include WLVQ-FM, Q-FM-96, WHOK-FM, K95.5, WHQK-FM, 105.7, WZAZ-FM, Channel Z, and WAZU-FM, The Big Wazoo.

All-talk shows and news represent an expensive format, Potter acknowledges, and not one that is an option for many stations. Yet it's just one of the many characteristics that make 610 WTVN stand out from the competition. Other factors that set it apart from its competitors include the largest coverage area of any Columbus radio station, covering most of the state of Ohio, and its ownership by Jacor Communications, one of the nation's leading owners and operators of radio stations. In addition to acquiring radio stations around the country, the Cincinnati-based parent company is purchas-

the Columbus Dispatch. Enhancing its news coverage is the station's affiliation with the ABC radio network, Associated Press, and ESPN radio.

NewsRadio 610 WTVN, which celebrated 75 years on the air in 1997, was named the outstanding radio news operation in the state of Ohio by the Associated Press in 1996 and 1997. In the last decade, the station has received 100 major news awards.

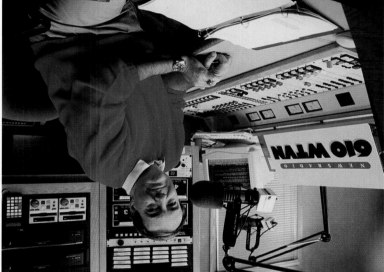

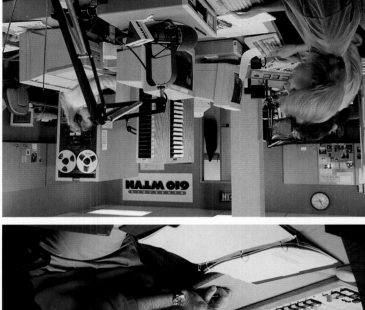

That commitment has been a hallmark of the station since its founding in 1922, and it's stronger than ever today. Known as the "news source," 610 WTVN has the largest news staff of any radio station in the state; its own traffic reporters, meteorologists, and weather radar in the studio; and some of the biggest radio talents in Columbus, including Bob Conners, dubbed the Morning Monarch by

NewsRadio 610 WTVN has some of the biggest radio talents in Columbus, including Bob Conners, dubbed the Morning Monarch by the Columbus Dispatch.

610 WTVN has the largest news staff of any radio station in the state, with its own traffic reporters, meteorologists, and weather radar in the studio.

THE STATION SUPPORTS MANY COMMUNITY ORGANIZATIONS, INCLUDING OHIO STATE UNIVERSITY ATHLETIC PROGRAMS. HERE, FANS GATHER FOR ONE OF 610 WTVN's "HINEYGATE" PARTIES PRECEDING AN OHIO STATE FOOTBALL GAME.

NEWSRADIO 610 WTVN WAS NAMED THE OUTSTANDING RADIO NEWS OPERATION IN THE STATE OF OHIO BY THE ASSOCIATED PRESS IN 1996 AND 1997.

ing syndicated networks, including the company that produces Rush Limbaugh's show. Such ownership ensures that Jacor stations will have access to the nation's top syndicated programs.

Jacor also has its own jingle/commercial production division. If a radio station needs a commercial for a local advertiser, it can tap into the service. To assist with communications and data transfer among its radio stations nationwide, Jacor recently purchased a satellite communications company. Besides enjoying the resources associated with a large organization, Jacor stations also enjoy a great deal of autonomy. The parent company gives local management free rein in developing programming that fits the needs of the local marketplace.

Because of its success, 610 WTVN has been able to attract top talent to its station and serves as a training ground for future general managers. The most successful radio station in Pittsburgh is managed by WTVN's former general sales manager, and several other general managers for major radio stations nationwide came from WTVN.

The station's professional affiliations include membership in the National Association of Broadcasters, Ohio Association of Broadcasters, and Radio Advertising Bureau.

CONTRIBUTING TO THE COMMUNITY

NewsRadio 610 WTVN is proud of its community involvement, which includes Secret Santa, a charity program started by 610 WTVN nearly 40 years ago. Through the program, 610 WTVN and sister stations generate cash to purchase toys for orphans and needy children. In 1997, thanks to Secret Santa, 8,400 children in Central Ohio received toys. The station also supports many other organizations, including Ohio State University athletic programs.

Originally founded in Columbus as WBAV, the station became WAIU

in the mid-1920s when the American Insurance Union, the nation's largest insurance company at the time, wanted to have its own radio voice. WAIU was broadcast from the American Insurance Union Citadel, now called the LeVeque Tower. WAIU soon became know for its "news bulletins at once."

In the future, 610 WTVN plans to continue to provide the highest quality of information and entertainment to Columbus listeners; provide the highest quality of advertising opportunities to the advertising community; and give employees the opportunity to succeed at the highest level of their abilities.

RANCO NORTH AMERICA

RANCO NORTH AMERICA BEGAN IN 1913, WHEN AN OHIO UNIVERSITY ENGINEERING graduate, E.C. Raney, founded the Automatic Reclosing Circuit Breaker Company. Raney's circuit breaker corrected dangerous short circuits that occurred in coal mines, steel mills, interurban railways, and oceangoing vessels. The com-pany drew its name from a product that—like many later Ranco offer-ings—made life simpler, safer, and easier.

When the icebox gave way to mechanical refrigeration in the mid-1920s, Raney introduced the world's first inexpensive household refrigera-tion control. By the end of World War II, any car with a fresh-air heat-ing system used a Ranco control. In the mid-1980s, Ranco extended its technological leadership in the heat-pump control market, developing the first microprocessor-based, electronic demand defrost control.

Today, Ranco North America is part of the HVACR group of Siebe Plc., a British-based organiza-tion with annual sales of more than $4 billion and strong market positions in products ranging from life support and safety equipment to appliance and process control devices. Through Siebe, Ranco can provide customers with partnerships that offer global expertise.

STANDARD FOR EXCELLENCE

Ranco designs and manufactures an extensive range of mechanical and electronic controls for three major markets: residential heating and air conditioning, commercial refrigera-tion, and automotive heating and air conditioning. Since its founding, the company has made more than a billion controls, and many Ranco products set the standard for excellence. Ranco is the world leader in reversing valves—the heart of the heat pump—and a leading producer of time controls. Ranco's K series of temperature con-trols is used by home appliance and commercial equipment manufacturers in more than 68 countries.

Ranco's company headquarters is northwest of Columbus in Plain City, the site of its 220,000-square-foot manufacturing facility as well.

With plants in Toronto, Brownsville, and Matamoros, as well as in Two Rivers, Wisconsin, company employ-ment totals nearly 2,000. Ranco is international; the company began ex-porting its products in 1922, initiated manufacturing in Europe in 1950, and today does business from Beijing to Boston and from Miami to Malaysia. For more than 80 years, Ranco has been an innovator and a leader in its field. Looking to the future, John Reid, Siebe HVACR president, states, "To compete in today's global market-place, we must redouble our efforts to become partners with our customers, getting close enough to understand how we can work together and achieve our mutual goals. We must aggressively pursue new product development, quality improvements, and reduced delivery lead times to be considered worthy of a partnership role and to provide true value to our customers." It is a goal that promises Ranco North America's continued success for many years to come.

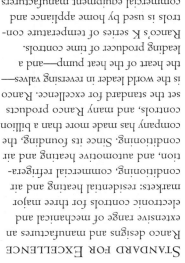

RANCO NORTH AMERICA MANUFACTURES A WIDE RANGE OF ELECTROMECHANICAL AND ELECTRONIC PRODUCTS.

RANCO NORTH AMERICA INCORPORATES LASER WELDING TECHNOLOGY IN THE MANUFACTURE OF SOME OF ITS PRODUCTS.

RANCO NORTH AMERICA'S COMPANY HEADQUARTERS IS NORTHWEST OF COLUM-BUS IN PLAIN CITY, THE SITE OF ITS 220,000-SQUARE-FOOT MANUFACTURING FACILITY AS WELL.

1926-1969

1926	T.G. BANKS SPECIAL PROJECTS DIVISION BANKS CARBONE CONSTRUCTION COMPANY
1926	NATIONWIDE INSURANCE ENTERPRISE
1928	MOTORISTS MUTUAL INSURANCE CO.
1929	BATTELLE
1929	BORDEN, INC.
1934	BIG BEAR STORES COMPANY
1934	WHITE CASTLE SYSTEM, INC.
1940	DOCTORS HOSPITAL
1946	TECHNEGLAS INC.
1947	CRANE PLASTICS
1947	NORSE DAIRY SYSTEMS
1951	COLUMBUS SYMPHONY ORCHESTRA
1951	UNITED MCGILL CORPORATION
1955	WORTHINGTON INDUSTRIES
1957	G.E. SUPERABRASIVES
1957	MADDOX-NBD, INC.
1960	McDONALD'S CORPORATION
1961	ALLIED MINERAL PRODUCTS, INC
1963	ARC INDUSTRIES, INC.
1963	LIMITED, INC.
1964	EXECUTIVE JET
1964	ISP FINE CHEMICALS INC.
1965	LIEBERT CORPORATION
1967	CONSOLIDATED STORES CORPORATION
1967	OCLC ONLINE COMPUTER LIBRARY CENTER, INC.
1968	ANHEUSER-BUSCH, INC.
1968	ATS OHIO, INC.
1968	LAKE SHORE CRYOTRONICS, INC.
1968	OLSTEN CENTRAL OHIO
1969	CHARLES PENZONE, INC./GRAND SALONS AND DAY SPAS
1969	SHONAC CORPORATION

T.G. BANKS SPECIAL PROJECTS DIVISION/
BANKS CARBONE CONSTRUCTION COMPANY

"I HAVE BEEN IN CONSTRUCTION ALL MY LIFE," SAYS T.G. BANKS, CHAIRMAN OF T.G. BANKS Special Projects Division. He pauses, and then adds, "actually, longer than that." His father was in the construction business for 51 years, and from the time Banks was 14, he was working for his father in the construction industry. Although doing construction work was not the 14-year-old's first choice of what to do with his summer vacation, the work was an apprenticeship that taught him much about construction. Says Banks, "I was brought up with the roots of quality, value, and service."

Today, Banks can draw upon his years of experience in construction and apply them to the two firms with which he is associated: Banks Carbone Construction Company and T.G. Banks Special Projects Division, which share common ownership. Banks Carbone handles large construction, construction management, and general contracting projects. In 1995, the company worked on projects totaling $74 million, earning it a ranking as the seventh-largest construction company in the Columbus area. Banks Carbone is also one of the area's largest minority-owned businesses in any field. Meanwhile, T.G. Banks Special Projects Division handles smaller projects, particularly renovations and new commercial projects.

While the two companies' tasks vary, many of the same considerations apply. "People want to get a good project for their money," Banks states. "Beyond that, they want to work with someone they feel they can trust, and who cares about both them and their project."

NATIONAL RECOGNITION
By the end of 1996, T.G. Banks Special Projects, formed in 1993 with T.G. Banks as president, had completed 73 projects, one of which brought the company's work to the attention of readers of *House Beautiful* and *The Remodeled Home* magazines. The project concerned a Columbus couple whose home lacked a great room that suited the interests of their six-member family. *House Beautiful* wrote, "So they turned to a local architect, and builder T.G. Banks, outlining their requirements: more elbowroom for their family—without sacrificing the charm of the 30-year-old house. The result is a family room that flows into the new kitchen and breakfast area."

That was not the first recognition the company had gained. Along with other honors, T.G. Banks Special Projects received the 1994 Craftsmanship of the Year award from the Building Industry Association of Central Ohio for one of its residential projects.

Similar standards are set by the Banks Carbone Construction Company, which handles new construction, renovations, and extensive restorations. In all its work, Banks Carbone structures its resources to meet the most demanding quality, cost, and time specifications.

HELPING TO SHAPE COLUMBUS
On a local level, Banks Carbone is involved with several construction projects that are changing the shape

T.G. BANKS, CHAIRMAN OF T.G. BANKS SPECIAL PROJECTS DIVISION

BANKS CAN DRAW UPON HIS YEARS OF EXPERIENCE IN CONSTRUCTION AND APPLY THEM TO THE TWO FIRMS WITH WHICH HE IS ASSOCIATED: BANKS CARBONE CONSTRUCTION COMPANY AND T.G. BANKS SPECIAL PROJECTS DIVISION, WHICH SHARE COMMON OWNERSHIP.

of Columbus. The company is a member of the construction management team for the new Ohio State University Arena—a $75 million project that includes a 20,000-seat arena for basketball and ice hockey. For this project, Banks Carbone has provided estimating services, value engineering, construction administration, quality assurance, project scheduling, and project controls. Also at Ohio State, the company is providing estimating services, value engineering, construction administration, quality assurance, project scheduling, and project controls for the new, $84 million Max M. Fisher College of Business building.

Banks Carbone is playing a similar role in the even larger, $120 million Hilltop Project. This venture is creating two buildings—each totaling 350,000 square feet—for the Ohio Department of Transportation and the Ohio Department of Public Safety.

On these and similar projects, Banks Carbone Construction Company operates through an integrated project team that ensures the project is completed on time and within budget.

THREE GENERATIONS OF EXPERIENCE

The roots of Banks Carbone can be traced back to 1926. In the three generations since its founding, the company has built a reputation for excellence in quality, craftsmanship, and service. Each decade brought new circumstances—new client needs and new techniques for construction and management. And Banks Carbone's management has kept pace both with the evolving requirements of the construction industry and with emerging technologies and management systems.

During its years in business, Banks Carbone has gained expertise in all phases of commercial, industrial, and institutional construction. Unlike many construction firms today, Banks Carbone principals take a hands-on approach to each project. They work with owners and architects in defining project specifications and scheduling, then provide supervision of both the operational and financial aspects of each project.

Throughout its history, Banks Carbone has received numerous awards for craftsmanship in applications ranging from new construction to extensive restoration/renovation projects. In each instance, Banks Carbone's blend of craftsmanship and technology has provided it with the continuing ability to answer a client's quality, efficiency, and cost-effectiveness goals.

According to Banks, what differentiates Banks Carbone Construction Company and T.G. Banks Special Projects from firms with similar interests is their ability to solve problems. "On any project," he says, "there is a potential for problems. You need the ability to resolve them. Often, it's a people-managing task. But regardless, you have to face challenges head on, meet them, and proceed."

ATIONWIDE INSURANCE ENTERPRISE—AS MUCH A PART OF COLUMBUS AS football in the fall—is a Fortune 500 company whose hallmark is providing leadership through change. ✳ Nationwide is one of the United States' leading insurers; its 1996 assets of $71 billion rank it among the country's

50 largest corporations. Nationwide provides financial service solutions for life's uncertainties: auto, home owner's, and life insurance; health and commercial insurance; and long-term savings products like annuities, mutual funds, and deferred compensation programs. The company has nearly 14 million policies in force, and its activities require the efforts of nearly 28,000 employees and 4,300 agents, as well as thousands of broker/dealers, financial planners, and registered representatives.

Founded in Columbus in 1926, Nationwide has an enormous presence in the Discovery City—one that will be enlarged further following Nationwide's decision, in mid-1997, to provide 90 percent of the financing needed to construct a downtown arena. The arena, to be located near the site of the old Ohio Penitentiary, is intended to be home to a National Hockey League team.

MASTERING THE NEEDS OF CHANGE

The arena for Nationwide's own range of activities is one characterized by continuing change—in customer needs, technology, and the marketplace. "Nationwide embraces change," states Chairman and CEO Dimon R. McFerson.

ONE NATIONWIDE PLAZA IS THE LOCATION OF THE NATIONWIDE INSURANCE ENTERPRISE CORPORATE HEADQUARTERS.

For example, most Americans under the age of 40 don't believe that Social Security will adequately provide for their retirement needs in the future. In response, Nationwide is offering investment solutions tailored to individual financial needs.

Additionally, as more customers have greater access to technology, the demand for additional services will increase. And the marketplace is changing. Says McFerson, "We are convinced that the long-term winning formula will be composed of

superior service, low cost, and rapid delivery of products that match our customers' needs."

Nationwide is utilizing this technological revolution to achieve these goals. For example, it is now possible for customers of auto, home owner's, commercial, and variable annuity products to contact a Nationwide representative or to access their accounts around-the-clock.

Today, the distinction among insurance companies, banks, and other financial institutions has blurred; in

fact, the rise of the global marketplace is blurring the distinction of national boundaries. And Nationwide is staking its claim in that global market. Through its Neckura subsidiary, Nationwide operates in Europe and, through reinsurance treaties, lends financial strength to insurers in more than 40 countries. In the years ahead, Nationwide plans to expand its presence abroad.

In these actions, Nationwide proceeds from an extremely sound financial base. The company carries the prestigious A+ rating from A.M. Best, and remains steadfast in its commitment to ensure the security of its customers' assets and savings.

An Advocate for Improvement

Nationwide does more than respond to change—it drives it, acting as an advocate for industry issues. Early in the national debate on the subject, Nationwide—believing no alternative was adequate to the task—announced the need for some form of federal health insurance for the elderly. Today, the company is the Medicare Part B administrator for 2 million residents of Ohio and West Virginia. Nationwide provides this service— and has done so since Medicare was enacted in 1966—on a cost-only basis.

Nationwide has long been an advocate of highway safety. On such matters as decreased highway speed limits, drunken driving, and air bag and seat belt use, Nationwide has been a leader in campaigning to save property and protect lives.

Nationwide is also an innovator— in its response to customer needs, its efforts to capitalize on technological change, and its advocacy of steps to improve health and safety. Promises McFerson, "We will continue to move with urgency to meet our competitive and market challenges. Our customers are expecting us to serve them in a variety of ways, and we must meet their requests."

A Varied Enterprise

Nationwide Insurance Enterprise conducts its activities through a variety of business organizations. Nationwide Financial Services, Inc. (NFS) and its primary subsidiary, Nationwide Life Insurance Company, provide an increasingly sophisticated array of customized solutions for financial needs. Currently, customers have dozens of investment options, including mutual funds managed by well-known fund houses.

Through Nationwide Property and Casualty Companies, Nation-

wide is the country's fourth-largest auto insurer and sixth-largest property insurer. In these activities, Nationwide has an enormous capacity to focus resources at the point of need—three days after Hurricane Fran struck North Carolina in 1996, Nationwide had more than 350 claims representatives and other professionals at the scene addressing the needs of those affected by the disaster.

That same concern shown for large-scale needs is directed to the individual's needs. Nationwide is recognized as providing best-in-the-business claims response, and plans to expand its role in urban markets through the opening of 12 sales/service centers.

Nationwide Insurance Enterprise includes a number of affiliate organizations—including GatesMcDonald, Wausau Insurance, and Scottsdale Insurance Company—each with its claim to distinction. GatesMcDonald is the nation's largest provider of unemployment and worker's compensation cost-control service. Serving

Dimon R. McFerson, Nationwide Insurance Enterprise chairman and chief executive officer (top)

Nationwide employees lend their elbow grease during the annual Community Care Day sponsored by the local United Way (bottom).

▲ JESSE CABUNGCAL

local and national employers, it provides the expertise to optimize each client's cost control of risk and benefit programs. Wausau Insurance, based in Wausau, Wisconsin, has pioneered managed health care in employee benefits. It is one of a very few property insurers capable of engineering highly protected coverages with its professional fire protection consultations, superior fire protection consultants, and fire protection laboratory. Scottsdale Insurance Company headquartered in Scottsdale, Arizona, is the country's second-largest excess and surplus lines insurer.

Other Nationwide units include Nationwide Advisory Services, Inc., a mutual fund organization; the Public Employees Benefit Services Corporation, the country's foremost marketer and administrator of deferred compensation plans for public employees; and Nationwide Communications, which owns and operates radio stations in eight markets throughout the country. In Columbus, Nationwide Communications owns and operates WNCI 97.9-FM, WCOL 92.3-FM, and WFII 1230-AM, broadcasting from Nationwide Plaza studios.

Calling Columbus Home

However far-flung its activities, Nationwide has always found its home in Columbus. Indeed, the company's headquarters has never strayed more than a few blocks from its first location—at 199 East Gay Street in the city's downtown. For some years, Nationwide's offices were in a converted mansion on East Broad, but in 1936, the company moved back downtown to 246 North High Street.

Nationwide began with a reasonable supposition and a small core of individuals who shared it. The supposition was that farmers who drove primarily on lightly traveled rural roads had fewer traffic crashes than persons who lived in cities—and thus merited lower insurance rates. Acting on that belief, organizers established the Farm Bureau Mutual Automobile Insurance Company on December 17, 1925, with three employees.

Within a few months, 1,000 policyholders had signed up, receiving well below prevailing rates. Nationwide soon spread beyond its original customer base of farmers and its original marketing territory of Ohio. By 1928, the company was operating

in the rural areas of West Virginia, Maryland, Delaware, Vermont, and North Carolina. By 1931, it had expanded to small towns. Three years later, Nationwide was selling its policies in cities. The product line also expanded, adding fire insurance in 1934.

The influence of Nationwide is reflected on the face of Columbus. Beginning in 1953 with Lincoln Village, Central Ohio's first planned-housing community, Nationwide has financed a series of local housing developments. These include Annehurst Village, a housing development in Westerville, started in 1964, and Green Meadows Village, begun in 1979 near Route 23 north of I-270. With the John W. Galbreath Company, Nationwide in the 1960s participated in the city's two largest urban renewal efforts, the 53-acre Market-Mohawk business section in downtown Columbus and the 47-acre Thurber Village development, immediately northeast of downtown.

Today, the Nationwide Plaza complex anchors the north end of Columbus' downtown, which was a blighted area until the company sparked a revitalization in 1974 by starting to build the city's largest office

McFERSON SHOWS HOW TO PROPERLY BUCKLE A CHILD CAR SAFETY SEAT DURING A NEWS CONFERENCE HELD TO PROMOTE THE PROPER USE OF THE SEATS.

building. Today, the plaza stands as evidence of the city's rebuilding and of Nationwide's contribution to that renaissance.

Nationwide Plaza consists of three separate towers of 40, 18, and 27 stories—a total of 2.3 million square feet. The Atrium, opened in 1989, is a focal point of the beauty in downtown Columbus, containing a tropical garden of thousands of exotic plantings, cascading waterfalls, peaceful pools, and a meandering stream.

Nationwide's size in Columbus extends beyond the prominence of Nationwide Plaza. The company is Central Ohio's largest private employer; its 8,500 Columbus employees share a payroll that exceeds $325 million. Financial impact extends beyond payroll: The company generates a cash flow of more than $22 billion that circulates through local banks.

A GENEROUS CITIZEN

Nationwide has played a notable role in support of local charities. In 1996, Nationwide employees contributed

$2 million to the United Way of Franklin County, an amount matched by the corporation. In addition, Nationwide's corporate blood donor bank provides 11 percent of Central Ohio's blood supply. Nationwide and its employees have also acted on behalf of the hungry: In one recent year, company employees donated nearly 350,000 meals to Franklin County's Operation Feed campaign, believed to be the largest corporate food campaign in the United States.

In 1997, Nationwide invested $20 million toward meeting the housing needs of the nation's low-income citizens. The investment, administered by Neighborhood Housing Services of America (NHSA), will be used to upgrade neighborhoods and increase home ownership in target areas.

Nationwide is also playing a leadership role in the planned relocation of the downtown science museum, Center of Science and Industry (COSI), where McFerson serves as the board chairman. The Nationwide Insurance

Enterprise Foundation has pledged $2.5 million to the creation of *Planet Ocean*, an interactive aquatic exhibit. In addition, Nationwide is cosponsor for the annual Red, White & Boom! Fourth of July event, which attracts 500,000 to the downtown area for what is billed as the Midwest's largest fireworks display.

In recognition of these and other such activities, McFerson was named the first recipient of the Greater Columbus Humanitarian of the Year award, presented at a banquet whose keynote speaker was Elizabeth Dole, president of the American Red Cross. He also was honored in 1997 with the Tree of Life Award from the National Jewish Fund for exemplary leadership and humanitarian service.

Nationwide Insurance Enterprise's commitment to community is equaled only by its commitment to customer service, the very reason the company has become an unparalleled success, and the reason it will continue to influence and protect lives for many years to come.

SOME 4,000 PEOPLE CELEBRATED IN FRONT OF NATIONWIDE'S HEADQUARTERS IN JUNE 1997 AFTER HEARING THE ANNOUNCEMENT THAT THE CITY WILL GET A NATIONAL HOCKEY LEAGUE FRANCHISE. THE TEAM WILL PLAY IN AN ARENA THAT NATIONWIDE WILL HELP BUILD.

The Motorists Mutual-American Hardware Insurance Group

ESTABLISHED IN 1928, MOTORISTS MUTUAL INSURANCE COMPANY WAS FORMED TO provide coverage for the growing number of automobiles that were beginning to dot the American landscape. In 1929 alone, more than 5 million vehicles were manufactured—by comparison, in 1898, only 200 were manufactured.

At the end of Motorists' first year, it had 48 policyholders, company assets of $14,956, and a surplus of $13,596.

Motorists grew along with the automobile industry, becoming a regional company doing business in Ohio, Indiana, Kentucky, Pennsylvania, and West Virginia. But in the mid-1980s, Motorists put a strategy into place that would ensure even greater growth than in the past.

The plan included growing its financial strength over a period of years, and the company's surplus surpassed the $300 million mark in 1997. An affiliation with American Hardware Insurance Group in 1993 created the opportunity for expansion into new territories and set the stage for the company to fulfill its growth mission. Like Motorists, American Hardware had a long history, tracing its founding to 1899 in Minneapolis. And although American Hardware was a financially troubled company, it had licenses in 48 states and did business in 32 states.

Differences in how the two insurers' products were marketed also presented opportunities. American Hardware sells its products through 115 employee sales representatives, while Motorists sells its products through a network of more than 2,800 independent insurance agents.

Today, the Motorists Mutual-American Hardware Insurance Group includes six companies: Motorists Mutual Insurance Company, American Hardware Mutual Insurance Company, Motorists Life Insurance Company, MICO Insurance Company, American Merchants Casualty Company, and AHM Insurance Agency, Inc.

Armed with the American Hardware affiliation, Motorists will continue to grow by providing superior products and customer service, maintaining financial strength, increasing market penetration, and expanding geographically. Overall company goals for 2001 include $1 billion in assets, $400 million in written premiums, and $400 million in surplus. Motorists may pursue additional affiliations, acquisitions, or mergers that offer a good match in the future.

Recently, the group began expanding into Wisconsin through American Merchants Casualty Company, which sells personal lines insurance. The products of Motorists Life were added in Wisconsin in 1997.

To reach its goals, Motorists also is increasing the number of agents writing its policies by assisting its agencies financially, providing them enhanced service, and helping them with recruiting efforts to put new producers into place. The company is proud of the loyal relationship it has established with its agents and its agencies, some of which have been associated with Motorists for more than 50 years.

Commitment to Quality

Today, there is a trend for companies to increase the emphasis on customer service in all lines of business, and the Motorists-Mutual American

ARMED WITH THE AMERICAN HARDWARE AFFILIATION, MOTORISTS MUTUAL INSURANCE COMPANY WILL CONTINUE TO GROW BY PROVIDING SUPERIOR PRODUCTS AND CUSTOMER SERVICE, MAINTAINING FINANCIAL STRENGTH, INCREASING MARKET PENETRATION, AND EXPANDING GEOGRAPHICALLY.

Hardware Insurance Group is no exception. The insurer's goal is built around the slogan Keep the Promise, according to Robert E.H. Rabold, Motorists' chairman, president, and chief executive officer. In addition to service, the company's promise is to provide "quality products, fair prices, prompt claims service, and the respect of every employee."

Motorists is also committed to providing ongoing training to its

agents and employees. Legislative and court rulings constantly change the nature of the insurance business, and agents and employees need to stay abreast of these changes.

As a part of its leadership role, Motorists is actively involved in legislative issues that affect the insurance industry, and it participates in various professional associations. Rabold has served as chairman of the Ohio Insurance Institute and, in 1998, will

serve as chairman of the National Association of Mutual Insurance Companies, which represents 1,400 insurance companies nationwide. On the legislative front, Garry Wharton, Motorists' secretary and corporate counsel, chaired the legislative committee of the Ohio Insurance Institute for a number of years.

Community involvement is also an important part of Motorists' history, and the company continues to support community events and organizations. The insurer has been a strong supporter of the Ohio State University through its sponsorship of the statewide OSU Football Radio Network, and has provided financial support for the creation of the Topiary Garden in downtown Columbus. Other organizations supported include United Way—Motorists consistently ranks as one of the top companies in Central Ohio in per capita giving and employee participation—and the Center of Science and Industry. "We want to be a visible, contributing part of the community," says Rabold.

As it pursues its growth strategy, the company also is committed to maintaining its financial strength and to providing the best possible service. Adds Rabold, "We feel very committed to our agencies, sales representatives, and policyholders. They are our lifeblood, and we want to do everything we can to support them and show that we appreciate them."

CLOCKWISE FROM TOP LEFT: MOTORISTS MUTUAL INSURANCE COMPANY GREW ALONG WITH THE AUTOMOBILE INDUSTRY, BECOMING A REGIONAL COMPANY DOING BUSINESS IN OHIO, INDIANA, KENTUCKY, PENNSYLVANIA, AND WEST VIRGINIA.

MOTORISTS MUTUAL INSURANCE COMPANY HELPED CREATE THE TOPIARY GARDEN IN DOWNTOWN COLUMBUS.

MEN OF VISION ESTABLISHED MOTORISTS MUTUAL INSURANCE COMPANY IN 1928 TO PROVIDE COVERAGE FOR THE GROWING NUMBER OF AUTOMOBILES THAT WERE BEGINNING TO DOT THE AMERICAN LANDSCAPE.

Lynn B. Timmerman

Charles C. Janes

Wilbur E. Benoy

Alvin Victor Donahey

Carl N. Crispin

A. E. Mittendorf

Joseph R. Gardner

COLUMBUS-BASED AND INTERNATIONALLY RECOGNIZED, BATTELLE IS ONE OF THE world's leading technology and research and development organizations. The institute touches the lives of the people of Greater Columbus every day through the products it creates; through its impact as a major area employer and as a

magnet that draws research, high-technology, and business activities to the region; and through the local companies its research and development efforts help create.

Battelle traces its name and its start to Gordon Battelle, described as a quiet, solid, and dependable businessman, whose 1929 bequest was designated for "a Battelle Memorial Institute . . . for the encouragement of creative research . . . and the making of discoveries and inventions." Today, the institute's staff of 7,500 covers the spectrum of scientific and engineering disciplines, works in more than 50 locations, and tackles more than 5,000 projects worth nearly $1 billion per year.

THE NAME BEHIND WHAT'S NEW
With all of its accomplishments, Battelle is not a household name. Its red brick headquarters is often mistaken for a part of the Ohio State University, which sprawls to the north. Unfamiliar, also, is the name of Chester Carlson, a bootstrap inventor who came to Batelle in 1944, looking for a collaborator to help him refine a technology. Together, Carlson and

Battelle created something that is familiar: xerography, which led to the office copier machine.

Batelle's developments have found their way into everyday life—the first typewriter correction fluid (sold originally as Sno-Pake), the cut-resistant golf ball, the compact disc, the first automotive cruise control system, and the UPC product labeling system, of which Battelle was part-creator. Then, there's Battelle's laser-based potato peeler and its heat resistant chocolate: doesn't melt in your hand, and doesn't melt in Arabia, as troops in Operation Desert Storm discovered.

A walk through Battelle underscores the range of its activities. In one room, its experts work to foresee the future: perhaps laptops powered

by the overhead light of an airplane seat or bridges that change color when their girders start to weaken. In another room, Battelle works to bring that future closer, with such products as an electronic, onboard automotive mapping device that provides current information on traffic jams or bottlenecks and recommends alternate routes. Commonly, Battelle works with industry—helping it map a broad future, develop a single product, or solve a puzzle in production.

Much of Battelle's work falls into the following markets: energy, environment, transportation, national security, digital transaction, automotives, chemical industry, pharmaceuticals, consumer products, agrochemicals, and medical products. Additionally, through technology development, commercialization, and transfer activities, Battelle collaborates with universities, industry, and the international community to expand the base of science and technological knowledge.

RESEARCH AND DEVELOPMENT
For much of its history, Battelle functioned as something of an R&D job shop—solving specific technical

INTERSECTION AHEAD
TURN RIGHT
1 KILOMETER

▲ LARRY HAMILL

problems for industry. Today, with market pressures to speed product introduction, it more often works as a square-one collaborator, defining and developing a product for market. For example, through a joint venture with the R.G. Barry Company, Battelle is developing and finding commercial applications for a microwavable polymer able to absorb, store, and slowly release heat. Its first application, known as the Heat Seat, is a stadium cushion that stays warm through four quarters of action.

Ideas are not just developed at Battelle; often, they are also spun off into companies that add to Columbus' technological capacity and employment. In 1986, for example, work undertaken at Battelle on full-text retrieval was spun off into a wholly owned subsidiary, Information Dimensions Incorporated (IDI), acquired by OCLC in 1993. IDI has remained the market leader in document manage-

ment for a decade, providing Global 2000 corporations and government bodies with software solutions that use documents to dramatically improve and control business processes.

Photonic Integration Research, Inc.—a joint venture among Battelle, Mitsubishi, and NTT—manufactures silica glass optical wave guide devices, used primarily by telecommunications companies and also supplied to aerospace, medical, and optoelectronics markets. Transmet, incorporated in 1979 to utilize technology developed at Battelle, is the world's largest supplier of rapidly solidified, very pure aluminum alloy particulates—used commercially in chemical and metallurgical processes, reflective roofing materials, and elsewhere.

Cybermark LLC—a joint venture among Batelle, Huntington Banks, and Sallie Mae—offers one of the first "smart cards" to feature a fully integrated hardware, software, and

service platform. It carries unique encryption and security features, and provides direct connection to the U.S. payment network. Cybermark's major field test is being conducted in Columbus, at Ohio Dominican College.

Battelle, through its Community and Education Relations Office, has a continuing engagement with Columbus-area educational institutions—kindergarten through graduate level—supplying human, financial, and material resources. The emphasis is on increasing student interest and achievement in math and science, creating innovative professional development opportunities for teachers, and working toward school improvement.

When Battelle opened in 1929, few in industry acknowledged the value of applied science. Today, when technology defines the limits of what is possible, Battelle works to see that those possibilities are realized.

CLOCKWISE FROM TOP LEFT:
TEAMING WITH R.G. BARRY, BATTELLE DEVELOPED AN INNOVATIVE HEAT-RETENTION MATERIAL TO KEEP THE MICROWAVABLE HEAT SEAT™ WARM FOR UP TO EIGHT HOURS.

MY BEST TOYS, INC. WORKED WITH BATTELLE TO DEVELOP SANDZ™, A NONTOXIC MATERIAL THAT MOLDS LIKE WET SAND—WITHOUT THE WATER.

BATTELLE LICENSED A NEW TECHNIQUE TO INCREASE CHOCOLATE'S RESISTANCE TO HEAT, WITHOUT CHANGING ITS FLAVOR OR TEXTURE.

OHIO DOMINICAN COLLEGE STUDENTS USE THE BATTELLE-DEVELOPED PANTHER CARD TO BUY BOOKS, PAY FOR MEALS, MAKE COPIES, ACCESS CAMPUS INFORMATION, OR PRINT A TERM PAPER.

BORDEN, INC.

ONE OF THE OLDEST AND BEST-KNOWN COMPANIES IN AMERICA—FOUNDED MORE than 140 years ago, in 1857—Borden, Inc. is in the midst of major transformation as it moves toward the new millennium. ✳ The company is realigning both its portfolio of businesses and its organizational structure. Borden people are redefining their jobs and how they carry them out. And Borden ownership has returned to a private entity, after nearly a century of publicly owned and traded stock.

Borden's transformation began with privatization in March 1995, when premier investment firm Kohlberg Kravis Roberts & Co. (KKR) completed its acquisition of all the company's shares. KKR quickly infused another $1 billion-plus directly to Borden to shore up its financial resources. This investment set the stage for rejuvenating Borden and capturing the value inherent in its businesses.

The story of Borden's transformation is unfolding largely in Columbus. The city has been the company's administrative headquarters since 1970 and its executive headquarters since 1994. Columbus is currently home to more than 1,000 Borden associates in functions including accounting, treasury, law, sales, marketing, human resources, information systems, research and development, operations, and general management.

Borden had a manufacturing presence in Columbus even earlier, with a dairy plant owned from the 1920s.

A NEW DIRECTION

Though long associated with milk and the dairy industry, Borden offers myriad packaged food and nonfood products to consumers, and is a major supplier of chemicals to industry. Borden's operations span the globe.

Since 1995, Borden management has transformed the organization, guided by a unique concept called Taking Ownership. Borden has evolved from a single company to a family of independent companies, each of them sharply focused on its own area of business, having its own chief executive officer and board of directors, and supported by its own operating resources and capital structure.

Essentially, teams of executives acting as entrepreneurs are empowered to run their enterprise. They have clear accountability for results, along with expanded decision-making authority. Authority and accountability extend downward through each operating company, and associate rewards are increasingly linked to their company's performance as well as personal contributions.

THE BORDEN FAMILY OF COMPANIES

The Borden Foods Corporation (BFC) is a company focused on grain-based meal solutions as its strategic growth platform for the future. Within this chosen area, BFC is already a leading North American producer of pasta and pasta sauce (including Classico,

BORDEN'S CORPORATE HEADQUARTERS IS LOCATED IN COLUMBUS.

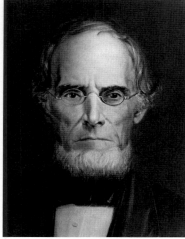

Catelli, Creamette, and other well-known brands).

Consumer-driven innovation, product differentiation, and brand emphasis lie ahead for BFC, along with the intent to acquire businesses that strengthen or broaden the current lineup. In mid-1997, the new and expanded BFC Innovation Centre was established in the Polaris section of Columbus to provide close interaction among R&D, marketing, and other BFC associates.

Another company, Wise Foods, Inc., is a leading producer of potato chips, pretzels, corn chips, popcorn, and other snacks distributed up and down the East Coast under the popular Wise, Moore's, and Quinlan principal brand names.

Elmer's Products, Inc. is a business that boasts two of the best-known brands in consumer adhesives: Elmer's Glue and Krazy Glue. New products are driving growth across the board, from fun and practical items for children to use at home and in school,

to high-performance adhesives, caulks, and sealants for professionals.

Borden Chemical, Inc. has in recent years been the largest generator of Borden income, and is a business with significant opportunities for domestic and international growth. Borden Chemical is the world's largest supplier of adhesives sold to the forest products industry for oriented strand board, particleboard, and other wood applications. The company also manufactures phenolic resins for foundries, oil and gas production, and other industrial tasks, and offers high-tech coatings and resins for fiber optics and electronics.

A new entity, reSOURCE PARTNER, INC., offers customers outside of Borden, not just within, a one-source resource for a wide range of infrastructure management services. These are the essential support activities that operate behind the scenes in most companies, from payroll and benefits processing to electronic commerce and customer support center services.

Borden Capital Management Partners is a small group providing specialized expertise to the Borden companies in finance, law, acquisitions and divestments, strategic planning, human resources, and corporate affairs. It also provides strong and active corporate governance functions.

What about dairy? In mid-1997, Borden management made the difficult decision, as part of the company's ongoing transformation, to sell its oldest and most identifiable business and to license the new owner to use Elsie the Cow, Borden's beloved icon for 60 years. Elsie continues to be a Borden asset, however, and available for corporate use and other products.

Remaining constant in the face of transformation is the Borden commitment to its communities, via corporate contributions and support for employee volunteerism. Children's Hospital and COSI are two among dozens of organizations supported.

Another constant is product quality. It dates back to Gail Borden Jr., who founded the company to process and market a sweetened, condensed milk that was pure, wholesome, and storable without refrigeration. Borden invented the product through perseverance and passion, after seeing children sicken and die from drinking fresh milk from infected cows aboard a transatlantic steamer in the early 1850s.

In the spirit of its founder, "If it's Borden, it's got to be good!" has been the company's quality endorsement for decades. And whatever transformation lies ahead, quality will always remain a Borden hallmark.

IN 1934, A FOOD INDUSTRY ENTREPRENEUR SET OUT TO CHANGE THE WAY SHOPPERS BOUGHT their groceries. At the time, grocery items were usually stocked behind a counter, and orders were filled by clerks while the customers waited. Customers had to go to three different locations to buy produce, meat, and bakery items. ✳ Wayne E. Brown

wanted to change all this. Brown wanted to create a shopping experience where customers had more control over their purchases, as well as a greater selection of merchandise. The birthplace of Brown's self-service concept was a former dance hall and roller rink on Lane Avenue near the Ohio State University campus. Called Big Bear, the 70,000-square-foot store became an immediate winner with customers, who could browse through aisles of merchandise and select their own items.

Some 64 years later, Big Bear, a division of the Penn Traffic Co., continues to offer customers the same innovation and quality found in that first store. "We have always tried to be on the leading edge. There were never any aspirations to be the biggest, just the best at what we do," says Phillip Hawkins, Penn Traffic Co. president.

Being the best includes selling only choice beef and pure apple cider

In 1934, Big Bear opened the first self-service supermarket in the Midwest in a former roller rink on Lane Avenue near the Ohio State University.

Today's Big Bear stores offer true customer convenience by combining numerous innovative products and services in one location.

in season. It also includes maintaining in-store bakeries, where items are baked fresh on the premises; offering the latest technological improvements; and hiring quality associates, many of whom retire with the company.

LISTENING TO CONSUMERS
The company's strategy involves responding to changing consumer

demands, which can be challenging, since trends are a moving target. Most recently, Big Bear has made available ready-to-go foods and hired in-store chefs to prepare fresh meals for customers who don't have time to cook anymore. Two locations in Columbus also contain sushi bars.

But for every customer who wants convenience, there is another who

wants to cook. These customers demand a vast array of spices, gourmet cooking items, international foods, and an in-store, full-service butcher shop. Other customers want shoe repair, coffee shops, banking, package shipping, photofinishing, and video rental services. Big Bear has complied with all these wishes; in fact, the company was the first retailer in the nation selected by Blockbuster Video for in-store video shops.

"The hard part about our business is not what we're going to do tomorrow, but how to add to what we did yesterday—because one store can't carry everything," Hawkins explains. But Big Bear tries; the company keeps tabs on consumer needs via consumer focus groups. "It all comes down to listening and trying to adapt our business based on what our customers say they want," says Hawkins.

Big Bear is constantly searching for ways to operate more efficiently so savings can be passed along to consumers. To that end, the company has implemented the latest technological systems, which include computers that control scheduling, refrigeration, lighting, in-store temperature, distribution, and inventory. The chain was the first to utilize motorized counters to transport merchandise from the cart to the cashier. It also was one of the first chains to accept credit cards.

In 1988, the company took the one-stop-shopping concept to another level when it combined its Harts dis-

count stores with grocery stores in some markets to form Big Bear Plus supercenters.

HOMETOWN SUPPORTER

Big Bear is proud to support the communities in which it does business by promoting numerous organizations and events. Over the years, the chain has been a major supporter of local libraries, Children's Hospital, and the Columbus Symphony Orchestra. The Mid-Ohio Food Bank, which provides service to much of Big Bear's area, also benefits from the company's community giving.

The company, which has 63 supermarkets and 15 Big Bear Plus combination stores in Ohio and West Virginia, has achieved its goals of

surviving and prospering in what supermarket analysts call one of the most competitive grocery markets nationwide. Big Bear goes head-to-head with some of the country's largest supermarket chains in many locations. It has seen other, less fortunate competitors lose the battle to succeed. But, due to quality products and excellent customer service, Big Bear has remained.

In the future, Big Bear shoppers can expect continuous improvement from the chain, which has become one of the most well known and respected businesses in Columbus. Its state-of-the-art supermarkets, found in convenient locations and staffed by quality people, will continue to serve Ohio with pride.

WHITE CASTLE SYSTEM, INC.

W HITE CASTLE®, KNOWN AS THE FIRST QUICK-SERVICE HAMBURGER RESTAURANT chain, is among the most readily recognizable symbols in America today, instantly identified for both its distinctive castlelike buildings and for the products it sells. ✹ For those who know it, White Castle System, Inc.

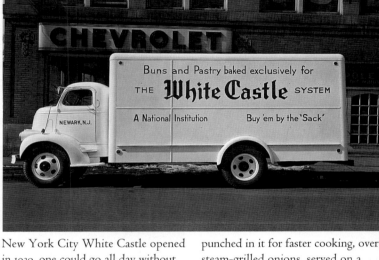

offers another association: that of a continuing story of American business success. Today, operating in one of the nation's most competitive fields, White Castle's position is solid: It ranks second in the nation in business volume per outlet, with a per-unit sales average of $1.1 million from more than 300 restaurants in 12 states.

Since 1934, when the organization moved its headquarters to the Capital City, White Castle has made Columbus its home. Today, White Castle System, Inc. is composed of its company-owned restaurants; White Castle Distributing, Inc.; and PSB, formerly Porcelain Steel Buildings. White Castle owns and operates three of its own bakeries, two meat processing plants, and two frozen sandwich production facilities.

COMMITMENT BRINGS SUCCESS

In larger terms, the success of White Castle has been the success of the industry. Today, the hamburger is the most American of foods—the breakfast, lunch, or dinner of choice for millions of people. This was not always the case. Indeed, when the first

New York City White Castle opened in 1930, one could go all day without ever seeing a hamburger sign. By introducing the hamburger to millions, White Castle helped create an industry.

In a field given to rapid change, White Castle has achieved success by adhering to a series of commitments that have remained constant over time. First, there is a commitment to a product. The White Castle core product consists of a square, frozen, 100 percent beef patty with five holes

punched in it for faster cooking, over steam-grilled onions, served on a whitebread bun with a pickle slice. That product has been little changed since 1921, when E.W. "Billy" Ingram and Walter Anderson spent $700 in borrowed funds to open their first restaurant in a 10- by 15-foot cement block building in Wichita, Kansas. That loan was rapidly repaid. Ever since, White Castle has operated without taking on long-term debt. As Ingram liked to state: "He who owes no money cannot go broke."

WHITE CASTLE OWNS AND OPERATES THREE OF ITS OWN BAKERIES IN CARTERET, NEW JERSEY; EVENDALE, OHIO; AND RENSSELAER, INDIANA. THIS TRUCK WENT INTO SERVICE FOR THE NEW JERSEY RESTAURANTS IN 1947.

WHITE CASTLE IS FAMOUS FOR ITS 24-HOUR A-DAY SERVICE, WHICH STILL HOLDS TRUE FOR MOST LOCATIONS (LEFT).

IN THE LATE 1990S, WHITE CASTLE INTRODUCED THIS EFFICIENT BUILDING DESIGN, SIMILAR TO THE ORIGINAL BUILT IN WICHITA, KANSAS, IN 1921 (RIGHT).

◄ WHITE CASTLE SYSTEM, INC.

A second commitment has been to restaurant design. White Castle's building style was copied from the Chicago Water Tower, whose battlements and turrets of stone were reproduced in porcelain enamel. Over the years, White Castle restaurants have featured facades of porcelain steel, stucco, and split concrete block. The castle style and white color have remained constant.

The White Castle subsidiary, PSB company, still fabricates many of the components for restaurant construction, including interior stainless steel kitchen fixtures. PSB operates a metal fabrication and powder painting facility in Columbus, and powder coating plants in Dayton and in Rome, Georgia.

Third, there is the White Castle commitment to employees. By policy, the company promotes from within. Every White Castle supervisor begins his or her career as an operator, cooking and serving hamburgers. All employees enjoy a package of company benefits introduced by White Castle long before such benefits became standard in the industry or were mandated by law. For example, in 1924, a cash bonus system was introduced, based on gross sales rather than on profits, and since 1927, company life insurance has been provided. Entry-level, full-time employees receive the same kinds of benefits as those provided to senior-level employees.

This commitment is reflected in another White Castle policy: The company has no domestic franchises, but operates solely through company-owned locations. As President E.W. Ingram III, the third generation of his family to head the enterprise, explains, "The reason is simple. We have a product and a philosophy that have been successful for 75 years. We have family pride in what we do. And we have a very special relationship with our employees because of the way our company is structured."

The family's commitment to employees is matched by its commitment to the communities in which White Castle operates. Since its establishment in 1949, the Ingram-White

Castle Foundation has made more than $7 million in donations, primarily to educational undertakings.

CUSTOMER LOYALTY

Of course, key to the success of White Castle is the commitment of White Castle's customers to the company's hamburgers and cheeseburgers. Commitment is too mild a word—to its customers, there is simply no substitute for the "Slyder®", as they affectionately call the White Castle core product. They often "Buy 'em by the Sack"—the phrase Billy Ingram coined to refer to a bag of 10 burgers.

White Castle keeps a story file known as the "Incredi-tales" as witness to the lengths to which its customers will go to acquire the product they crave. These include air drops, a 15-hour wait in line, and a trip to the South Pole, to name a few. The company also publishes the top 10 customer-submitted recipes each year from its annual recipe contest. All the recipes begin with a sack of 10 White Castle hamburgers. White Castle East Indian Bobotie is one of the more than 200 recipes submitted each year to celebrate National Hamburger Month, sponsored by White Castle.

Customer loyalty led to another company undertaking. White Castle operates in 16 metropolitan areas; often, when customers moved, they found that they could not obtain

their favorite meal in their new location. Some would order dozens of hamburgers to be delivered by air express. Because White Castle burgers are steam grilled, they retain moisture, which allows them to be frozen and reheated in a microwave. In 1987, this led to the creation of White Castle Distributing, Inc., which supplies frozen White Castle hamburgers, cheeseburgers, and chicken sandwiches to grocery stores across the country.

All of this is a formula for growth. The company plans to expand its roster by adding 150 new restaurants in the next decade. This will give even more customers the chance to realize the truth of the company slogan: White Castle, What You Crave.

CLOCKWISE FROM TOP LEFT:
IN THE EARLY 1980s, WHITE CASTLE BEGAN TO ADD DRIVE-THROUGH SERVICE.

WHITE CASTLE HAS RECENTLY BECOME A FRANCHISEE FOR CHURCHS FRIED CHICKEN RESTAURANTS.

WHITE CASTLE CAN BE FOUND AT SELECTED GASOLINE STATION/CONVENIENCE STORE LOCATIONS.

Doctors Hospital

SINCE ITS FOUNDING AS A 25-BED FACILITY IN 1940, DOCTORS HOSPITAL'S HISTORY has been one of growth, change, and innovation. The result: Doctors Hospital's emergence as one of the largest osteopathic teaching centers in the United States and the only health care system in Franklin County accredited by both the

American Osteopathic Association and the Joint Commission on the Accreditation of Healthcare Organizations.

Anchoring this wide service network are two acute care hospitals in Columbus, numerous clinics and family physician offices, and a hospital staff with more than 400 physicians and 2,000 allied health professionals and associates. Doctors Hospital serves as the central site for CORE (Centers for Osteopathic Regional Education) and is also Central Ohio's 17th-largest employer.

"As Columbus becomes one of the country's most dynamic cities, Doctors Hospital continues to enhance services and systems to meet the ever changing needs of the greater Central Ohio community," says hospital President and CEO Richard A. Vincent.

Quality Health Care for the Whole Family

In 1996, Doctors Hospital completed the largest renovation and enhancement program in its history. The enhancements at both facilities ensure its dedication to providing health care access for the whole family. Doctors is Columbus' only hospital capable of caring for the entire family—from newborns to senior citizens.

Doctors Hospital North, a tertiary care center in Columbus' Victorian Village, offers medical and surgical capabilities including open-heart surgery and the latest cardiac catheterization technology; the area's largest hospital-based dialysis center; total joint replacement; vascular, urological, neurological, and gynecological surgery; and state-of-the-art imaging.

Doctors Hospital West, the city's only west side hospital, also provides a range of medical and surgical capabilities and the latest radiologic technology. It also houses the Pediatric Center, Columbus' only pediatrics unit in a general acute care hospital, and the Maternity Center, a mother/infant delivery center boasting state-of-the-art obstetrical technology backed by the hospital's 57 years of experience in delivering babies. Within the Maternity Center is the Neonatal Special Care Unit, staffed around the clock by neonatal specialists.

Additionally, Doctors Hospital West offers the Licklider Rehabilitation Unit, where seriously ill or injured patients receive medical treatment and physical, occupational, and speech therapy; the Rehabilitation Institute for Business and Industry, a comprehensive outpatient program for industrial injury prevention and treatment; and the inpatient Mental Health Unit.

According to Vincent, "Doctors Hospital's mission is shaped by the osteopathic philosophy of whole-person, primary, preventive health care for the entire family." Dedicated to providing the highest standards of patient care, appropriate technology, and outstanding medical education, Doctors Hospital is prepared to lead the community in providing affordable, quality health care, accessible to all, as well as programs and services for the training of osteopathic physicians and other health care professionals.

CLOCKWISE FROM TOP: RECENTLY EXPANDED AND RENOVATED, DOCTORS HOSPITAL WEST FEATURES A STATE-OF-THE-ART MATERNITY CENTER WITH 12 PRIVATE BIRTHING SUITES AND A NEONATAL SPECIAL CARE UNIT.

THE NEW DOCTORS HOSPITAL NORTH FEATURES A PATIENT-FRIENDLY FRONT ENTRANCE WITH A CONVENIENT OUTPATIENT REGISTRATION AND FAMILY WAITING AREA.

WITH SERVICES RANGING FROM PEDIATRICS TO OPEN-HEART SURGERY, DOCTORS HOSPITAL IS CENTRAL OHIO'S ONLY HEALTH CARE SYSTEM CAPABLE OF CARING FOR THE ENTIRE FAMILY.

CRANE PLASTICS

IN 1997, CRANE PLASTICS MARKED 50 YEARS AS AN INNOVATOR IN THE MANUFACTURE OF high-quality, customized plastic profile extrusion. This process forms plastic materials into long, continuous shapes, which, once cut and finished, reach the consumer as vinyl siding, door and window weather stripping, and other products. Crane markets to the

building products, transportation, appliances, electrical equipment, and office machines and furniture industries.

Crane Plastics is a family-owned business, Columbus-born and -bred. The company started in 1947, when Robert S. Crane set up two hand-built extrusion machines and began production. Now, Crane's operations include 120 extrusion machines, 750 employees, and 400,000 square feet of manufacturing space. Brothers Robert S. Crane Jr. and Jameson Crane guided the company for 40 years, and now a third generation of Cranes directs company affairs: Tanny Crane is president and Mike Crane is executive vice president.

Crane Plastics pursues three major areas of business: the manufacture and sale of its own vinyl siding; contract manufacturing of engineered components for original equipment manufacturers; and the marketing of such proprietary products as synthetic decking, vinyl gutter guards, plastic seawall, and vinyl stadium seats.

INNOVATION AND PARTNERSHIP

Crane has solid standing as an industry innovator. It pioneered the extruding of rigid-vinyl plastic, thus helping create today's high-quality, maintenance-free vinyl siding industry. Crane pioneered the manufacture of specialty-engineered products, such as office-wiring raceways and cooling tower splash bars. In addition, Crane has been an industry leader in manufacturing vinyl-clad window products.

At Crane, the key word is partnership. A successful business relationship, Crane believes, is mutually beneficial, building success for both the company and its customers. Reflecting this, the key phrase for Crane employees is "Don't think parts, think partners."

At Crane Plastics, innovation is built in at every step. In design, Crane engineers work directly with the customer to create the part that makes the better product. In materials selection, Crane continually searches for materials that improve product function, lower costs, and provide tighter tolerances. In production, Crane ensures quality by undertaking each step of manufacturing in-house, thus reducing cost, saving materials, and eliminating assembly.

Crane Plastics believes the rewards of enterprise should be shared. As their share, Crane customers receive the benefits that grow from excellence in manufacturing. Crane employees share through the Working/Sharing Partnership, the company's unique profit-sharing plan. This plan helps create a team effort at Crane, encouraging each employee to be "a part of the company . . . not apart from the company." And Crane's employee group shares with the community. It has consistently ranked among the

top per capita contributors to the United Way among major Columbus employers.

Crane Plastics enters its second half-century with the belief that its commitments to product excellence and partnering will continue to make it a respected name in its field. As company literature states: "You can see the difference in our profiles."

Clockwise from top: Crane employees proudly shoulder a Crane vinyl product, PermaCap®, designed to fit over wood stadium bleachers to extend their usability.

Timber Tech®, engineered wood/plastic composite decking panel, is a new idea in recreational living from Crane. Decking won't rot, split or warp, and tongue-in-groove construction eliminates deck gaps and exposed fasteners common to other material.

From left: Tanny Crane, president and chief executive officer; Mike Crane, executive vice president; and Jameson Crane, chief executive officer of the Crane Group of associate companies, show off an early prototype of a Crane product.

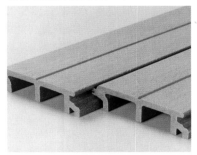

TECHNEGLAS, INC.

WHEN THE COLUMBUS-BASED FIRM TECHNEGLAS, INC. SELECTED ITEMS TO PLACE IN a time capsule to mark its 50th anniversary in June 1996, one item stood out as unusual: a current copy of *TV Guide*. It's not so unusual, though, when one considers that Techneglas is the largest U.S. manufacturer of the glass

used in the production of color television picture tubes, and has been a key supplier to the television industry for about as long as that industry has existed. Indeed, the time capsule Techneglas used was one of its own products—glass for a 35-inch television screen.

The company designs, manufactures, and sells glass funnels (the rear half of a color television tube) and glass panels (the front portion of the tube), supplying them to North American color picture tube manufacturers, including Sony, Zenith, Panasonic, RCA, Hitachi, Philips, and Toshiba. Techneglas produces enough glass to manufacture 20 televisions each minute—and accounts for about 65 percent of the North American color television glass market.

A WORLDWIDE, NICHE MARKET

Two circumstances shape the field in which the company works, says Techneglas President and CEO Tim Hickey. First, it's a niche market. "The number of customers we serve is very small. Actually, we serve seven customers in North America, who make color picture tubes," Hickey says. Numerically, it's a small market, but

geographically, it's a global one. "Our customers compete around the world," he adds, "and we have to keep them cost competitive in that international market."

Second, it's technically demanding. "The faceplate of a screen has to be optically perfect, like eyeglass lenses, without blisters or blemishes. It must have built-in X-ray protection to safeguard the viewer, and, dimensionally, it must be extremely precise to allow for high resolution of the pictures," Hickey explains.

TECHNICALLY DEMANDING

In television glass manufacturing, glass is subjected to extreme variances

in temperature and pressure, which must be precisely controlled. As a result, Techneglas' facilities are highly automated and computer driven. The manufacturing process includes the precise mixing of raw materials into a batch, and heating the batch in state-of-the-art furnaces to produce molten glass. Next comes automated measuring of molten glass to exact and consistent quantities, forming the molten glass by centrifugal force or presses, cooling the glass, grinding and polishing, and a visual inspection before the funnel or panel is ready for shipment.

Techneglas' origins trace back to 1946, when the company, then a

THE TECHNEGLAS COMPLEX, LOCATED ON COLUMBUS' SOUTH SIDE, OCCUPIES MORE THAN 44 ACRES OF LAND TO HOUSE ITS PRODUCTION FACILITIES AND CORPORATE HEADQUARTERS.

TECHNEGLAS HAS PRODUCED TV GLASS IN COLUMBUS SINCE 1949. THE FACILITY HAS UNDERGONE NUMEROUS EXPANSIONS AND REVISIONS TO RESPOND TO THE NEEDS OF THE EVOLVING TV INDUSTRY (LEFT).

STATE-OF-THE-ART MACHINERY IS USED EXTENSIVELY IN THE PRODUCTION PROCESS TO MEET EACH CUSTOMER'S DEMANDS (RIGHT).

KURT DIECKMANN

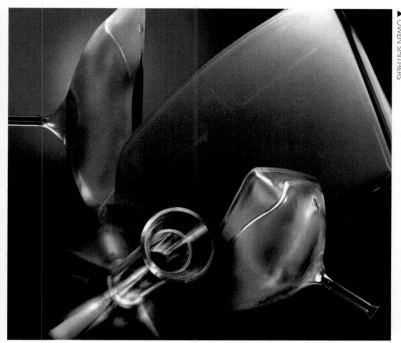

OWEN SMITHERS

division of Owens-Illinois, began making glass for black-and-white television sets. This was at the dawn of the television age: 1946 was the year in which RCA introduced the first mass-produced television sets, selling them for $375 each—equivalent to about $1,800 today.

In 1988, Owens-Illinois entered into a joint venture with Nippon Electric Glass of Japan (NEG) to allow the company to invest in the emerging large-size market (30 to 36 inches). In 1993, the company became a wholly owned subsidiary of NEG and was renamed Techneglas.

Today, Techneglas employs more than 3,200 people in its three manufacturing facilities—Columbus and Perrysburg, Ohio, and Pittston, Pennsylvania. With more than 1,400 local employees, Techneglas is among the 30 largest employers in Franklin County, where it spends approximately $100 million a year on wages, purchased goods and services, and local contractors.

RECOGNIZED FOR ENVIRONMENTAL PROTECTION

Techneglas is committed to environmental protection, and has won recognition for its efforts. In 1994, Techneglas' Columbus plant became the first television glass manufacturer

in the world to convert all of its glass-melting process to an oxygen/gas-firing system, thus drastically reducing the pollutants created in manufacturing. More recently, the Columbus plant received a White Glove Award for waste minimization for its system for removing glass and loose abrasives from the water used in polishing.

The Pennsylvania Environmental Council honored Techneglas, Inc. with the fifth annual Environmental Partnership Award for its achievement of excellence in environmental protection and conservation in northeastern Pennsylvania. In addition, Pennsylvania's Department of Environmental protection selected Techneglas for the 1995 Governor's Waste Minimization Award in the large-business/pollution-prevention category.

The company's concern for the physical environment is matched by concern for the working environment: Techneglas' Columbus plant received the 1995 Outstanding Employer Award from the National Association of Rehabilitation Professionals in the Private Sector for its installation of a health and wellness center designed to reduce reinjury to employees returning to work.

For Techneglas, the future is one of expanding opportunities and increasing demands. The company

has the technical capability to manufacture glass panels and funnels for high-definition television (HDTV) and evolving display markets.

Whatever decisions the company makes will occur in a context of accelerating technical change. "In the past," Hickey said at the time of the 50th anniversary, "we had the relative luxury of making changes over time. But that will not be the case in the new century. Technology is moving at warp speed now, and we will either keep up with the challenges and changes, or we will be out of business. I have no doubt that we at Techneglas are up to the challenges that await us tomorrow."

CLOCKWISE FROM TOP LEFT: TECHNEGLAS IS NORTH AMERICA'S LEADING MANUFACTURER OF GLASS FOR COLOR TELEVISION PICTURE TUBES.

CONTROL ROOM TECHNICIANS CONTINUOUSLY MONITOR PRODUCTION INFORMATION, MAKING PRECISE MACHINERY ADJUSTMENTS TO MAINTAIN PRODUCTION QUALITY.

COMPUTER-CONTROLLED MACHINES USE HIGH-INTENSITY HEAT TO SEAL THE FUNNEL NECK ONTO THE MAIN BODY OF THE UNIT.

NORSE DAIRY SYSTEMS

WORK CAME TO AN ABRUPT HALT ONE DAY AT NORSE DAIRY SYSTEMS (NDS)— meetings were adjourned, memos left half-written, production activities stopped. Throughout NDS's Joyce Avenue plant, employees abandoned their tasks and headed out—to the company-sponsored Las Vegas Night.

The reason for the festivities: Norse Dairy Systems had met its business target for the quarter, and the Las Vegas Night provided a pause in normal company activities to acknowledge the success of the company and its employees.

AN INDUSTRY LEADER

Norse Dairy Systems, headquartered in Columbus, markets packaging, filling machines, and ice-cream cones to companies that manufacture and distribute frozen ice-cream products. These manufacturers, which include Nestlé and Good Humor-Breyers, produce such novelty items as sundae cones, sold in grocery stores, convenience stores, and theme parks; push-up tubes, sold at public events; and frozen treats, sold by ice-cream trucks that wind their way through local neighborhoods.

Currently, Norse Dairy Systems sells its products to hundreds of customers throughout North and South America and along the Pacific Rim. To these customers, NDS leases nec-

essary equipment, and supplies packaging components. For example, if a customer wants four-ounce cups with Power Rangers printed on them, Norse Dairy Systems supplies the cups and the lids, all manufactured to run on NDS equipment. In addition, NDS backs the entire operation with whatever marketing support and field service support the customer needs.

ALL-IN-ONE APPROACH

NDS's all-in-one approach is a key competitive advantage. Ice-cream manufacturers who invest capital to purchase their own equipment often must conduct an extensive search for competent servicing. Those who broker their own operations—buying cups from one vendor, lids from a second, and printing from a third— are faced with the problems of coordination and of assigning responsibility if anything goes wrong.

Often, Norse Dairy Systems draws upon its expertise to develop a new product for a customer. As Nick Kosanovich, vice president for

marketing, explains, "Someone may say, 'I really need to upgrade my cone,' and we'll come back with ideas: 'How about wrapping it in a foil sleeve that looks like a blizzard and calling it Snowstorm?' " As part of the effort, customers gain access to NDS' manufacturing equipment and expertise in package design and consumer trends to create products to meet their needs.

Norse Dairy Systems' roots run deep. The cones it produces, for example, date from innovations developed by Carl Taylor, the engineering student who acquired a fondness for the handmade sugar cones he encountered at the 1904 St. Louis World's Fair. To speed production, Taylor invented a machine that formed and baked these cones inexpensively. Cream Cone, the company Taylor founded, was acquired by what is now Norse Dairy Systems, and today, Norse is the leading supplier of sugar cones to the industrial market.

Recently, NDS acquired the Indianapolis-based Zimmer Custom-Made Packaging, whose products

NORSE DAIRY SYSTEMS, HEADQUARTERED IN COLUMBUS, MARKETS PACKAGING, FILLING MACHINES, AND ICE-CREAM CONES TO COMPANIES THAT MANUFACTURE AND DISTRIBUTE FROZEN ICE-CREAM PRODUCTS.

include flexible packaging, such as the wrap used to hold ice-cream sandwiches and stick novelties. Norse Dairy Systems now employs approximately 500 people.

A Good Place to Work

Like any privately owned company, Norse Dairy wants to see rising sales and healthy profits. But the company has another ambition as well. As Kosanovich explains, "Most compa-

nies, if they are publicly owned, are too worried about the short-term results to look to the long term. True, you have to make a profit, but you can also make a difference in people's lives."

One company objective, according to Kosanovich, is that NDS be among the nation's 100 best companies for which to work. This ambition follows the 1995 purchase of a former division of the Nestlé Ice Cream

Company; following this acquisition, a number of new benefits were introduced for the company's staff. For example, all employees receive NDS's monthly financial report, and all employees share in the company's incentive plan.

In keeping with its goal of community involvement, Norse Dairy Systems supports local charities, both with its dollars and with its time. The company was a $10,000 sponsor of the Mid-Ohio FoodBank Golf Classic. In 1996, the company and its employees donated 33,365 meals to the Operation Feed Community Food Drive, which, on a per capita basis, was the largest contribution in Franklin County. In addition, the company also donates its employees' time: Each month, Norse chooses a charity to which 10 employees give two hours of their time, contributing their efforts at company expense.

The difference between NDS and many other companies is one of attitude. "Most companies," Kosanovich says, "don't celebrate their victories enough." Whether finding innovations to better serve its customers or pausing to celebrate the efforts of its staff, NDS is poised to continue its pattern of success well into the future.

WHETHER FINDING INNOVATIONS TO BETTER SERVE ITS CUSTOMERS, OR PAUSING TO CELEBRATE THE EFFORTS OF ITS STAFF, NDS IS POISED TO CONTINUE ITS PATTERN OF SUCCESS WELL INTO THE FUTURE.

NORSE DAIRY SYSTEMS SELLS TO MANUFACTURERS SUCH AS NESTLÉ AND GOOD HUMOR-BREYERS, WHICH PRODUCE SUCH NOVELTY ITEMS AS SUNDAE CONES, SOLD IN GROCERY STORES, CONVENIENCE STORES, AND THEME PARKS; PUSH-UP TUBES, SOLD AT PUBLIC EVENTS; AND FROZEN TREATS, SOLD BY ICE-CREAM TRUCKS THAT WIND THEIR WAY THROUGH LOCAL NEIGHBORHOODS.

CELEBRATING ITS 50TH SEASON IN 2000-2001, THE COLUMBUS SYMPHONY Orchestra has set itself a challenge for the new millennium: To realize its full potential as a world-class orchestra by performing newly commissioned works, pursuing recording opportunities, and achieving national recognition.

The Columbus Symphony Orchestra's rise has been steady. For a decade after its founding in 1951, the institution was known as the Columbus Little Symphony. But by 1988, it had received major orchestra status from the American Symphony Orchestra League as being one of the 50 largest-budget orchestras in North America. Today, its $8 million budget is the 23rd largest in the country.

A RISE TO EXCELLENCE

The Columbus Symphony Orchestra's growth has been the consequence of many factors, including its artistic leadership, the community's commitment to creating a first-rate cultural institution, a young and energetic corps of professional musicians, and the Symphony's thoroughgoing efforts to build an audience for classical music in Columbus.

Currently, the Symphony—through an exceedingly full schedule of more than 200 performances—reaches a live audience of 300,000 each year. The schedule includes 18 weekends of classical concerts, six weekends of pops performances, 16 programs of family- and student-oriented performances in the historic Ohio Theatre, and six weeks of Picnic with the Pops and Popcorn Pops concerts at its summer outdoor venue, Chemical Abstracts Service.

WORLD-RENOWNED CONDUCTOR

Artistic direction comes from Music Director Alessandro Siciliani, who, when he began his tenure in 1992-1993, was the first internationally known conductor to lead The Columbus Symphony Orchestra. Maestro Siciliani brings impressive credentials to his post. He is one of only four conductors ever to receive the Amerigo Vespucci Award, given to Italian conductors of international stature. Siciliani has appeared as guest conductor with such leading orchestras as the Atlanta Symphony; the National Symphony in Washington, D.C.; Grant Park in Chicago; the Symphony orchestras of Munich, Dresden, Dallas, Pittsburgh, Stockholm, and Hong Kong; and the National Arts Centre Orchestra of Ottawa. He has also conducted operatic productions for many of the country's leading companies, including the Metropolitan Opera and the New York City Opera.

The Columbus Symphony Orchestra reflects the continual growth and transformation of Columbus and its increasing cultural sophistication and aspirations. The Symphony's path was set to a large degree in 1983, when its board of directors established a plan to develop The Columbus Symphony Orchestra as a major cultural asset. Since then, local leaders have been actively engaged, contributing their time, influence, and financial patronage. Simultaneously, the Symphony has established a broad base of support, with more than 9,000 individual donors and 1,500 volunteers. Fund-raising efforts include an annual gala that raises as much as $250,000—featuring such renowned artists as Marilyn Horne and Marvin Hamlisch, violinist Itzhak Perlman, pianist Van Cliburn, and tenor José Carreras—and the first ever Annual Music Educator Awards, recognizing music educators who positively influence the lives of children and adults throughout Central Ohio.

The Columbus Symphony Orchestra also has the advantage of youth—not only as an institution, but also in terms of the age of its musicians. It is a younger-than-average orchestra—one that is still taking risks and expanding the limits of its abilities. At present, the Symphony boasts 53 full-time musicians, and presents an average of 88 musicians for classical performances. Vacancies for full-time positions are filled through national

CLOCKWISE FROM TOP:
RECENTLY LAUDED BY THE *Chicago Tribune* FOR HIS "INSPIRED CONDUCTING" IN A STUNNING GRANT PARK MUSIC FESTIVAL DEBUT, MAESTRO ALESSANDRO SICILIANI HAS TAKEN THE COLUMBUS SYMPHONY ORCHESTRA TO WORLD-CLASS STATUS.

THE SYMPHONY MAINTAINS A STRONG COMMITMENT TO THE TRAINING OF CENTRAL OHIO'S FINEST YOUNG MUSICIANS, SPONSORING THREE TRAINING ORCHESTRAS AND A 90-MEMBER YOUTH ORCHESTRA REPRESENTING MORE THAN 20 HIGH SCHOOLS IN CENTRAL OHIO.

THE SYMPHONY PLAYS TO CONSISTENT ACCLAIM FROM SOME OF THE FINEST ARTISTS IN THE WORLD.

CHAS KRIDER

CHAS KRIDER

D.R. GOFF, PHOTO COURTESY OF CAPA

PICTUREAMERICA

auditions, allowing the Symphony to engage the best of the nation's talent.

Along with these elements—gifted artistic leadership, corporate and community support, and talented and enthusiastic musicians—The Columbus Symphony Orchestra is also distinguished by the skill with which it reaches and builds audiences and provides education.

AN EMPHASIS ON EDUCATION

In building an audience, The Columbus Symphony Orchestra presents such events as Concerts for Families, Popcorn Pops Concerts, Lollipop Concerts, and Picnic with the Pops. At a time when entertainment is increasingly segmented by age, many of these events offer something that can be shared by the entire family.

Since the 1960s, the Symphony has sustained a notable commitment to musical education—both of future musicians and of area youngsters. The Columbus Symphony Orchestra is recognized by arts educators as one of the finest teaching orchestras in the country. Its relationship with schools in the community has created additional learning opportunities for kids through the SEATS Program (Symphony Education and Audience Training in the Schools), which has been nationally recognized as a model for other orchestras. The Symphony's programs reach more than 60,000 children and adults in 20 counties each year.

Each season, The Columbus Symphony Orchestra sponsors three youth training orchestras and a Young Musicians Competition. The youth orchestras provide a quality performing experience for Central Ohio's gifted young instrumentalists; cur-

rently, the Youth Orchestra—more than 90 players drawn from 20 high schools—performs an extensive concert series each season. In recognition of its excellence, the Youth Orchestra has been invited to perform at the International Festival of Youth Orchestras in Banff, Canada, in April 1998. For younger musicians, the Columbus Symphony Cadet Orchestra (grades 7-10) and the Junior Strings (grades 4-8) provide preparation for the Youth Orchestra.

By giving world-class performances filled with musical excitement, building audiences for classical music, and helping to train today's young musicians, The Columbus Symphony Orchestra has created a great present and an exciting future—a future destined to include newly commissioned works, recordings, and the nation's premier venue, Carnegie Hall.

CLOCKWISE FROM TOP LEFT: THE COLUMBUS SYMPHONY ORCHESTRA PRESENTS AN ANNUAL GALA, OFFERING COLUMBUS AN UNPRECEDENTED OPPORTUNITY TO EXPERIENCE SOME OF THE FINEST TALENTS IN THE WORLD—INCLUDING VIOLINIST ITZHAK PERLMAN, TENOR JOSÉ CARRERAS, PIANIST VAN CLIBURN, AND, MOST RECENTLY, ENTERTAINERS MARILYN HORNE AND MARVIN HAMLISCH.

THE SYMPHONY PRESENTS MORE THAN 200 PERFORMANCES EACH SEASON IN THE BEAUTIFUL AND HISTORIC OHIO THEATRE.

THE COLUMBUS SYMPHONY ORCHESTRA RECOGNIZED MUSIC EDUCATORS WHO POSITIVELY IMPACT THE LIVES OF CHILDREN AND ADULTS THROUGHOUT CENTRAL OHIO AT THE FIRST EVER ANNUAL MUSIC EDUCATOR AWARDS IN MARCH 1997. PICTURED ARE WINNERS (FROM LEFT) GEORGE EDGE, MURIEL WEAVER, CAROL WELK, AND JOHN DELIMAN.

PICNIC WITH THE POPS, THE SYMPHONY'S POPULAR SUMMER CONCERT SERIES, PRESENTS SIX WEEKENDS OF FUN, FOOD, FIREWORKS, AND FANTASTIC MUSIC UNDER THE STARS ON THE LAWN OF CHEMICAL ABSTRACTS SERVICE IN COLUMBUS.

UNITED McGILL CORPORATION

OUNDED IN 1951 AS A METAL-FABRICATING AND CONTRACTING COMPANY SERVING customers in Central Ohio, United McGill Corporation has experienced enormous growth and diversification in nearly a half century of existence. Today, the corporation has 600 associates and a nationwide network of manufac-

turing plants and sales offices, and is an industry leader in engineering and manufacturing products for air handling, air pollution control, noise control, and pressure processing.

Despite its continuing growth, the locally owned company has remained committed to its customers. Drawing from its origins in contracting, United McGill maintains a tradition of working closely with customers to serve their special needs.

WORKING CLOSELY WITH CUSTOMERS

Engineering has always been one of United McGill's strengths. The company focuses on solving the customer's problems, custom-designing many of its products for a specific application. Even when providing standard products, its technical salespeople will work with the customer to value-

engineer an efficient application of those products. And because United McGill constantly refines and tests its designs, the customer gets innovative products with proven track records.

United McGill's highly trained workers use the latest fabrication techniques to transform the engineering staff's designs into finished products. On turnkey projects, installation or construction services are provided. At all stages of a job, United McGill's technical and manufacturing personnel work to meet the customer's specifications, schedule, and applicable code requirements.

DIVERSE PRODUCT LINE
United McGill supplies air-handling systems to the commercial construction industry. It pioneered the manufacture of spiral duct and fittings—products that continue to set the industry standards for performance and economy. Today, the company provides an extensive line of duct system components and related products such as sealants and adhesives.

United McGill is also recognized as a technological leader in the field of air pollution control. Over the years, it has helped customers in a broad range of industries meet chang-

ing environmental standards with such air pollution control products as electrostatic precipitators, fabric filters, regenerative thermal oxidizers, and spray-dry scrubbers.

In addition, United McGill solves noise control problems in HVAC systems and industrial applications. With decades of experience and a state-of-the-art acoustical laboratory, the company can help customers create safe and quiet work environments. Products include silencers, acoustical panels, acoustical curtains, and a variety of noise control materials.

Finally, United McGill designs and manufactures specialized equipment for pressure-processing applications. Its autoclaves are essential to many bonding, vulcanizing, laminating, and sterilizing operations, and its vacuum dryers are used in chemical, pharmaceutical, and food-processing operations.

With a high degree of experience and success in each of its fields, it's not hard to see why United McGill has become an industry leader and a major presence in the city of Columbus. The corporation's commitment to customer satisfaction and continued improvements in its products will ensure United McGill's success for many years to come.

MADDOX-NBD, INC.

At Maddox-NBD, designing buildings is only a part of the big picture. The primary focus has always been on solving problems and creating a better environment. "Our firm's overall philosophy has remained constant for more than 40 years," says Jerry Maddox, president. "Our firm's earlier history as Brubaker/Brandt and Holroyd & Myers has provided a strong foundation. We are grateful for our past and we build each day for our future."

On each project, the client's program is the driving force. That program is executed by a staff of highly qualified professionals, many of whom have been with Maddox-NBD for more than 25 years. The staff of 45 keeps the firm on the cutting edge of its profession and is able to provide personal attention to each client. Such dedication has seen results, according to Executive Vice President Bob Nichols, who says, "We are honored by the fact that we have clients who have been with our firm for more than 40 years."

SHAPING THE SKYLINE
In serving a broad base of clients, Maddox-NBD has helped shape the rapidly changing Columbus skyline.

The firm has executed major design projects, including Rhodes State Office Tower, Motorist Insurance, and Port Columbus International Airport. In addition, Maddox-NBD has designed buildings for such organizations as Worthington Industries, Ohio University, Grange Insurance, Online Computer Library Center, and Otterbein College. Currently, the firm is involved with projects across the United States—from the Rocky Mountains to the eastern seaboard, and from Lake Erie to Florida.

In recent years, Maddox-NBD has become recognized as a national leader and innovator for the design of gerontological environments in the senior living industry. Clients include First Community Village, Wesley Glen, Ohio Masonic Home, Maple Knoll, HCF, Omnilife, Otterbein Homes, Humility of Mary, and Episcopal Retirement Homes. Some of the firm's broad-based projects include the Student Recreation Center for Ohio University, and the headquarters for the Ohio Department of Agriculture and the Ohio Department of Transportation.

"Columbus and the state of Ohio have certainly been good to us," says Chris Bendinelli, vice president of Maddox-NBD. The company's success, he believes, is due to its leadership in each walk of life. "We have enjoyed building professional friendships and win-win situations with numerous businesses and governmental and educational leaders throughout the state," he says. "Columbus and Ohio will continue to be the road to the future during the 21st century."

CLOCKWISE FROM TOP RIGHT: MADDOX-NBD HAS DESIGNED BUILDINGS FOR SUCH ORGANIZATIONS AS OHIO UNIVERSITY, WHICH ADDED A STUDENT RECREATION CENTER TO ITS CAMPUS.

ONE OF MADDOX-NBD'S BROAD-BASED PROJECTS INCLUDES THE OHIO DEPARTMENT OF AGRICULTURE.

IN RECENT YEARS, MADDOX-NBD HAS BECOME RECOGNIZED AS A NATIONAL LEADER AND INNOVATOR FOR THE DESIGN OF GERONTOLOGICAL ENVIRONMENTS SUCH AS MAPLE KNOLL VILLAGE.

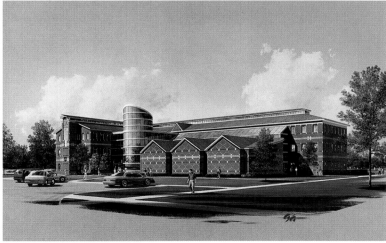

A 1997 NEWS RELEASE ANNOUNCING WORTHINGTON INDUSTRIES' INTERNATIONAL expansion described the company as a leading manufacturer of metal and plastic products, headquartered in Columbus and operating 66 facilities in 22 states and eight countries, employing 12,000 people, and reporting annualized sales of approximately $2 billion.

What the press release didn't say, and what the company won't boast of, is that the Worthington story is required reading at leading American graduate business schools, including Harvard. The Worthington story began in 1955, when founder and Chairman Emeritus John H. McConnell borrowed against his four-year-old Oldsmobile to purchase a load of steel, and created what would become a multinational enterprise. The story continues with Worthington's phenomenal growth, which has taken place during years of general decline in the industry and has been achieved without laying off a single employee.

CONTINUING FINANCIAL SUCCESS

Worthington's success is reflected in its financial record. The company has posted a profit every year it has been in business, and has carried out 11 share splits since Worthington's stock became public in 1968. An investment in company stock made in 1968, with dividends reinvested, would have increased by more than 10,000 percent today; additionally, the cash dividend has increased every year.

Worthington Industries operates in three business segments. The first is processed steel products, and the company is the nation's leading intermediate flat rolled steel processor, covering the most extensive range of products and services in the industry. In the custom products segment, the company is one of the top 10 plastic injection molding companies in North America. Worthington's precision metals segment supplies extremely close tolerance, critical metal parts to the automotive industry, and the company designs, produces, and manufactures the industry's broadest line of railcar castings out of the largest single-site steel foundry in the country.

Worthington Industries' growth has been achieved in a number of ways. The company has gained market share by focusing on quality and service, has aggressively invested in new facilities and equipment, developed new products and services, expanded geographically to penetrate new markets, and pursued selected acquisitions and joint ventures.

While the full story of the growth of Worthington Industries continues to be written, experts, employees, observers, and stockholders alike regularly attribute the company's success to its commitment to several key areas, all of which boil down to successful interpersonal relationships.

The relationship between the company and its employees is based on the guiding Worthington Philosophy, which maintains that people, not machines or technology, are the most important factor in the success

CLOCKWISE FROM TOP:
FOUNDER AND CHAIRMAN EMERITUS, JOHN H. McCONNELL (LEFT) WITH WORTHINGTON CHAIRMAN AND CEO, JOHN P. McCONNELL

WORTHINGTON STEEL'S BLANKING PRODUCTION PROVIDES SAVINGS FOR THE COMPANY'S CUSTOMERS THROUGH MATERIAL, FREIGHT, INVENTORY, AND CARRYING COSTS. THE BLANKS SHOWN HERE WILL BE FORMED INTO RIMS FOR AUTOMOBILE WHEELS.

WORTHINGTON'S STEEL FACILITY IN DELTA, OHIO, OFFERS PICKLED, SLIT, AND HOT DIPPED GALVANIZED STEEL PRODUCTS.

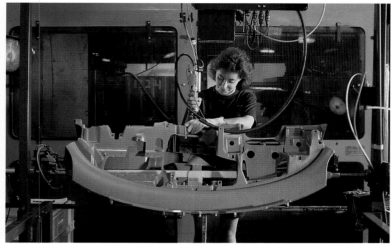

of any enterprise. This philosophy is grounded in Worthington's Golden Rule, which states: We treat our customers, employees, investors, and suppliers as we would like to be treated.

A COMMITMENT TO PEOPLE

Worthington's commitment enables its employees to share in the fruits of their labor, while keeping their interests in line with the larger goals of the company and its shareholders. Through the company profit sharing plan, a fixed percentage of earnings is shared and distributed each quarter to all nonunion employees, regardless of position. Further, an open-door policy encourages employees to question management, offer suggestions, and put forward ideas for improving operations. The system works well: Employee turnover is virtually nonexistent, and Worthington has been included in both editions of the best-selling book *The 100 Best Companies to Work for in America*.

Worthington's commitment to employees has been matched by its commitments to customer service, total communication, and the production of the highest-quality products. Employees are constantly reminded that without the customers' needs for Worthington products and services, the company would soon cease to exist. Worthington products consistently earn overall acceptance rates exceeding 99 percent, and such Worthington customers as Ford, General Motors, General Electric,

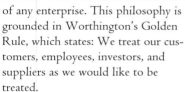

and others have recognized the company with their highest quality awards.

An oft-repeated tenet at Worthington is that the first goal of the company is to make money for its shareholders. Worthington may be unique in the extent to which it connects this goal with its commitment to total communication and openness with its customers. This commitment is reinforced at all levels of the company, and responsibility for maintaining these essential open lines of communication is shared by every member of the Worthington team.

While founded on steel processing, Worthington has expanded its reach into new product lines, new industrial processes, and new markets located around the globe. Acquisitions and partnerships have rapidly expanded Worthington's ability to serve old clients in new ways and to develop new clients in emerging industries.

In many ways, the success and maturation of Worthington Industries has run parallel to the coming

of age of the company's hometown of Columbus. The only major city in America's northeastern quadrant to grow steadily since World War II, Columbus is now described by many as a prototype of the next generation of great global cities.

Worthington has benefited from the region's combination of excellent location, quality of life, balanced economy, educational resources, and proximity to abundant natural resources. In recent years, the Greater Columbus region has supplemented these more traditional strengths with a new commitment to developing technology-based growth companies and is becoming a vibrant hub for international trading companies.

When asked about growth, McConnell always stated, "We've only scratched the surface." As McConnell's son, current Chairman John P. McConnell, leads Worthington Industries into the next century, the company will continue to dig deeper for new ways to serve its stockholders, employees, and customers.

GE Superabrasives

THINK OF DIAMONDS AND AT ONCE IMAGES ABOUND OF A TREK TO AFRICA, OR A mysterious trip to the far reaches of India, or even an excursion in the rugged back country of Australia. But the modern explorer has to go no farther than the Columbus suburb of Worthington. Here lies the headquarters and principle manufacturing facility for GE Superabrasives, the inventor and leading manufacturer of diamond and other superabrasives.

The treasures there are not the long-sought-after gems; rather, they are industrial diamonds valued for their ability to grind, shape, and polish the parts and materials used in practically every industry.

Industry Leader

GE Superabrasives has been the industry leader for more than four decades. The leadership began in 1955 with the news that GE had created the first manufactured diamond, and was reinforced by subsequent high-pressure/high-temperature creations of cubic boron nitride, polycrystalline diamond (PCD), and polycrystalline cubic boron nitride (PCBN). GE has been first with virtually every new scientific achievement in its industry.

These products represent a full market basket of industrial superabrasives that can machine, grind, and drill in ways never before possible. Use of superabrasives permits higher productivity and the development of new processes using hardened steel, carbides, ceramics, glass, superalloys, and other materials. Space-age materials and combinations can now be incorporated into modern manufacturing operations because superabrasive tools can efficiently and effectively produce finished components.

Touching Everything

To gain a full appreciation of the impact GE Superabrasives has had across all industry, the consumer must understand how many different ways the company's products touch their lives. Every car has hundreds of parts ground or finished by superabrasives. The car's decorative, high silica-aluminum wheels were probably machined with PCD, as were the pistons and engines. Its brake drums and rotors were finished to size with PCBN. The glass windows were pencil-edged with diamond, while the cams and crankshafts were precision ground with cubic boron nitride.

Many other industries show the signs as well, from the superalloys and thermal sprays machined with PCBN in jet engines to the concrete airport runways grooved for safety and traction with diamond saw blades. The results can be seen in a piece of fine furniture sculptured with diamond or a sturdy oil rig using a diamond bit to drill for oil in the North Sea.

At GE Superabrasives, increased emphasis on technology has led to dramatic improvements in both product offerings and in the ways those products are used. GE Superabrasives, in conjunction with GE Corporate Research & Development, has created new coatings, diamond types, and sizes for virtually every industrial requirement. The diamond of today is manufactured with more perfect shapes, hardness, and improved ability to match a specific application need. The GE Application Development laboratories in Worthington and in Europe are intricate research

GE Superabrasives has its world headquarters and primary manufacturing facility in the Columbus suburb of Worthington.

MBS™ diamond is used in a wide range of tools to cut and drill hard stone and concrete.

centers dedicated to solving problems for industry and to creating effective manufacturing operations. An experienced staff of technical experts is continually working with end users to create parameters and answer application questions.

Manufacturing facilities are located in both Worthington and Dublin, Ireland. These two sites support a global sales and marketing team that extends through 25 countries and serves a worldwide customer base. GE Superabrasives sells more than 70 percent of its products to markets outside the United States.

QUALITY IS CENTRAL

Quality has always been central to GE Superabrasives' business philosophy. From early approaches to quality team building and Commitment to Quality programs, through ISO 9000 accomplishments and certification, to the present Six Sigma approach, GE has always been a world-class quality leader. The current effort, Six Sigma, is considered one of the most excellent quality concepts ever undertaken within the industry. Sigma is a measure of defect frequency based on a million opportunities. A typical American company operates at around three sigma, which is about 66,800 defects per million opportunities. GE Superabrasives' goal is to be six sigma by the year 2000. That means only 3.4 defects per million. The

efforts are under way, and GE's previous quality accomplishments serve as a springboard to achieve this ambitious goal.

A GOOD NEIGHBOR

GE Superabrasive associates devote time and effort to community and volunteer projects. Associates have been frequently recognized by the Red Cross for their participation in blood drives, and regularly donate their time to such volunteer activities as UNCF, United Way, and other community works.

GE Superabrasives has an outstanding safety record and is responsible for countless initiatives for environmental efforts. GE has received many awards from federal, state, and city associations acknowledging its

environmental leadership. The company has been heavily involved with the community in fire and emergency response procedures, and has held on-site seminars and classes for local fire companies and emergency teams for training in both fire and hazardous materials response.

CORPORATE STRENGTH

GE Superabrasives is a business within the General Electric Company, and as such shares in the corporate brand identity, research and development, and management leadership for which General Electric is so well known. These strengths impart characteristics of industrial leadership, quality, and a power of diversity that sets GE Superabrasives apart from its competition.

BORAZON™ CUBIC BORON NITRIDE IS A MANUFACTURED CRYSTAL, SECOND IN HARDNESS ONLY TO DIAMOND.

GE SUPERABRASIVES' SIX SIGMA QUALITY MANUFACTURING PROGRAM DELIVERS WORLD-CLASS PRODUCTS (LEFT).

HIGH MAGNIFICATION SHOWS THE OUTSTANDING QUALITY OF PREMIUM INDUSTRIAL DIAMOND CRYSTALS (RIGHT).

MCDONALD'S

O**N OCTOBER 20, 1960, A SIMPLE BUT DISTINCTIVE RED-AND-WHITE DRIVE-THRU** restaurant introduced Columbus to the 15-cent hamburger and the All American Meal at Hamilton Road and Broad Street. From these humble beginnings of one restaurant and $250,000 in annual sales, McDonald's

now serves more than 4 million customers per year in more than 110 restaurants throughout the greater Columbus marketplace. McDonald's secret to success is simple: QSC&V (quality, service, cleanliness, and value). The ideals that were established by the very first McDonald's continue to be the vision for each and every McDonald's, whether it's in Chillicothe or on Sawmill Road. It means delivering "Fast, accurate, and friendly service" to each and every customer.

A UNIQUE PARTNERSHIP
Ray Kroc, founder of McDonald's, said, "None of us is as good as all of us." The Columbus market is a strong example of that philosophy, as the first four restaurants to open in the market were owned by the corporation (McDonald's Operating Company), making Columbus one of the first in the country to have restaurants owned and managed by the company.

The vast majority of restaurants are owned and operated by local entrepreneurs, who make significant contributions to their local schools,

churches, and communities. Many Columbus-area owner/operators (such as John Stiving, Ron Fewster, Chris Wilson, Willard Congrove, and Jim Petruzzi) initially worked for the corporation, and now utilize their knowledge to serve in their local communities.

It's been estimated that one of every eight persons in the labor force has worked for McDonald's. On any given day in Columbus, there are more than 5,500 McDonald's employees, drawn from all walks of life, serving

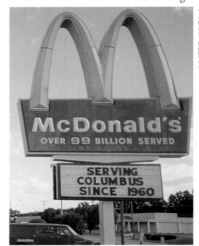

thousands of customers. Seventy percent of McDonald's restaurant managers began as crew people, and more than half of McDonald's Corporation's middle and senior management, as well as franchisees, began behind the counter in restaurants.

Columbus has been a pathway for many individuals who have provided significant contributions to the country. Ed Rensi started as a grill man in a Columbus restaurant and retired at the end of 1997 as the president of the U.S. company. Carl Osborne became one of the first African-American owner/operators of a McDonald's in February 1971. Del Wilson leads operations for eight U.S. regions, representing more than $4 billion in revenue. Raymond Mines served as the Columbus regional manager, and now serves as the senior vice president, chief franchise relations officer overseeing diversity programs and owner/operator relationships with the corporation on a national basis. Mike Harden, regional vice president, helped pioneer and lead the development of a just-in-time production system, which is being introduced to the rest of the country. And many others contribute to the company in fields ranging from merchandising to product development to Ronald McDonald House Charities.

NATIONAL CONTRIBUTIONS
To succeed in marketing, Kroc believed, McDonald's had to reach out and respond to each market. Marketing ideas had to come from his partners in the field—the owner/operators. The Columbus marketplace is a leader in the McDonald's system by being a constant test market for new products and ideas. Past successes included testing of Chicken McNuggets in the late 1970s; the first salads in 1984; McChicken in 1987; and pizza in 1991. Several local pro-

CARL WARD, OWNER/OPERATOR OF THE FIRST MCDONALD'S RESTAURANT IN COLUMBUS, STANDS IN FRONT OF HIS RESTAURANT WITH REPRESENTATIVES OF THE MCDONALD'S CORPORATION STAFF, OWNER/OPERATORS, AND RESTAURANT MANAGERS AND CREW.

▼▲ TERRY GILLIAM

motions have also been accepted nationally, and, in 1996, the Columbus market created its own advertising campaign, "Welcome to My Restaurant," which featured local restaurant managers stressing their commitment to QSC&V and delivering the best possible service to every customer on every visit. The success of this campaign prompted the national advertising agency to integrate many of the local elements into a 1997 national campaign featuring the slogan "My McDonald's."

RONALD McDONALD HOUSE CHARITIES

The Columbus Ronald McDonald House celebrated its 15th birthday on March 17, 1997. Located next to Children's Hospital in downtown Columbus, the house provides free or low-cost room and board for approximately 1,200 families a year that have children requiring extended hospital care. The initial concept and planning began in 1978, with a committee that included two owner/operators who are still active with the house, Dick Halstead and Dave Young. The house opened with 15 rooms; today, expansion has provided for 30 bedrooms and an operating budget of more than $300,000. To help meet the house's budget needs, many McDonald's restaurants hold fund-raising events, such as the Doug Fellers' organization, which has raised more than $40,000 since 1988 with its

annual Zanesville Fish 'N Fun event, and Joe Mortellaro's franchise, which teamed up with the MI/Schottenstein company to raise more than $70,000 in 1997 in an annual golf classic.

When Kroc died in 1984, the company created Ronald McDonald Children's Charities (RMCC) to continue his legacy of giving back to communities by helping children and families. Known today as the Ronald McDonald House Charities (RMHC), the local Central Ohio organization has provided grants totaling more than $500,000 to many local organizations, including the March of Dimes, Help Me Grow, YWCA, Hannah Neil Center, Kids 'n Kamp, Special Olympics, City of Chillicothe Parks

& Recreation, North Side Child & Family Development Center, and United Negro College Fund. All owner/operators collect moneys through canister donations in their restaurants, and more than $100,000 per year in grant moneys is distributed through the Ronald McDonald House Charities.

McDonald's food is served at the Polaris Amphitheater, Columbus Motor Speedway, Spring Nationals in Kirkersville, Pumpkin Festival in Circleville, and Nationwide Building downtown—and it's enjoyed as part of children's birthday parties at Play-Places all over the city. McDonald's is not just a restaurant; it's a way of life in Columbus.

JOHN MASON, LITTLE TURTLE RESTAURANT MANAGER, WAS THE STAR OF A LOCAL AD CAMPAIGN, WELCOME TO MY RESTAURANT, WHICH INSPIRED A NATIONAL AD CAMPAIGN DURING THE SUMMER OF 1997 (LEFT).

FOUNDED IN 1978, THE RONALD McDONALD HOUSE SERVES MORE THAN 1,200 FAMILIES EVERY YEAR WITHIN CENTRAL OHIO (RIGHT).

THE CLASSIC DRIVE-THRU RESTAURANT IN GAHANNA CELEBRATES McDONALD'S HERITAGE WITH ITS DISTINCTIVE, NOSTALGIC LOOK.

ALLIED MINERAL PRODUCTS, INC.

IN ITS EARLY DAYS, ALLIED MINERAL PRODUCTS RAN A SIMPLE OPERATION. FOUNDER William Winemiller and partner Robert Scott worked out of Winemiller's garage, mixing minerals in drums rolled across the floor, then shoveling the mix into bags for sale. ✳ Winemiller and Scott were making refractories—not a material

CLOCKWISE FROM TOP RIGHT: FOUNDED IN 1961, ALLIED MINERAL PRODUCTS, INC. PRODUCES 60,000 TONS OF REFRACTORIES ANNUALLY, AND ITS WORKFORCE OF 220 INCLUDES 30 GRADUATE ENGINEERS.

FROM ITS HEADQUARTERS IN COLUMBUS, ALLIED MINERAL OPERATES WORLDWIDE.

JON K. TABOR, PRESIDENT AND CHAIRMAN OF THE BOARD (SEATED), JOINED ALLIED MINERAL IN 1970 AS THE SOLE MEMBER OF ITS SALES FORCE. JOHN L. TURNER, EXECUTIVE VICE PRESIDENT AND GENERAL MANAGER, JOINED A FEW MONTHS LATER, AND—WITH TABOR—COVERED NORTH AMERICA UNTIL ADDITIONAL SALESMEN WERE HIRED BEGINNING IN 1972.

generally produced in the average garage; indeed, not a material generally known to the public, even though refractories are essential to the making of much of what consumers buy and use.

Simply stated, refractories are materials that resist heat, resist corrosion, and retain their physical shapes and chemical identities under extreme conditions.

Allied Mineral makes monolithic refractories used to line high-temperature furnaces in foundries and steel mills. Its customers include the makers and shapers of steel, enterprises that cast copper into plumbing fixtures or superalloys into jet engine blades, and numerous iron foundries making engine blocks and other auto parts—and even a few mom-and-pop operations that cast trinkets sold as souvenirs. Today, Allied Mineral operates worldwide—roughly one-quarter of its 1996 sales of $55 million went overseas.

TECHNICAL INNOVATION
Allied Mineral's growth has been driven by technical innovations. Winemiller and Scott developed MINRO-SIL® RAM 1001, now the major silica refractory used in North and South America, Australia, Taiwan, Korea, Southeast Asia, and South Africa.

Allied Mineral was among the first to apply DRI-VIBE® refractories to induction furnaces and many other industrial applications, and also developed low-moisture, high-density castables used in the steel and foundry industries. By simultaneously developing more conventional refractories, Allied Mineral created the most complete product line in its field.

In the 1970s, Allied Mineral was unique in that 90 percent of its output was intended for electric induction melting operations. As industry moved away from fossil fuels in response to environmental concerns, it moved in the direction of Allied Mineral's products. Then, in the 1980s, Allied expanded its sales into the steel industry, utilizing technology licensed from Japan.

In 1992, Allied Mineral ventured into the aluminum melting field, purchasing an ownership interest in Matrix Refractories of Chicago; Allied completed the purchase of 100 percent of Matrix in June 1997. Allied Mineral also formed a joint venture company in Newell, West Virginia, in 1989, to process minerals imported from China and other locations. North American Processing Co. (NAPCO) is jointly owned by Allied Mineral and Frank and Schulte of Germany, which provides world-

wide sourcing of the needed minerals, while Allied Mineral provides the operations know-how as the managing partner.

Allied Mineral began exporting in 1977. In 1983, it received the President's E Certificate for Exports, and, in 1986, the E Star Award for continued outstanding contribution to the Export Expansion Program of the United States. In 1996, the company initiated a joint venture operation in Italy, and has plans to begin manufacturing in South Africa in 1997, China in 1998, and Brazil shortly thereafter.

THE RIGHT MIX
The challenge in making refractories lies less in mixing the minerals than in knowing what to mix. Allied Mineral Products makes more than 300 different refractories. New compositions are prompted by customer need, and these technical challenges are handled by the staff of Allied Mineral's William F. Winemiller Research Center, where new products are developed.

Allied Mineral's dedication to research and customer service fuels the success of the company, which is adding 85,000 square feet of warehouse space in 1997. That success will continue, as Allied Mineral has proved it can take the heat.

EXECUTIVE JET

N 1964, EXECUTIVE JET MADE HISTORY BY BECOMING THE FIRST COMPANY TO operate business jets commercially. Since then, the company has grown to be the world's largest manager of business aircraft, servicing businesses coast to coast and abroad; soon, Executive Jet will have a presence in all four corners of the globe.

Leading the way for the international expansion is Executive Jet's highly acclaimed, shared-aircraft ownership program called NetJets, which provides companies a less-expensive way of owning and using business jets. Through the program, companies or individuals purchase shares in an aircraft, creating the benefits of owning an aircraft, but providing many operating efficiencies as well.

In a typical scenario, customers can buy a one-eighth interest in a $6 million business jet for $750,000. In exchange for purchasing that share and paying a fixed, monthly management fee, they are entitled to 100 occupied hours of jet use per year, guaranteed at the time they specify. The savings vary among clients, which include small, private firms; affluent individuals; retired executives; small, fast-growing public companies; and large Fortune 500 businesses.

Although Executive Jet continues to provide a full range of business aviation services, including aircraft sales and maintenance, the company has derived much of its success from NetJets, which was founded in 1987. "The program knows no geographic boundaries," says Scott Liston, Executive Jet vice president of customer service and charter sales. In June 1996, with

AL WHICKER

the help of two European partners, the company launched NetJets Europe, which is based in Lisbon. Executive Jet is also expanding the program in the Far East, the Middle East, and Latin America.

THE RIGHT PLACE FOR THE RIGHT IDEA

Since its founding by Retired Brigadier General O.F. "Dick" Lassiter, Executive Jet's fleet has grown to include more than 100 aircraft. In 1997, the company added 32 aircraft, and during the next seven years, plans call for adding no fewer than 25 aircraft per year.

Lassiter, who was familiar with military uses for transporting people, anticipated there would be civilian

applications as well. Columbus provided a logical starting point. The city is near the former Rickenbacker Air Force Base and current Wright Patterson Air Force Base, which provides Executive Jet with a skilled labor pool. Other attractions include the city's geographic proximity to half of the U.S. population, and the city's favorable economic climate.

With its recent expansion, Executive Jet is experiencing growing pains at its original facility on North Hamilton Road, and will move to a larger facility at Port Columbus. The company's continuing growth attests to the fact that Executive Jet provides an innovative solution to the travel needs of the business community.

CLOCKWISE FROM TOP:
THE EXECUTIVE JET FLEET RANGES FROM COMFORTABLE, SMALL CABIN JETS TO MID-SIZE TRANSCONTINENTAL AIRCRAFT, TO LARGE, OPULENT LONG-RANGE JETS.

EXECUTIVE JET'S GROUNDBREAKING FRACTIONAL OWNERSHIP PROGRAM IS THE MOST COST EFFECTIVE, TIME SAVING BUSINESS TRAVEL SOLUTION. THE NETJETS PROGRAM OFFERS ALL THE BENEFITS OF OWNING A CORPORATE JET, AND MORE, AT A FRACTION OF THE COST.

WITH A FLEET OF MORE THAN 100 JETS, NETJETS OWNERS HAVE ACCESS TO THE AIRCRAFT TYPE THAT BEST SUITS THEIR TRAVEL REQUIREMENTS.

AL WHICKER

ARC Industries, Inc.

RC Industries, Inc. is a Columbus-area agency that, like many employment services, provides a broad range of contract services to Central Ohio enterprises. But unlike a traditional employment agency, ARC Industries is a nonprofit organization chartered by the State of Ohio and affiliated with

the Franklin County Board of Mental Retardation and Developmental Disabilities.

Through ARC Industries, adults with mental retardation and/or developmental disabilities receive the opportunity to increase their independence, self-sufficiency, and productivity; to minimize the effects of their disabilities; and to attain a better quality of life. Currently, ARC Industries brings useful, remunerative work to more than 1,200 such employees, who are unique in more than their physical and mental capabilities: The exuberance they bring to each job and the pride that ARC Industries employees display in their work are truly refreshing.

One area business benefiting from this enthusiastic work ethic is Nationwide Insurance. Nationwide's Corporate Distribution Center in Columbus is a workplace where attention to detail and deadlines is key. Among those mastering that detail and cheerfully meeting those deadlines are 50 to 75 employees provided through ARC Industries' on-site crew program.

Social Service Plus Good Business

ARC Industries is also special in that it is a thriving business, unlike most social service agencies. In 1996, ARC Industries generated $4.9 million in revenues, which reflects a fourfold increase over the last 10 years. To remain competitive in these technologically advanced times, ARC Industries also offers its own Web page at www.arcind.com, and can now communicate with customers via E-mail.

In addition to Nationwide Insurance, ARC Industries' current roster of customers includes Sunworthy Wallcoverings, a division of Borden Decorative Products; Countryside Products; Simpson Strong Tie; Ross Laboratories; Consolidated Stores; Wal-Mart; MacMillan/McGraw

Hill; Schottenstein Stores; and the U.S. Postal Services and Distribution Fulfillment Services.

Such employers rate highly the services provided by ARC Industries employees. Paula Igo, employment manager of Consolidated Stores Distribution Center, is enthusiastic in her support of ARC Industries and the performance of its on-site work crews. "We are very pleased with our relationship with ARC Industries," says Igo. "To maintain our production schedules, we have to be able to count on our employees. We've had

outstanding performance from the on-site work crews. Teams are well-trained and managed, enthusiastic and totally reliable. ARC Industries provides us with exactly what we need, every day."

In its work, ARC Industries meets all appropriate government standards. Accredited by the Commission on Accreditation of Rehabilitation Facilities (CARF) and certified by the State Use Committee of Ohio and the U.S. Department of Labor, ARC Industries offers widely diverse services including job placement,

An ARC Industries on-site work crew assembles teaching materials for distribution.

An ARC Industries on-site work crew member packages a customer's product.

on-site work crews, and subcontract services.

Job placement opportunities and on-site work crews are handled through ARC Industries' employment services department, which fulfills service contracts with area businesses and agencies by sending groups of trained, supervised employees to the customer's site. The on-site work crews provide a range of services, including light industrial, assembly, inspection, janitorial, paper collation, packaging, and apparel ticketing. The department also assists with job placement opportunities for individuals showing an interest in, and an aptitude for, independent work.

ARC Industries' four production facilities provide more than 100,000 square feet of production and warehouse space for subcontract services, including shrink wrap, poly bagging, blister packing, boxing, and prepackage assembly services.

Hand assembly is a highlight of ARC Industries' services, including such projects as hand packaging of construction brackets and garden tools assembly, and all the cutting, sorting, coding, packaging, and shipping of wall covering samples required for a national account's distribution system.

At ARC Industries, employees build products for direct sale; most notably, unique, handcrafted gift items through SunApple and Company. In addition, ARC Industries Products Division completes work subcontracted from other manufacturers.

Meeting Customer and Client Needs

For success in the business world, ARC Industries employs industrial engineers who furnish accurate estimating, bidding, and timely quotes for potential and repeat customers. All ARC Industries production managers are members of the American Production and Inventory Control Society (APICS). They work with customers to ensure that each project is properly organized for timely completion. Production management produces scheduling options that best fit the

purchaser's recurring needs. Production management teams meet weekly with the sales staff and production teams to assess existing contracts and to schedule new jobs.

To succeed with employees, ARC Industries' engineers are knowledgeable both about federal labor guidelines and the provisions needed for the special capabilities of ARC Industries' employees. Versed in engineering and human factors analysis, they design processes to adapt the employees' skills to the tasks required by the customer. A rehabilitation engineer and technicians develop jigs and fixtures that permit participation by even the most mentally and physically challenged individuals.

At the completion of each project, customers are invited to rate ARC Industries' sales staff and workers on

their promptness and the quality of their work. Consistently, ARC Industries' customers respond with rankings in the mid-90th percentile.

Such results have driven the consistent growth of ARC Industries, and are an endorsement of ARC Industries' mission: meaningful work for its employees and cost-effective, high-quality services to customers.

Empowered by the dignity of work, the skills, dependability, and determination of the agency's motivated employees make them important assets to any employer interested in productivity and cost-containment. This comprehensive program of job training, placement, and supervision is a partnership in which everyone—employers, employees, the agency, and the community—ends up on the winning side.

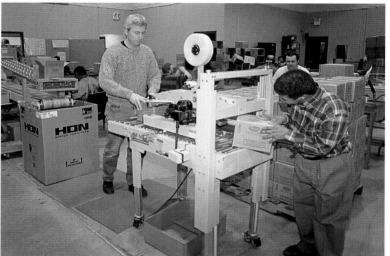

An ARC Industries employee uses a packaging machine at one of ARC Industries' four production facilities.

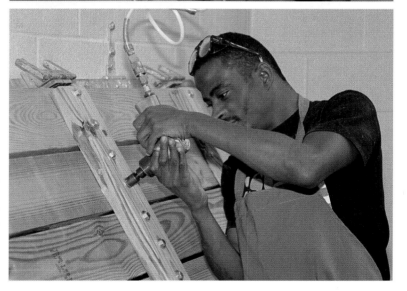

ARC Industries builds picnic tables for the Department of Natural Resources.

The Limited, Inc.

I N 1963, A YOUNG ENTREPRENEUR NAMED LESLIE H. WEXNER BORROWED $5,000 FROM his aunt and opened his first store, The Limited, at Kingsdale Shopping Center in the northwest suburb of Upper Arlington. The store's first-day sales were $473. His goal was to make $10,000 a year and buy a new car every three years.

Wexner's shop became the flagship of one of the world's largest specialty retailers, recently reporting annual sales approaching $9 billion. Today, The Limited, Inc. has full or partial ownership of 13 retail businesses, ranging from lingerie to sporting goods; operates approximately 6,000 stores; and has more than 120,000 associates.

A Retail Pioneer
Building on the success of The Limited, the company diversified and added new brands. Some were homegrown at The Limited, Inc. headquarters, such as Express (1980) and Bath & Body Works (1990). Others, such as

Lane Bryant (1982), Victoria's Secret (1982), and Abercrombie & Fitch (1988), were acquired.

The company has a history of pursuing marketing niches and seizing new retail opportunities as they present themselves. For example, when Victoria's Secret Catalogue realized that sales in Japan were $40 million in 1996, compared to $1.5 million in 1995, the division quickly opened a telephone center there. Additional international expansion is expected in the near future.

In 1987, when Wexner saw a void in the market for men's and young girls' fashion apparel, Structure and Limited Too were born. The com-

pany also tapped into the burgeoning personal care industry in 1990 with the creation of Bath & Body Works, which had sales of $1 billion in 1997. In 1995, The Limited, Inc. added sporting goods to the mix with the purchase of Galyan's Trading Company, a high-energy, emerging sporting goods retailer.

Whether created or acquired, The Limited, Inc. is known for taking a retail concept and turning it into a distinctive national brand that builds customer loyalty. Victoria's Secret is the world's dominant lingerie brand, with more than $3 billion in sales annually. Lane Bryant is a leading apparel retailer for women who wear size 14 or above. Abercrombie & Fitch, which once was an upscale sportswear and sporting goods retailer, is today a leading casual American lifestyle brand targeting the young, hip customer.

Wexner summed up the company's strategy in a recent annual report: "Once we recognize a market opportunity, and develop a brand to fill it, we put the full force of the business' marketing, merchandising, sourcing, store design, finance, and distribution skills behind it. And,

FOUNDED IN 1963 BY LESLIE H. WEXNER, TODAY THE LIMITED, INC. IS ONE OF THE WORLD'S LARGEST SPECIALTY RETAILERS.

once the concept has been tested, refined, and its potential proven, we move. In fact, no one moves faster."

Recently, some of The Limited's brands were spun off into public companies in recognition of their growth and market following. They include Abercrombie & Fitch and Intimate Brands, consisting of Bath & Body Works, Cacique, Victoria's Secret Stores, Victoria's Secret Catalogue, and Gryphon Development, a leading producer of cosmetics, fragrances, and personal care products.

In addition to its retail divisions, The Limited, Inc. owns Mast Industries, an international contract manufacturer, importer, and distributor of apparel. The company also leases real estate, creates and designs stores, and offers credit services to its customers through Alliance Data Services, which is 40 percent owned by The Limited.

A Commitment to Helping Others

Community involvement is an important tenet of The Limited's culture. Whether through financial giving, serving on a board, or rolling up their sleeves and getting involved, Limited associates and the corporation as a whole are major contributors to the community. The company has chosen to focus its support on organizations that reflect the values and concerns of its associates and customers. Targeted are programs that are responsive to the needs of women, children, and education.

Programs and organizations The Limited, Inc. works with, or on behalf of, include the United Way, Village to Child, American Red Cross, Choices Center for Victims of Domestic Violence, Center for New Directions, YWCA, Children's Defense Fund, Big Brothers/Big Sisters, Girl Scouts of America, Adopt-a-School program, Ohio's Center of Science & Industry (COSI), and United Negro College Fund.

Leading The Limited's efforts is Wexner, a tireless supporter of community causes. He played a major role in the relocation of Ohio's Center of Science & Industry, suc-

ceeded in greatly increasing Columbus' number of $5,000-plus donors to the United Way by being one of the city's first major donors, and made possible Children's Hospital's Wexner Pediatric Center. Wexner also serves on the board of trustees of his alma mater, Ohio State University, and has been very involved in maintaining the integrity of its campus through the

funding of several major new buildings, including the campus' new business school building and the creation of the Wexner Center for the Arts.

For the future, The Limited, Inc. will continue to be known for the characteristics that built the company into the world's dominant specialty retailer: vision, leadership, innovation, and community responsibility.

SOME OF THE LIMITED'S NEW BUSINESSES WERE HOMEGROWN AT THE COMPANY'S HEADQUARTERS, SUCH AS EXPRESS IN 1980, AND OTHERS, SUCH AS VICTORIA'S SECRET, WERE ACQUIRED.

IN ADDITION TO ITS MANY SPECIALTY CLOTHING BRANDS, THE LIMITED, INC. TAPPED INTO THE BURGEONING PERSONAL CARE INDUSTRY IN 1990 WITH THE CREATION OF BATH & BODY WORKS.

ISP Fine Chemicals Inc.

HAT DO PHARMACEUTICALS, INSECT SEX ATTRACTANTS, AND HAIR SPRAY RESINS have in common? Each plays a useful part in our everyday lives, and all are produced at the ISP Fine Chemicals plant in Columbus. ✳ The scientists and researchers at ISP's Columbus operation are experts in producing com-

plex synthetic and organic chemicals and polymers used in the pharmaceutical, agricultural, personal care, and other fine chemical markets.

ISP Fine Chemicals was founded in 1964, when Dr. Kenneth Greenlee acquired the assets of Ohio State University's American Petroleum Institute Project, which he had directed. Greenlee transformed the former university project into a catalog research chemical business. Originally named Chemical Samples, the company built its reputation by supplying fine organic chemicals and analytical standards to government, university, and industrial research laboratories.

Advanced Capability

Today, the Columbus operation of ISP Fine Chemicals sits on a 100-acre tract on the western edge of Columbus. Acquired by ISP Corporation in February 1993, the operation employs nearly 100 individuals with expertise in research and development, manufacturing, engineering and maintenance, environmental, health and safety, quality assurance, regulatory affairs, and finance and administration. Work at the plant is directed by Dr. Paul Taylor, former director of process research for ISP in Wayne, New Jersey, who came to head operations in Columbus after the acquisition.

The plant has some highly unusual capabilities: It can manufacture compounds at -150° F, and contains modern bulk drug finishing areas, high vacuum distillation expertise, and sophisticated batch polymerization equipment. Products are manu-

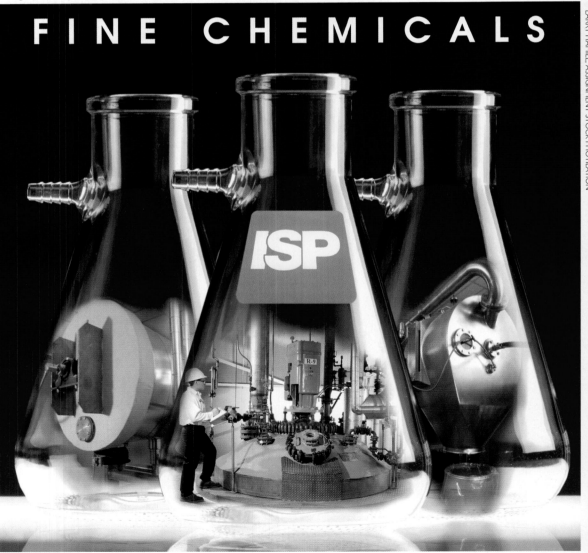

FINE CHEMICALS

factured in glass-lined or stainless steel reactors and purified by extraction, crystallization, or distillation. In addition to a line of proprietary products, the plant makes materials on a custom or contract basis.

SAFE PEST CONTROL

Early on, the plant developed technology to produce pheromones, complex organic compounds that are sex hormones, or attractants, for insects. These compounds create an environmentally friendly way to monitor and control a target species of insect populations. In minute quantities, pheromones attract insects for population monitoring and trapping; in larger quantities, they disrupt the insects' reproductive cycles. For example, Z-9-Tricosene is the pheromone for the common housefly, and it is used worldwide as an attractant in conjunction with insecticides in fly traps. Though used in small quantities, pheromones can have enormous beneficial impact. Through history, many useful plants have been subject to devastation by particular insect pests—the boll weevil, for example, was a recurring threat to cotton crops.

Today, this hazard is combated by Grandlure, a pheromone produced exclusively by ISP in Columbus. In 1997, more than 5 million acres of cotton plants will be treated, using just 220 pounds of Grandlure. In the last 15 years, this substance, combined with other management techniques, has essentially eradicated the boll weevil in the southeastern United States. Credit for that accomplishment goes largely to Dr. Terrence Holton, director of research and development for ISP, who over the last 25 years has refined the synthesis of this very complex mixture, and is considered a world expert in developing new synthetic routes to pheromones.

Such expertise has brought ISP's Columbus site recognition as a world leader in bulk pheromone production. The site produces commercial quantities for the Mediterranean fruit fly, tomato pinworm, gypsy moth, pink bollworm, and codling moth, as well as the housefly and boll weevil.

▲ STATE AERIAL COMMERCIAL PHOTOGRAPHY

EXPERTISE IN PHARMACEUTICALS

In 1983, the plant expanded activities, beginning production of pharmaceutical intermediaries and bulk active drugs. These compounds become part of the complex molecules used in antibiotics, cholesterol-reducing drugs, antihistamines, analgesics, heart drugs, antivirals, and chemotherapy medications formulated and marketed by pharmaceutical companies. As the cost of bringing new drugs to market rises, major pharmaceutical companies focus on research and development, outsourcing their need for bulk intermediates. ISP Fine Chemicals fills this market niche. Today, ISP Fine Chemicals both produces these materials commercially and manufactures the clinical trial quantities needed to test drugs under development.

Nationally, ISP Corporation, the parent company of ISP Fine chemicals, Inc., is a major producer of pharmaceutical excipients, beverage treatment products, agricultural adjuvants, sunscreens, cosmetic preservatives, hair spray resins, dental care products, shampoo ingredients, and other personal care products.

Other fine chemicals produced at the Columbus plant include prepolymers, paper coatings, specialty film coatings, agricultural intermediates, and additives and catalysts used to produce specialty polymers with unique characteristics.

ISP Fine Chemicals is sensitive to its surroundings—both the physical environment and the Columbus community. The company is a member of the Ohio Chemical Council, SOCMA, CMA, and Columbus Emergency Planning Advisory Committee, and is an active voluntary participant in Ohio Prevention First, an initiative by Governor George Voinovich to reduce hazardous wastes by 50 percent by the year 2000. Locally, ISP is a sponsor of COSI Connect, which financially assists grade school visits to the Columbus Center of Science and Industry, and provides mentoring for aspiring young scientists.

ISP has grown rapidly since its 1993 acquisition. The existing plant is at full capacity, with plans to double that capacity by the year 2001. In a community known for leading-edge technologies and creative enterprise, ISP Fine Chemicals takes pride in its past achievements and has a vision for further development of the fine chemical business in Columbus.

THE ISP FINE CHEMICALS PLANT, BUILT IN 1979, IS LOCATED ON 100 ACRES ON THE WEST SIDE OF COLUMBUS (TOP).

INTERMEDIATES AND ACTIVE INGREDIENTS USED IN THE PHARMACEUTICAL, AGRICULTURAL, AND OTHER FINE CHEMICAL INDUSTRIES ARE MANUFACTURED AT ISP'S COLUMBUS SITE (BOTTOM).

ASK ANY SUCCESSFUL BUSINESSPERSON WHAT'S INDISPENSABLE TO DAILY OPERATIONS. The answers are likely to be computer network . . . E-mail . . . fax . . . phone system . . . because in today's information age, connectivity is the essential need. In fact, it goes even deeper than that: It's constant access to data and

communications tools that delivers uncommon business efficiency.

In other words, systems availability is the business lifeline—that's what keeps business in business. It's the critical need to support this lifeline that makes the future so bright for Columbus-based Liebert Corporation. Protecting the business lifeline, specifically the systems that manage and control critical operations, is Liebert's business.

The company started in 1965, when Ralph C. Liebert pioneered the first computer cooling systems. Over the years, the company literally invented the computer support and protection industry by creating new products and developing innovative technology. Liebert currently offers

environmental control and power protection products, plus a variety of site monitoring products, and all are backed by an industry-leading service organization.

RESPONDING, BUILDING FOR THE FUTURE

Business computing has undergone dramatic changes in the last decade. As the traditional mainframe computer, protected in its "big glass house" environment, evolved into networked client-server applications, Liebert reassessed its core competencies. It was the beginning of a new era in which the company redefined its business to

focus on protecting mission-critical operations. There was an opportunity for Liebert anywhere sensitive electronics were used to manage and control such functions.

Those opportunities led to a significant expansion of traditional Liebert markets, plus new applications for protecting telecommunications, industrial automation, and medical imaging industries. Product lines tripled and several sales channels were added. Today, Liebert's worldwide presence includes global manufacturing capabilities and several hundred sales and service locations in more than 80 countries.

Now, business lifelines have taken a new form, and Liebert is there: building and sustaining long-term customer relationships, and lending support before, during, and after product installation.

AT THE HEART OF IT ALL

Liebert's longevity and considerable success is the result of many factors, the most significant of which is a very involved Liebert team. Committed to a world-class standard for products and customer support, this team has continually demonstrated a can-do attitude in a rapidly changing environment.

A tribute to Liebert associate involvement is the fact that more than 50 percent of the current workforce actively participates in Associate Action Teams (AAT). AAT task forces are charged with continually improving Liebert's processes and practices, while focusing on a promise to keep the Liebert brand synonymous with highest-possible value.

Optimum value is also rooted in an aggressive total quality management (TQM) effort. At Liebert, TQM goes beyond slogans, buttons, and posters. Commitment to continuous improvement is woven into daily

LUCENT TECHNOLOGIES' COLUMBUS WORKS IS THE PRIMARY MANUFACTURER FOR WIRELESS SYSTEMS SWITCHING EQUIPMENT IN SUPPORT OF THE FAST-GROWING WORLDWIDE CELLULAR INDUSTRY. LIEBERT POWER PROTECTION EQUIPMENT IS USED IN A NUMBER OF APPLICATIONS THROUGHOUT THE COMPANY'S FACILITY (TOP LEFT).

THE RIVERSIDE CAMPUS OF THE GRANT/ RIVERSIDE METHODIST HOSPITALS IN COLUMBUS DEPENDS ON 36 INTERCONNECTED LAN'S FOR ON-LINE COMMUNICATIONS THROUGHOUT THE 1200-BED FACILITY. MONITORING AND CONTROL OF ALL 93 LIEBERT UPS POWER SYSTEMS IS VIA SNMP COMMUNICATIONS SOFTWARE, A CRITICAL FEATURE FOR TESTING BATTERIES AND SCHEDULING THEIR REPLACEMENT (TOP RIGHT).

THE LITTLE GLASS HOUSE, WHICH PROVIDES DATA-CENTER QUALITY ENVIRONMENTAL AND POWER PROTECTION FOR REMOTE NETWORK EQUIPMENT, AND THE INTELECOOL, WHICH MAINTAINS A SAFE OPERATING CLIMATE FOR ISOLATED TELECOMMUNICATIONS SWITCHGEAR, ARE TWO EXAMPLES OF LIEBERT'S INNOVATION THAT HAVE CONTRIBUTED TO GROWTH IN NEW MARKETS (BOTTOM LEFT AND RIGHT).

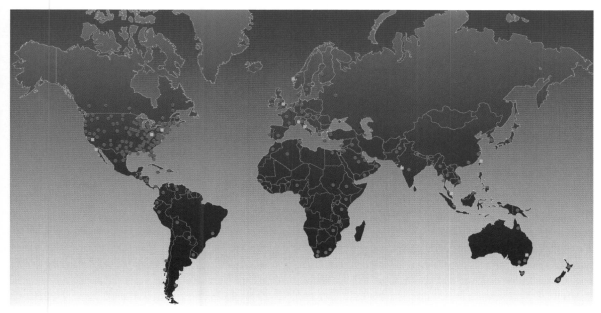

operations throughout the organization. In fact, intensive quality training is mandatory for all staff. To underscore its commitment to quality, the company defines goals in its mission and vision statements that challenge customers to measure progress in terms of error-free performance and exceeding expectations.

The quality score card is constantly growing—numerous awards, some on a consecutive-year basis, have been received from the Ohio Manufacturers' Association (the Governor's Award) and the Association for Quality and Participation.

Liebert also regularly competes for top honors in the Emerson Electric Co. Quality Award Program. The management of Liebert's parent organization, Emerson, strongly encourages divisions to compete, and the criteria are as stringent as any independent program. As a result, Liebert frequently goes head-to-head with the other industry-leading divisions of Fortune 100 Emerson Electric—and wins in these competitions, as well.

It's Working

Liebert's sales records continue to be broken on a regular basis. Wally O'Dell, Liebert's president since 1991, offers insight: "Clearly, our current 20 percent growth rates are the result of great effort in areas of associate

involvement, quality systems, and customer focus. But, I also strongly believe the decision to redefine traditional Liebert business lines is the strategy of the decade for our company. Today, we address the unique needs of new forms of computer-based operations—telecommunications, industrial automation, and medical imaging. The support needs of electronics, particularly those used in applications categorized as mission-critical, ideally fit our core competency. We fully intend to seek out and respond to these emerging opportunities."

This growth is a reflection of customer confidence and loyalty, creating a very optimistic outlook for

the future. Although the company enjoys significant market share in many of its target industries, Liebert is not a take-it-for-granted company. Customer satisfaction surveys are constantly being taken. The feedback received is vital information, because it updates performance benchmarks and asks the most appropriate audience, Liebert's customers, to rate their experience with the company and its products.

Liebert's ability to protect the business lifeline will continue to win at the customer level, keeping the company growing and sustaining it as a solid corporate citizen that proudly calls Columbus home.

Newly opened manufacturing facilities in mainland China and Eastern Europe add to existing facilities in Ireland, United Kingdom, Italy, India, Australia, Mexico, and three locations in the United States (top).

Though Liebert believes quality is ultimately measured by customers, the company was proud to receive the Governors Award from the Ohio Manufacturers Association for Quality and Associate participation, and the Quality Award from Emerson Electric Co. (bottom).

CONSOLIDATED STORES CORP.

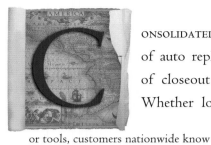

CONSOLIDATED STORES CORP. BEGAN IN 1967 AS A SMALL, WHOLESALE DISTRIBUTOR of auto replacement parts. Today, the company is the nation's largest retailer of closeout merchandise and the largest operator of mall-based toy stores. Whether looking for housewares, electronics, sporting goods, toys, jewelry,

or tools, customers nationwide know to shop at Consolidated's nearly 2,000 Big Lots, Odd Lots, and K•B toy stores for quality, brand-name items at savings ranging from 30 to 70 percent off the regular retail price.

Appealing to value-minded, middle-income shoppers has been the guiding principle for the company since its beginning in the wholesale business. Consolidated has been able to attract these customers by offering an ever changing array of manufacturers' overruns, discontinued product lines, and out-of-season goods.

Over the years, Consolidated has grown both through acquisitions and by branching out into new business lines. From wholesaling, the company expanded into the closeout business with the opening of its first store in 1983, followed by a foray into

the single-price-point business when the All for One stores (selling all merchandise for one dollar) opened in 1991.

In the early 1990s, the company also realized that toy departments were outperforming other areas in its stores. This realization led to the acquisition of Toy Liquidators in 1994, and KayBee Toy Stores and Toy Works in 1996. With these acquisitions, Consolidated doubled its revenues, gained a presence in all 50 states and Puerto Rico, and emerged as the nation's second-largest toy retailer.

Existing KayBee and Toy Liquidators stores retain their names, while new stores in this division are called K•B Toys, K•B Toy Outlet, or K•B Toy Works. Located in major shopping malls, neighborhood strip cen-

ters, and outlet centers, these stores sell a large variety of current toys (in addition to closeout merchandise), which differentiates them from Consolidated's core Odd Lots and Big Lots stores.

Exploring new product lines has also resulted in company growth. In 1996, Consolidated began testing fur-

ODD LOTS, LIKE THE ONE IN HILLIARD, OFFERS A BROAD RANGE OF CONSISTENTLY CHANGING CLOSEOUT MERCHANDISE AT PRICES UP TO 70 PERCENT LOWER THAN DISCOUNT STORES (TOP).

IN CONSOLIDATED'S ODD LOTS AND BIG LOTS STORES THE "IT'S THE PRICE" CAMPAIGN TOOK THE COMPANY BACK TO ITS ROOTS, BY SIMPLIFYING ITS VALUE MESSAGE. THE CAMPAIGN ALSO ADDED A GREAT LOOK TO CONSOLIDATED'S STORES (BOTTOM).

niture in some stores. Today, there are freestanding Big Lots Furniture stores, as well as numerous in-store furniture departments. Food may be the next expansion area for the company, which already carries some food items. In 1997, Consolidated began testing frozen foods in several markets.

STRONG VENDOR RELATIONSHIPS

Consolidated's expansion into new product lines has been facilitated by the relationships it has fostered over the years with its vendors. In the early days, company buyers had to pound the pavement to secure closeout merchandise. Today, the company has an arsenal of about 3,000 vendors who supply items on a regular basis.

Vendors know that Consolidated can liquidate their product overruns and discontinued lines without upsetting their regular lines of trade with other retailers. Consolidated has a reputation for legitimizing the closeout business, unlike many of its competitors. Even with this growth, however, buyers are still encouraged to maintain their entrepreneurial spirit to find special closeout deals.

At the store level, managers are encouraged to adjust their merchandise mix to meet the needs of their specific area. Although that spirit may be harder to hold onto today because of Consolidated's size, it is a tenet that is revered throughout the company. One saying Chairman William G. Kelley is fond of repeating is, "If you stop thinking like a small business, you'll become one."

A CUT ABOVE THE REST

Consolidated is a success story in a retail industry that has been plagued by bankruptcies, downsizings, and consolidations. The company reported a net income of $84 million on revenues of $2.7 billion in fiscal 1996, up from a net income of $64.4 million on revenues of $1.4 billion in fiscal 1995.

Consolidated has a reputation for providing a great return for shareholders and great values for customers. The company is also known for its commitment to its more than 50,000 associates and to the communities in which they live and work. Following the recent expansion of its Columbus distribution center, 50 percent of new workers hired qualified as economically or physically disadvantaged. The company is also actively involved in the Literacy Initiative, primarily through a computer-based work skills program called Read and Achieve, which helps improve adult literacy.

Columbus is the perfect home for Consolidated, due to the availability of a skilled labor force for its high-tech, state-of-the-art distribution center; the city's superb location from a distribution perspective; and the responsiveness of city and state officials in providing incentives for expansion.

As Consolidated continues its tradition of success, the company will also maintain its commitment to providing value for middle-income customers. Says Kent Larsson, Consolidated's senior vice president of marketing, "We're in the business of saving people money."

THERE IS A K•B TOY STORE IN ALMOST EVERY ENCLOSED SHOPPING MALL IN THE COUNTRY, PROVIDING VALUE-PRICED TOYS IN A CONVENIENT, EASY-TO-SHOP ENVIRONMENT.

OCLC Online Computer Library Center, Inc.

FREDERICK G. KILGOUR AND THE PRESIDENTS OF OHIO'S COLLEGES AND UNIVERSITIES originally founded OCLC Online Computer Library Center, Inc. in 1967 to help the state's 54 academic libraries share resources and reduce costs. Today, more than 25,000 libraries in 63 countries use OCLC computer services to manage their library collections and services and provide information to their users.

A nonprofit, membership organization, OCLC's goals are to further access the world's information and to reduce information costs. To satisfy the first part of its mission, OCLC has increased the availability of library resources through its electronic, shared cataloging, and interlibrary lending systems and databases. It provides patrons, researchers, and scholars access to a wide range of databases, some of which were developed by OCLC, to assist with their information needs. OCLC was the first organization to provide database-searching capabilities to end users.

To accomplish the second part of its mission, OCLC offers services that help libraries reduce their costs. This includes providing systems that allow libraries to operate more efficiently. It also involves helping libraries leverage their investment by providing them with technology that they can use over an extended period. One example of this is OCLC software that allows a library to access the World Wide Web and other resources through its existing computer system, thus extending the life and capability of its own local computer hardware.

PREPARING FOR THE FUTURE

Guided by its mission, OCLC's current strategic plan focuses on service integration, innovation, international expansion, and education.

To keep its members and users on the cutting edge, OCLC offers advanced education and knowledge exchange for librarians and information specialists through the OCLC Institute, established in 1997.

OCLC is working to integrate its services so that they are linked electronically. The organization also will continue to innovate and take advantage of new technologies. OCLC is currently looking at new options for electronic archiving of library materials as the volume of electronic documents at libraries continues to increase.

Opportunities also abound in cyberspace. OCLC, which owns the Dewey decimal classification system, is examining ways to automatically catalog information available on the Internet since no library type of classification currently exists.

OCLC is working to make access to information available on a global basis. The organization now serves

OCLC ONLINE COMPUTER LIBRARY CENTER, INC., ORIGINALLY FOUNDED IN 1967 TO HELP OHIO'S 54 ACADEMIC LIBRARIES SHARE RESOURCES AND REDUCE COSTS, TODAY SERVES MORE THAN 25,000 LIBRARIES IN 63 COUNTRIES.

more than 25,000 libraries in 63 countries. That means being operational 24 hours a day, seven days a week, 365 days a year.

An ultimate goal is to attract all major universities from around the world to become members of OCLC. The organization now has an office at Tsinghua University in Beijing, China. It is also working with Russian librarians to establish a version of OCLC in that country. The collaborative efforts are useful because members contribute records to the database. In addition, most research libraries in the United States obtain much of their material from abroad.

POISED FOR THE FUTURE

OCLC has prospered in Columbus, thanks to a number of computer-based organizations that make Columbus their home, and to the Ohio State University and other colleges and universities, which provide a steady talent pool. The organization can be labeled as one of the region's significant public/private ventures. The Ohio College Association and the Ohio legislature, which granted

$500,000 to help found OCLC, joined forces to create a worldwide organization that today is totally self-supporting, has provided member libraries more than $1 billion in services, and saves them millions of dollars in costs.

Other key accomplishments for the organization include the creation of WorldCat, the OCLC Online Union Catalog, the most consulted database in higher education. The database, which grows at the rate of 2 million records annually, describes books, journals, audiovisual media, maps, archives/manuscripts, sound recordings, music scores, and computer files, and includes a list of member libraries that hold the items. At current growth rates, WorldCat will contain more than 43 million records by the year 2000.

Because it has a track record of improving and democratizing access to information, OCLC holds a prominent position in helping the nation move to an information-based society. OCLC remains dedicated to its broad public purpose of furthering access to information and reducing information costs.

ANHEUSER-BUSCH, INC.

BEER IS ONE OF THE OLDEST AND MOST CELEBRATED BEVERAGES; FOR CENTURIES, SKILLED brewmasters have been combining grains, malts, hops, and yeast to create the brew that is a welcome tradition in many cultures. In Ohio today, the beers most often served at sporting events, family cookouts, and wherever people congregate are

those produced at the Anheuser-Busch, Inc. brewery in Columbus.

In 1996, nearly half the beer sold in Ohio—61.9 million cases—was brewed at Anheuser-Busch's Columbus brewery, which produces Budweiser, Bud Light, Michelob, Michelob Light, Busch, Busch Light, Busch NA, Natural Light, and O'Doul's for distribution throughout Ohio, Michigan, Indiana, and West Virginia.

Following a two-year construction effort, the brewery opened in 1968 on 250 acres to the north of Columbus. It was the sixth brewery in the Anheuser-Busch network, and has played a major role in helping the company maintain its position as the world's leading brewer. Operations at the site have been progressively enlarged and improved: capacity was doubled in 1976 and, currently, the brewery is undergoing a five-year modernization and expansion.

MODERNIZATION AND EXPANSION

The first phase of this project, creation of an automated warehouse, was completed in 1996. The effort created the most advanced storage system of any brewery in the world. Within this warehouse, full pallets of beer are transported by automated guided vehicles (AGVs) to an automated storage facility. From storage, AGVs move pallets to the truck dock for shipping to Anheuser-Busch's network of wholesalers. This system reduces warehousing costs and guarantees customers the freshest beer possible.

Due for completion in 1997, the next phase of modernization will enlarge the draught beer cold storage area to accommodate the expanding Anheuser-Busch product line. The entire draught beer packaging line will be replaced in early 1998.

Down the line, brewery capacity will be increased by 900,000 barrels

a year by automating the brew house and fermenting operations. Here, modernization will create fully automated control of milling, mashing, and brew-kettle operations. The cooling, settling, and distributing of the wort—the liquid which, once fermented, becomes beer—will be automated, as will primary fermentation and transfer to the lagering cellar.

This $118 million modernization ensures that the Columbus brewery will continue to make a major contribution to the economy of Central Ohio, in part, because local contractors are used whenever possible. More important, the modernization makes the brewery more competitive, helping to ensure steady employment for Anheuser-Busch workers.

The Anheuser-Busch brewery is one of the area's largest private employers, with more than 950 employees whose aggregate wages and benefits top $58 million. An additional

FOLLOWING A TWO-YEAR CONSTRUCTION EFFORT, THE BREWERY OPENED IN 1968 ON 250 ACRES TO THE NORTH OF COLUMBUS. IT WAS THE SIXTH BREWERY IN THE ANHEUSER-BUSCH NETWORK AND HAS PLAYED A MAJOR ROLE IN HELPING THE COMPANY MAINTAIN ITS POSITION AS THE WORLD'S LEADING BREWER.

IN 1996, NEARLY HALF THE BEER SOLD IN OHIO—61.9 MILLION CASES—WAS BREWED AT ANHEUSER-BUSCH'S COLUMBUS BREWERY, WHICH PRODUCES BUDWEISER, BUD LIGHT, MICHELOB, MICHELOB LIGHT, BUSCH, BUSCH LIGHT, BUSCH NA, NATURAL LIGHT, AND O'DOUL'S FOR DISTRIBUTION THROUGHOUT OHIO, MICHIGAN, INDIANA, AND WEST VIRGINIA.

1,117 people, with salaries and benefits totaling $48.7 million, are employed by the 27 independent wholesalers who distribute Anheuser-Busch beers to 20,300 retail accounts throughout Ohio.

A Diversified Operation

Anheuser-Busch is not in Columbus—or Ohio—just for the beer. Under the umbrella of Anheuser-Busch Companies, Inc., it operates a range of other activities, the best known of which is Sea World of Ohio, in Aurora, one of the Midwest's most popular attractions. Sea World draws crowds with Shamu the whale, seven live shows, and more than 20 animal attractions, including the Dolphin Cave, where visitors can experience firsthand encounters with bottlenose dolphins.

Anheuser-Busch creates homes for businesses as well as dolphins. The Busch Corporate Center, an award-winning business/industrial park developed on 155 acres near the brewery by Busch Properties, Inc., provides leased office, warehouse, and light industry space to approximately 160 companies.

The Columbus plant of Anheuser-Busch's Metal Container Corporation provides nearly all the metal cans required by the Columbus brewery. The facility, with 205 employees, produces 2.4 billion cans annually.

Its operation is tied to the work of the Anheuser-Busch Recycling Corporation, the nation's largest recycler of used aluminum, which maintains a recycling plant in Marion.

"Making Friends Is Our Business"

More than a century ago, Adolphus Busch, the industry innovator who founded the Budweiser brand, coined the phrase "Making Friends Is Our Business." Probably no promotion makes more friends for the company than its Clydesdale horses. These majestic champions tour the country, appearing at the Ohio State Fair and elsewhere, to remind spectators of the quality associated with "the King of Beers." In addition, Anheuser-Busch extends hospitality in Columbus with brewery tours; nationally, the company operates a network of Busch Gardens and Sea World theme parks.

IN OHIO TODAY, THE BEERS MOST OFTEN SERVED AT SPORTING EVENTS, FAMILY COOKOUTS, AND WHEREVER PEOPLE CONGREGATE ARE THOSE PRODUCED AT THE ANHEUSER-BUSCH, INC. BREWERY IN COLUMBUS.

In Columbus, Anheuser-Busch is both host and benefactor. A recent survey ranked Anheuser-Busch among the nation's top 20 corporate contributors. In recent years, it has contributed more than $1 million to local organizations, including the Columbus Symphony, Columbus Zoo, Columbus Public Schools, and Boys Club of Columbus. Anheuser-Busch's commitment to the community also includes a continuing involvement with Ohio's minority communities. The business funds scholarship programs, youth development organizations, athletic and cultural programs, civil rights efforts, and economic development efforts through business and banking relationships with minority-owned firms.

Busch believed in making friends; he also believed in brewing the finest beer. It's a combination long welcomed by the Buckeye State, as well as by the nation.

ATS Ohio, Inc.

FOR MANY MANUFACTURING COMPANIES THAT ARE LOOKING FOR STATE-OF-THE-ART, custom-designed factory automation systems, the search ends at ATS Ohio, Inc. Founded in 1968, the Columbus-based business has made a name for itself by creating systems that enable its customers to remain on the cutting edge of production efficiency and profitability.

Well aware of its customers' needs for both value and flexibility, ATS Ohio, which recently received ISO 9000 certification, designs systems that are cost effective, modular, and expandable. Whether businesses are searching for power- and free-pallet-based assembly and test systems; precision link transport systems; stand-alone robotic assembly work cells; vision inspection systems; material handling and palletizing systems; or consumer packaging systems, at ATS Ohio they will find the best quality, service, support, and innovation in the factory automation systems industry today. Typical contracts for ATS Ohio range from $250,000 to $10 million.

ATS Ohio is equipped with a staff of mechanical designers, electrical engineers, systems engineers, technicians, and machinists who possess the necessary industry knowledge to solve even the most complex problems faced by manufacturers.

Total Solution Capability

ATS Ohio maintains a competitive advantage through its total solution capability. The company can assist clients from conception to completion of a project, including the design phase, development, toolmaking and machining, programming, integration, assembly, installation, training, and support. The company prides itself on its hands-on operator and classroom training, which occurs at ATS Ohio and at the customer's facility, and its documentation packages, which are so complete that most customers are able to maintain the automated systems in-house. Documentation packages include a comprehensive operations and maintenance manual as well as mechanical drawings, electrical drawings, and professionally commented application source code.

The company's superior performance is evidenced by the fact that 75 percent of ATS Ohio's business comes from repeat customers. Continued customer demand is driven by history, according to General Manager Joseph A. Moreno Sr., who says, "Customers are looking for a supplier who has a proven track record, and that is one of the key elements that we are able to offer them at ATS Ohio."

Typical customers are Fortune 500 companies, and automotive manufacturers represent nearly half of ATS Ohio's client base. Other industries served include computer and peripherals; semiconductor; electrical and appliance; consumer packaging; electronics; and telecommunications.

LOCATED JUST NORTH OF COLUMBUS, THE ATS OHIO MANUFACTURING FACILITY WAS EXPANDED TO 77,000 SQUARE FEET IN 1996 (TOP).

WITH MORE THAN 2,000 EMPLOYEES IN LOCATIONS ACROSS NORTH AMERICA, EUROPE, AND THE FAR EAST, ATS, INC. HAS THE RESOURCES TO MEET ITS CUSTOMERS' SPECIFIC NEEDS (BOTTOM).

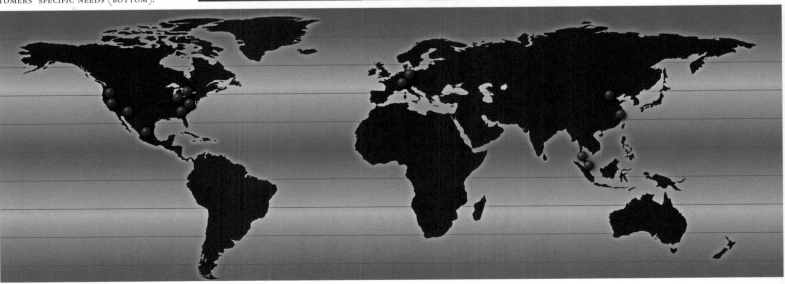

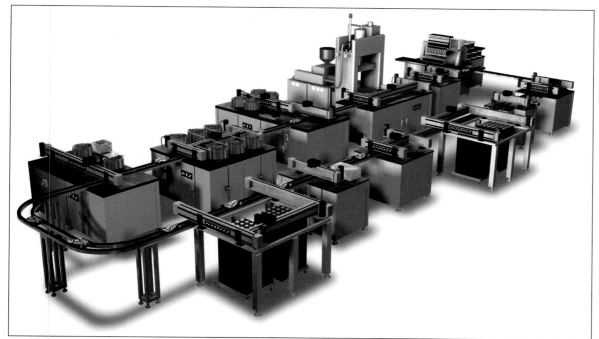

ATS Ohio is responding to the global needs of its customers. The company has installed systems throughout North America, Europe, and Asia. ATS Ohio is pursuing other opportunities as its domestic customers expand internationally.

ADEPT AND RESPONSIVE

Operating out of a 77,000-square-foot facility on Enterprise Drive, ATS Ohio has experienced annual growth in revenue of approximately 20 percent during the past five years. Contributing to that success is the company's project-manager-based organizational structure. A number of project managers, who have several years of experience at the company, are the linchpins of the business. They are responsible for complete project coordination, including manufacturing, purchasing, fabrication, assembly, and all engineering disciplines. Another organizational strength is the company's relatively small and tightly knit group of approximately 150 employees. The smaller size enables the company to be adept and responsive to its customers' needs.

Contributing to the company's leadership ranking are innovation, dedication, and the capability to deliver systems in a timely manner. Much credit goes to the area's workforce;

ATS Ohio has found a steady labor pool of skilled workers from local universities and technical schools, and company officials praise the strong work ethic and stability found in Central Ohio workers.

Also playing a positive role in ATS Ohio's growth is its ownership by Canadian-based ATS Automation Tooling Systems Inc., a fast-growing company that had 1996 sales of nearly $200 million, up approximately $60

million from the previous year. ATS Ohio is able to utilize the innovations and technology of its parent, such as a new, proprietary robot that is known for its speed, scalability, and low costs.

Return on investment is imperative in any industry. ATS Ohio will continue to build on its hallmarks of dedication, innovation, capability, and quality to provide value for its customers and its employees.

LAKE SHORE CRYOTRONICS INC.

ESTABLISHED IN 1968, WESTERVILLE-BASED LAKE SHORE CRYOTRONICS IS AN INTERnational leader in developing innovative measurement and control solutions. Founded by Dr. John M. Swartz, a former professor of electrical engineering at Ohio State University, and his brother David, Lake Shore's Scientific Division

produces equipment for the measurement of cryogenic temperatures, magnetic fields, and the characterization of the physical properties of materials in temperature and magnetic environments. The Industrial Division, formed in 1990, serves the process industry by providing heavy-duty velocity- and position-measuring devices.

Although Lake Shore's products are technical in nature, they touch people's lives in many ways. The operation and efficiency of electric motors, computer systems, medical imaging systems, cellular telephones, compact disc players, speakers, floppy disks, paper, raw metal, tires, and satellites in space are all enhanced by Lake Shore's measurement and control equipment.

ON THE CUTTING EDGE
With a focus on utilizing innovative technology to improve the measurements of scientists and industry, Lake Shore maintains a long-standing com-

LAKE SHORE'S NEW 60,000-SQUARE-FOOT HEADQUARTERS IN WESTERVILLE (TOP)

HIGH PERFORMANCE DIGITAL TACHOMETERS, ENCODERS, PULSE GENERATORS, AND INSTRUMENTATION FOR ACCURATE AND RELIABLE MEASUREMENT OF MOTION ON INDUSTRIAL MACHINERY (BOTTOM).

mitment to research and development, which makes up approximately 16 percent of the company's annual revenues.

Not only has the innovation that has resulted from that research and development positioned Lake Shore as the market leader of proven products, but it has earned the company numerous awards, patents, and research and development grants. The Scientific Division has received numerous patents and industry-related awards for its development of cutting-edge products. In fact, on five different occasions, among several thousand applicants, Lake Shore products have been on the list compiled by *Research & Development* magazine of the top 100 scientific innovations of the previous year.

Recently, the company received a grant of nearly $500,000 from the U.S. Air Force through Wright-Patterson Air Force Base to develop a new semiconductor characterization system. This system will help researchers around the world evaluate new semiconductor materials in order to improve the performance of integrated circuits for faster computers, wireless electronic products like cellular phones, and military applications.

SERVING SCIENCE AND INDUSTRY
Lake Shore traces its roots to cryogenic temperature sensors, an offshoot of John Swartz' interest in semiconductor physics. Initially, these products were manufactured in the basement of his home in Minerva Park, while David Swartz handled the sales and marketing from his home in Buffalo. In 1973, both operations were consolidated in Columbus.

For much of its history, the company has focused on cryogenic sensors used for the precise measurement of temperatures from near absolute zero to room temperature. Lake Shore started its instrumentation group in 1980, designing and manufacturing products to monitor Lake Shore's cryogenic temperature sensors and to precisely control the cryogenic temperature environments that researchers use to study the physical properties of materials. In 1987, Lake Shore formed a systems group that incorporates sensors, instruments, software, and other components to develop complete systems focused on characterizing the magnetic properties of materials.

Lake Shore systems help researchers worldwide study giant magnetoresistance; high-temperature and organic superconducting materials; molecular-based magnets; rare earth and transition metal materials; spin glasses; amorphous magnets; and many other magnetic and nonmagnetic materials. The company's systems also help quality control engineers and researchers at industrial companies characterize a variety of permanent magnet and magnetic media materials. These include audio, video, and digital tapes; flexible media; magneto-optical materials; magnets for AC and DC electrical motors; and audio speakers.

Lake Shore's fast-growing Industrial Division recently changed the industry standard for tachometers, which measure precision rotational speed between a large roll on a machine and the electronic drive controlling the power requirements to the process. Utilizing a new, patented, magneto-resistive technology with innovative designs, the RIM & SLIM Tach Series of digital tachometers has led such top motor and drive manufacturers (OEMs) as General Electric, Allen-Bradley, Reliance Electric, and Siemens to switch to Lake Shore from other tachometer manufacturers.

A recipient of the governor's Excellence in Exporting Award, Lake Shore is a key international player, annually exporting approximately 40 percent of its products. In the future, the company anticipates expanding its distribution into the emerging global markets in China and the Far East, in Eastern Europe, and throughout Latin America. Within the next five years, exports will exceed 50 percent of Lake Shore's sales. In short, Lake Shore's success at developing advanced technology is bringing millions of dollars from international markets into the Central Ohio community.

Lake Shore is positioned to introduce several new technologies for diversifying the measurement and control devices currently offered. To prepare for this future growth, in 1997, Lake Shore relocated to a new, 60,000-square-foot complex, equipped with enhanced manufacturing capacity and upgraded research and development facilities.

Lake Shore's scientists and engineers are dedicated to developing tomorrow's precision measurement technology and to providing customers with high-value solutions through the company's products. The result

will be enhanced productivity and quality for the end user's process. Lake Shore also plans to increase its staff to develop new products, broaden existing product lines, and expand its worldwide distribution channels.

Summing up the Lake Shore philosophy, John Swartz concludes, "Lake Shore will maintain appreciable growth by continuously improving our internal systems, our staff, and our product lines, and by introducing new technologies as we see their potential importance in our spheres of influence."

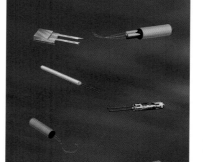

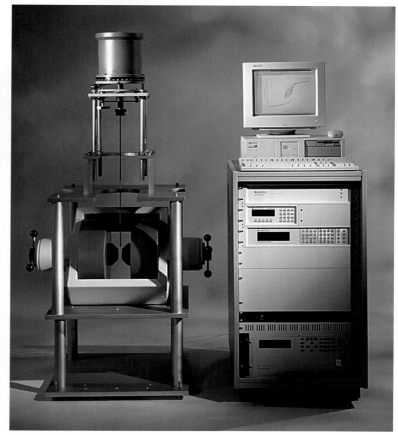

CHARLES PENZONE, INC. / GRAND SALONS AND DAY SPAS

OR MOST OF HIS LIFE, CHARLES PENZONE HAD A VISION OF THE ULTIMATE BEAUTY salon, where customers could go for pampering, relaxation, and head-to-toe beauty services, including hair design, facial treatments, massage therapy, and hand and foot care. In 1991, his vision became a reality. ✸ After successfully

operating a chain of smaller salons in Central Ohio for 22 years, Penzone consolidated six locations and opened the 18,000-square-foot Grand Salon—the largest beauty salon and day spa in the world. Despite the skeptics who said it couldn't be done, especially in Central Ohio, the Dublin-based salon was an instant success and was named 1993 Salon of the Year by *Modern Salon*, a leading industry publication.

In 1996, Penzone opened a second Grand Salon, consolidating three locations to serve the expanding northeastern quadrant of Central Ohio, specifically the communities of

Gahanna and New Albany. This 20,000-square-foot salon, which features waterfalls, private elevators, palm trees, soothing music, and an atrium, recently received a special distinction award from *Modern Salon* for salon design.

A LEAGUE OF ITS OWN

"These are not beauty parlors in any sense of the word. These are $3.5 million, world-class facilities, which are run like businesses," says Penzone, whose company and Grand Salons operate under the name Charles Penzone, Inc. While some doubted that two large facilities could be sup-

ported by the Columbus market, the company was confident that its day spa concept, where both male and female customers could seek refuge from their hectic schedules, would work. The company was right.

The two Grand Salons are strategically located within easy distance of any spot in Central Ohio. The company's steady and growing clientele is also served by a small, 1,100-square-foot hair salon in trendy German Village called Max, The Salon, which opened in 1996.

What keeps attracting clients? Certainly the luxurious, beautifully designed settings help. Despite their large size, the salons were carefully designed to give clients the illusion of a small, intimate setting. The full range of services is appealing, as well. The Grand Salons feature a 40-page catalog, detailing every type of beauty service imaginable. Special services include A Quick-Fix Package, which offers a European facial, nutrient manicure, basic whirlpool pedicure, and makeup application during a three-hour, 15-minute session. Another option is The Grand Experience. Included in the eight-hour service is a continental breakfast, aromatherapy hot oil massage, paraffin body treat-

CHARLES PENZONE'S DUBLIN-BASED SALON, OPENED IN 1991, WAS AN INSTANT SUCCESS AND WAS NAMED 1993 SALON OF THE YEAR BY *Modern Salon* MAGAZINE, A LEADING INDUSTRY PUBLICATION (TOP).

"THESE ARE NOT BEAUTY PARLORS IN ANY SENSE OF THE WORD. THESE ARE $3.5 MILLION, WORLD-CLASS FACILITIES, WHICH ARE RUN LIKE BUSINESSES," SAYS CHARLES PENZONE (BOTTOM LEFT AND RIGHT).

ment, facial, lunch, manicure, deluxe pedicure, hair service, and makeup consultation and application.

The quality of the staff of more than 300 skilled technicians is another component that keeps clients coming back for more. Charles Penzone's hair stylists, manicurists, skin care technicians, massage therapists, and pedicurists must go through rigorous in-house training after they are hired. Regardless of their previous experience, newly hired associates are required to attend training for six to 14 months. Established associates, too, must attend at least eight advanced training sessions annually.

STATE-OF-THE-ART TECHNOLOGY

Both Grand Salons rely on a state-of-the-art computerized system to help manage day-to-day operations. The system books appointments, performs payroll operations, and tracks inventory, among other functions. To assist with customer retention efforts, in-house technology allows the company to monitor each client's number of visits and types of services utilized. Charles Penzone is known for setting industry standards with its computer systems and business management techniques.

In recognition of his innovation and success, Penzone, who was born and raised in Columbus, was recently named one of the top 20 salon owners in the United States. He also was

appointed by Governor George V. Voinovich to the seven-member Ohio State Board of Cosmetology, the group that sets the standards for the state's cosmetology industry, which includes 114,000 practitioners. The company also has enjoyed widespread media coverage, including features in *People*, *Midwest Living*, and numerous trade publications, as well as on such national broadcasts as *The Today Show* and *Inside Edition*.

Even though it operates the two largest salons and day spas in the world, the company does not

plan to rest on its laurels. As it looks toward the future, more expansion is expected locally and beyond the boundaries of Central Ohio.

Charles Penzone has a reputation for longevity in an industry known for high turnover. The company will continue to build on its stellar past by innovating and revamping to ensure success in the future. "We're relentless in trying to improve our particular operation," says Penzone. "We are constantly upgrading our system to make tomorrow better than yesterday."

CLOCKWISE FROM TOP LEFT:
THE 20,000-SQUARE-FOOT NEW ALBANY GRAND SALON, WHICH FEATURES WATERFALLS, PRIVATE ELEVATORS, PALM TREES, SOOTHING MUSIC, AND AN ATRIUM, RECEIVED THE 1997 SALON OF THE YEAR AWARD FROM *Modern Salon* MAGAZINE.

IN 1996, PENZONE OPENED A SECOND GRAND SALON, CONSOLIDATING THREE LOCATIONS TO SERVE THE EXPANDING NORTHEASTERN QUADRANT OF CENTRAL OHIO, SPECIFICALLY THE COMMUNITIES OF GAHANNA AND NEW ALBANY.

THE GRAND EXPERIENCE, AN EIGHT-HOUR SERVICE, INCLUDES A CONTINENTAL BREAKFAST, AROMATHERAPY HOT OIL MASSAGE, PARAFFIN BODY TREATMENT, FACIAL, LUNCH, MANICURE, DELUXE PEDICURE, HAIR SERVICE, AND MAKEUP CONSULTATION AND APPLICATION.

SHONAC CORPORATION

IN JULY 1991, THE DOORS OF THE FIRST DSW SHOE WAREHOUSE OPENED AT 3901 WEST Dublin-Granville Road. The brainchild of the Columbus-based Shonac Corporation and its president, Stephen Nacht, DSW was not simply a new shoe store, but a new approach in shoe retailing. ✹ Brought about by a changing market climate, the

opening of DSW Shoe Warehouse was just the latest in a long line of shoe business developments that have kept the Nacht family at the forefront for three generations.

A FITTING BUSINESS

By the time the first DSW Shoe Warehouse began welcoming customers, Shonac Corporation had decades of industry experience through its leased shoe departments and discount shoe outlets. In fact, Nacht had grown up in the business; his father, George Nacht, started selling shoes in the 1920s. But the younger Nacht headed off to Ohio State University with other ideas in mind. "I intended to be a lawyer," he says. "Then, after each year of college, I wanted to be a lawyer less—and in the shoe business more."

Following college, Nacht signed on with the Shoe Corporation of America; later, he bought a half interest in a shoe box company in Boston. After four years in Boston, he sold his holdings and returned to Columbus. His return came just as his father received an offer both thought worthy of consideration.

"The Schottenstein family was talking to my dad about going into a lease arrangement. My father was 61," Nacht recalls. "It was not something he wanted to start alone."

Together, they leased space in Schottenstein's Department Stores for on-premise, retail shoe operations. Forming Shonac Corporation—a simple combination of the Schottenstein and Nacht family names—they opened their first department in Euclid in February 1969. Two decades of fairly steady expansion followed. By 1990, however, opportunity had leveled off. Growth in the shoe business focused on athletic shoes; elsewhere, sales were stagnant.

Says Nacht, "We weren't selling anything unique. New companies were coming into the market, and we were sharing our business with them."

A NEW DIRECTION

By launching DSW Shoe Warehouse, Shonac gained access to a fresh market. Rather than matching styles and wits with discount retailers Famous Footwear and Picway, the company positioned itself against the mall anchors. Targeting the more affluent, brand-conscious buyers meant a major change in stock. While Shonac's discount stores offered a mix of cancellations and buyouts, with DSW, the company switched to first-run,

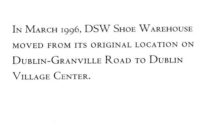

IN MARCH 1996, DSW SHOE WAREHOUSE MOVED FROM ITS ORIGINAL LOCATION ON DUBLIN-GRANVILLE ROAD TO DUBLIN VILLAGE CENTER.

current-style, name-brand shoes, purchased from 400 sources and brought to customers the same season they reached the market.

The DSW Shoe Warehouse idea—an unsurpassed selection of quality shoes at discount prices—has brought resounding praise. A Detroit magazine named it the "best shoe store" in the city; in Indianapolis, DSW was cited for "the best shoe bargains." And readers surveyed in Cleveland and Columbus ranked it their favorite.

Nacht does not claim the idea as original, but points out that no one has developed the idea as far as he and Shonac. "We're the only ones doing this with more than five stores," he says. Since that first outlet opened in Dublin, DSW Shoe Warehouse has grown into a chain of 39 stores spread through 22 states, from New York to California. Six additional stores will open in 1998, toward a goal of 50.

Each DSW store presents an upscale, warehouse environment, with 25,000 to 55,000 shoes displayed in rows that rise only a few feet. This permits customers an easy view of the store's entire selection, which includes handbags, socks, hosiery, and other items.

New Market Brings Flexibility

The warehouse approach put Shonac in the driver's seat regarding its growth potential. "If you operate in space leased from department stores," Nacht

notes, "then you have to wait until someone opens a department store to add one of your own." With DSW Shoe Warehouse, Shonac could pick and choose its own locations and store opening schedule.

And DSW brought balance to Shonac. Paired with its leased operations, Nacht observes, "We have two strong drivers; we're not wholly dependent on one or the other."

Along with its DSW operation, Shonac maintains its base in discount shoes, leasing and operating nearly 100 shoe departments in Schottenstein and Value City stores in the Midwest, Southeast, and East. Shonac employment now tops 1,000, and wherever possible, the company promotes from within. "They know the company,

they know shoes, they know the buyer," Nacht says.

"To be in the shoe business," Nacht adds, "you have to love shoes— have experience with shoes and how they fit. You have to know the history of styles. Styles tend to come back 15 to 20 years later. I was selling Hush Puppies in the 1950s; I'm selling Hush Puppies today."

Styles may return, but the shoe industry itself has changed. "It used to be large chains/small independents," says Nacht. "Nobil is gone; Thom McCan is gone; the independents are gone. Now, it's department stores plus Wal-Mart." Plus Shonac—thanks to new ideas, decades of experience, and a solid appreciation for the shoe business.

Clockwise from top left: Each DSW store presents an upscale, warehouse environment, with 25,000 to 55,000 shoes displayed in rows that rise only a few feet.

The DSW Shoe Warehouse idea— an unsurpassed selection of quality shoes at discount prices—has brought resounding praise.

DSW offers first-run, current-style, name-brand shoes, purchased from 400 sources and brought to customers the same season they reach the market.

HETHER THEY ARE IN FINANCE, INSURANCE, DISTRIBUTION, OR MANUFACTURING, when Central Ohio businesses need staffing, they turn to Olsten Central Ohio. The largest privately held staffing service in the area, Olsten has been providing quality service and assignment employees for 30 years. ✴ Seventy-five

percent of the largest employers in Columbus are Olsten clients. From its 12 locations, 85 staff members coordinate the activities of more than 2,000 assignment employees at 500 companies annually in the Greater Columbus area, including the outlying areas of Lancaster, Newark, Marion, Delaware, Marysville, and Bellefontaine.

Whatever the assignment—warehouse, distribution, assembly production, information systems, administration, or office support—Olsten sends qualified individuals who are ready to contribute to a company's productivity.

Setting Olsten apart from the competition is its dedication to delivering superior service to clients and its commitment to its assignment employees. Before an applicant is assigned to any job, an Olsten representative works closely with the client to understand specific job requirements. "We can't just take an order for a word processor. We have to understand the hardware, the software, and the nature of the work," says Bobbie Ruch, president of Olsten Central Ohio. Sometimes that includes

sending a staff member to the work site to do the job. In some instances, Olsten representatives are based at the work site on an ongoing basis to help oversee assignment employees.

LONG-STANDING CLIENT RELATIONSHIPS

Over the years, Olsten has established long-term relationships with many of the area's largest employers, some of which have been clients since the franchise's founding by George C. Ruch Sr. and Betty Lou Ruch. Those relationships were cemented by Olsten's commitment to innovation in meeting its clients changing needs. For example, if a client installs a new software system, Olsten will make that software part of its training. Olsten can also provide hiring, screening, recruiting, and a full range of human resource services for its clients.

Contributing to Olsten's success is its affiliation with Melville, New York-based Olsten Corp., an international company with systemwide sales of more than $4 billion and 650,000 employees. Because of its size, Olsten franchises benefit from testing techniques, technology, and the ability to share ideas and concepts.

COMMITMENT TO EMPLOYEES

Olsten goes to great measures to ensure that applicants have the skills required for a particular job. That includes carefully screening applicants, who include new college graduates, individuals reentering the workforce, people desiring job flexibility, and those seeking a career change or work after retirement, to ensure that they match clients' needs. The company first performs a complete background check, then conducts a series of skill tests that are unique to Olsten.

Other measures include following up within the first hour of assignment employees' start times to verify they have arrived, and that the initial introduction to the job is going well. Before the conclusion of the first day, an Olsten representative will call the supervisor for an update of the day's events. The employee is contacted at home that evening to receive his or her assessment of the workday.

Olsten also prides itself on the way it treats its assignment employees, which includes providing benefits and job counseling. Olsten's alliance with large employers in the area and its steady supply of assignments also makes its services appealing.

Olsten does the majority of its business—45 percent—in the administrative/office support sector. Distribution and production assembly represent about 35 percent, while professional services, specifically in the areas of accounting and information technology, make up the remaining 20 percent. As it looks to the future, Olsten plans to expand its range of skilled assignment employees to include more in the office automation, accounting, and information technology sectors. Olsten also plans to include more assignment employees with legal backgrounds to further position the company as a one-stop shop for clients. Other growth areas will be in human resources, job searches, and consulting.

Under the leadership of Ruch, Olsten Central Ohio also plans to continue its legacy as a pioneer in the staffing service industry by setting testing and service standards. Also important to Olsten is its continuing tradition of community involvement, notably with many community service organizations based in Central Ohio.

OLSTEN CENTRAL OHIO HAS BEEN PROVIDING QUALITY SERVICE AND ASSIGNMENT EMPLOYEES SINCE 1968.

JOE JOHNSON, THE COLUMBUS DISPATCH

1971-1991

1971	CARDINAL HEALTH
1971	COCA-COLA USA
1971	COMMUNICOLOR
1971	TIME WARNER COMMUNICATIONS
1972	BridgeStreet ACCOMMODATIONS
1972	MPW INDUSTRIAL SERVICES, INC.
1972	RED ROOF INNS, INC.
1973	COMMERICAL MOVERS, INC.
1973	TRACEWELL SYSTEMS
1974	CENTRAL OHIO TRANSIT AUTHORITY
1974	STERLING COMMERCE
1975	TOSOH SMD, INC.
1976	CUTLER-HAMMER
1976	PIZZUTI DEVELOPMENT, INC.
1977	WYN MOLDED PLASTICS INC.
1978	SCHULER INC.
1979	BAKER & HOSTETLER LLP
1979	HONDA OF AMERICA MFG. INC.
1979	SQUIRE, SANDERS & DEMPSEY L.L.P.
1980	CORE MATERIALS CORPORATION
1983	APPLIED INNOVATION INC.
1983	CROSSMANN COMMUNITIES OF OHIO/DELUXE HOMES
1983	LCI INTERNATIONAL
1984	BISYS FUND SERVICES
1985	STAR BANK
1986	TOMASCO MULCIBER INC.
1986	TS TECH NORTH AMERICA
1987	THE NEW ALBANY COMPANY
1989	EXECUTIVE OFFICE PLACE
1991	EXXCEL CONTRACT MANAGEMENT
1991	LS II ELECTRO-GALVANIZING CO.

CARDINAL HEALTH, INC.

EW FIELDS ARE AS CLOSE TO THE CENTER OF PUBLIC ATTENTION AS HEALTH CARE, which affects consumers and taxpayers in many different ways. In recent years, few health care companies have drawn as much attention as Cardinal Health, which—with 1997 sales of $11 billion—has rapidly established itself as one

of the leading pharmaceutical service providers in the United States.

Cardinal Health was founded in 1971 as a food wholesaler, and first entered the pharmaceutical distribution business in 1979 with the acquisition of a small drug distributor in Zanesville, Ohio. In 1988, Cardinal divested its food operations in order to focus exclusively on pharmaceutical distribution.

Cardinal Distribution is one of the leading distributors of pharmaceuticals and health products in the country. Cardinal Distribution's nationwide network of 27 facilities enables the company to offer economical, streamlined delivery to its retail, hospital, and other health care provider customers throughout the United States. The company's growth

is attributable to its ability to provide customers with coast-to-coast distribution capabilities, competitive pricing, unsurpassed order fill rates, next day delivery, diversified product lines, product consistency, and superior information systems.

In recent years, Cardinal Health formed two specialty distribution operations to address particular needs of certain segments of the health care marketplace. National Specialty Services, Inc. was founded by the company in 1992 to deliver pharmaceuticals and medical supplies to physician practices, and therapeutic plasma products to hospitals, outpatient clinics, and surgery centers. CORD Logistics, Inc. was initiated by Cardinal in 1996 to provide pharmaceutical companies with an integrated solution for warehousing, distribution, inventory management, information systems, customer support, and financial services.

GROWTH THROUGH ACQUISITION AND DIVERSIFICATION

Since its initial public offering in 1983, Cardinal Health has completed

17 business combinations that have enabled the company to expand its distribution operations nationwide and significantly augment its portfolio of complementary pharmaceutical services.

The company's most recent business combinations, according to Robert D. Walter, chairman and chief executive officer, "all relate to simplifying the process of pharmaceutical distribution for all participants along the supply channel, better organizing data and disseminating relevant information to supply-chain partners, improving the capacity for pharmacist intervention, and developing important marketing programs with our customers. This strategy should help our customers drive further improvements in patient care and, ultimately, reduce costs across the health care continuum."

In late 1995, Cardinal completed a merger with Medicine Shoppe International, Inc., a leading franchiser of apothecary-style pharmacies with more than 1,200 franchises in the United States and eight foreign countries. Fiscal 1997 sales of Medicine Shoppe stores aggregated more than $1 billion, ranking the franchiser among the largest retail pharmacy operations in the country.

A merger with Pyxis Corporation, a leading manufacturer of point-of-use systems that automate the distribution, management, and control of pharmaceuticals and medical supplies in hospitals, nursing homes, and other health care provider facilities, was completed in May 1996. Pyxis, known for its innovative products and high-quality customer service, counts more than 3,000 hospitals and other health care providers as customers.

Cardinal began repackaging pharmaceuticals for its customers in 1987 with the start-up of National

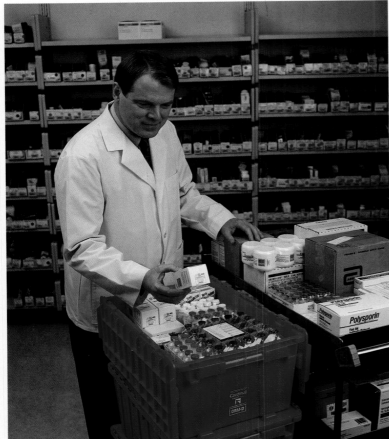

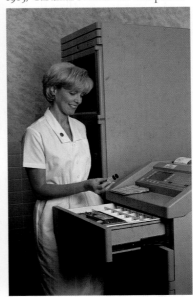

PharmPak Services, Inc., which is today the largest pharmaceutical repackaging operation in the country. In October 1996, Cardinal complemented its packaging capabilities with the acquisition of PCI Services, Inc., a leading international provider of integrated packaging solutions to the pharmaceutical industry. The company operates nine state-of-the-art facilities in the United States and three foreign countries that are capable of meeting a wide range of packaging requirements.

Owen Healthcare, Inc., which merged with Cardinal Health in March 1997, is a world-leading provider of fully integrated, contract hospital pharmacy management services with approximately 400 hospital customers. Trained to control costs and provide improved service levels to patients, physicians, and nurses, Owen pharmacists manage all aspects of the hospital pharmacy, which include staffing, purchasing, medication dispensing, and providing clinical services and information technology.

For its retail, hospital, and other customers, Cardinal provides new solutions to the challenging task of managing their businesses in today's complex health care environment. For Kmart Corporation, as one example, the company provides comprehensive pharmaceutical distribution and repackaging services for all of the entity's 1,600 in-store pharmacies. As part of this unique agreement, Cardinal

actually owns and helps to efficiently manage the retailer's inventory, utilizing the company's purchasing and inventory management expertise to help Kmart's pharmacies achieve improved profitability. For large integrated health networks, such as Duke University Medical Center and Sharp HealthCare, Cardinal has developed specific solutions, using services that involve multiple subsidiaries, including pharmaceutical distribution, information systems, automated pharmaceutical dispensing, and pharmacy management.

AN ENTREPRENEURIAL OUTLOOK

Cardinal Health, located in a new headquarters facility in Dublin, Ohio, employs approximately 700 associates in the Columbus area and 11,000 associates worldwide. The company actively promotes an ownership mentality among its employees to maximize their focus on creating long-term value. Walter comments, "Cardinal has always been very entrepreneurial in its approach to running the business, and we want to ensure that this spirit continues."

Indeed, that entrepreneurial spirit may lie behind the comment of one

leading investor publication: "We sense that Cardinal is a company that continually redefines its business, constantly pushing the envelope to exploit new growth avenues." Through that redefining process, Cardinal Health will continue to expand its role in health care—the one field that affects all people.

COCA-COLA USA

A T A HIGH SCHOOL FOOTBALL GAME IN WORTHINGTON, A CARIBBEAN RESTAURANT in Short North, a basement TV room in Dublin—all over the Greater Columbus area, Coca-Cola beverages are part of the scene. ✴ As a brand name, Coca-Cola is among the best known in the country; indeed, Coca-Cola

is a symbol recognized around the world. The flavor is also immediately recognizable to most, but the secret formula that makes up the heart of that taste is known to very few. Something else known to a surprising few is that the syrup used to make Coca-Cola classic, diet Coke, Sprite, and other products of The Coca-Cola Company is blended in the Discovery City.

A Coke and a Smile
In the Columbus Coca-Cola Syrup Production Facility, located on a

22-acre site on Watkins Road, 175 employees blend the famous syrups, which are then distributed to Coca-Cola Bottling operations and to fountain drink operators throughout the Midwest and beyond—Ohio, Illinois, Indiana, West Virginia, Kentucky, Michigan, Pennsylvania, and Missouri.

Coca-Cola USA has been operating the Columbus Coca-Cola Syrup Production Facility since 1971. In a move that corresponded with its silver anniversary, Coca-Cola USA announced that it would be expanding its Columbus operation, making

it the largest of the 10 syrup production facilities Coca-Cola USA maintains in the United States.

The ceremony at which that announcement was made featured the participation of Greg Lashutka, mayor of Columbus; Jo Anne Davidson, speaker of the Ohio House of Representatives; and Thomas S. Blackstock, vice president, manufacturing, Coca-Cola USA. Speaking at a construction site at the facility, Lashutka told Coca-Cola employees and invited guests, "Our city is proud that— more than 25 years ago—Coca-Cola USA decided Columbus was the best place in this region to build a plant that plays such an important role in the production of many of the world's best-known soft drinks."

Davidson described the expansion as a recognition of the economic strengths of the city of Columbus, and added, "The commitment Coca-Cola has made to our state by virtue of this expansion recognizes the dedication of the citizens of Columbus in helping to make our capital city a productive environment for industry."

Columbus' central location, noted Blackstock, was a prime factor

IN 1996, COCA-COLA USA ANNOUNCED A 110,000-SQUARE-FOOT EXPANSION OF THE COCA-COLA SYRUP PRODUCTION FACILITY IN COLUMBUS AT A CEREMONY THAT FEATURED THE PARTICIPATION OF (FROM LEFT) GREG LASHUTKA, MAYOR OF COLUMBUS; STATE SENATOR BRUCE JOHNSON; JO ANNE DAVIDSON, SPEAKER OF THE OHIO HOUSE OF REPRESENTATIVES; AND THOMAS S. BLACKSTOCK, VICE PRESIDENT, MANUFACTURING, COCA-COLA USA (TOP).

IN THE COLUMBUS COCA-COLA SYRUP PRODUCTION FACILITY, 175 EMPLOYEES BLEND THE FAMOUS SYRUPS, WHICH ARE THEN DISTRIBUTED TO COCA-COLA BOTTLING OPERATIONS AND TO FOUNTAIN DRINK OPERATORS THROUGHOUT THE MIDWEST AND BEYOND (BOTTOM LEFT AND RIGHT).

THE SYRUP USED TO MAKE COCA-COLA CLASSIC, DIET COKE, SPRITE, AND OTHER PRODUCTS OF THE COCA-COLA COMPANY IS BLENDED IN THE COLUMBUS FACILITY.

duction Facility strives to maintain a safe and healthful environment. The operation is committed to recycling its waste materials, and works diligently to meet or exceed all relevant state and federal environmental standards.

The Columbus Syrup Production facility has a direct impact on the Central Ohio economy, contributing more than $10 million in goods, services, and payroll. An additional $3.2 million is spent locally on purchased services, raw materials, and supplies.

This local presence is important to Coca-Cola USA; and thanks to its presence in Columbus, area residents are also buying local, every time they say, "Always Coca-Cola."

COCA-COLA'S EXPANSION PLANS IN COLUMBUS COINCIDED WITH ITS 25TH ANNIVERSARY IN DISCOVERY CITY.

in that decision. He explained that "as a distribution point to major population centers and source for a skilled workforce, Columbus has been extremely important to our U.S. business over the past 25 years. We have enjoyed growing with Columbus, and look forward to continued, mutual growth for many years to come."

The 110,000-square-foot expansion will increase the facility's current 205,000-square-foot production facility by half. As the first phase of the expansion, a total of 48,500 square feet will be added to accommodate the installation of new tanker truck bays, a receiving warehouse, and additional parking. The full expansion will include new mixing tanks, processing equipment, packaging lines, a shipping warehouse, and office improvements.

PART OF THE COMMUNITY

The Coca-Cola Syrup Production Facility is not simply located in Columbus; it is an active corporate citizen, contributing to the well-being of the city and region. Internally, the facility strives to provide a quality work experience for its employees; externally, it supports a wide range of community, charitable, athletic, and educational activities. This aid comes in many forms; for example, during natural disasters the Columbus Syrup Production Facility and its employees have responded by providing disaster relief aid throughout the state—in particular, by providing bottled water to areas where the usual sources of drinking water have become contaminated.

For both its employees and its neighbors throughout the state of Ohio, the Columbus Syrup Pro-

COMMUNICOLOR

AT ONE TIME, THE MOST NOTABLE ASPECT OF MASS MAILINGS WAS SIMPLY VOLUME. Several years ago, Communicolor produced a single mailing for Publisher's Clearing House that consisted of 47 million pieces. But the business of direct marketing is changing, due to the ever higher degree of personalization

made possible by computers. Newark, Ohio-based Communicolor, which creates more than 1 billion pieces of literature a year for direct marketers, is on the leading edge of these changes.

To illuminate the transformation taking place within the industry, Michael Spaul, senior vice president and general manager of Communicolor, reaches for a direct mail piece, one an automaker has distributed to the owners of its cars. Each printed and fully personalized piece gives information specific to one of the automaker's 4,400 dealerships. The mailing also carries six coupons—drawn from a pool of 300 possible offers—selected to target the likely needs and interests

of the individual to whom the mailer is addressed.

"The aim of today's direct mailing industry is to make mailing recipients feel they are getting not a mass-produced circular, but a letter of interest that was written, produced, and mailed specifically to them," says Spaul.

A CHANGING INDUSTRY

Achieving that aim requires better-quality printing, complex programming and data manipulation for personalization, higher grades of paper, and quicker turnaround times. A decade ago, Communicolor had six to eight weeks to generate a mailing; today, a customer might be unhappy with anything longer than 10 days.

Long-term employee James Hardy, director of manufacturing, joined the company a quarter century ago as a journeyman printer. In the years since, computers and the revolution in desktop publishing have brought remarkable changes to printing operations, Hardy's included. When he joined Communicolor, all press adjustments were made manually. Today, 90 percent of those adjustments can be made at a central console,

based on information supplied by video cameras mounted on the press.

A positive aspect, Hardy notes, is that quality is rising. "What people used to call 'junk mail' was cheap paper and low-quality printing. Today, the work Communicolor does resembles what you would see coming off a commercial press and requires mass coordination of details as well as expertise."

At Communicolor, all these changes make life more complicated—and more interesting. Communicolor has been an integral part of the direct mail industry since 1964. Specializing in the production of effective, innovative promotional packages for direct marketing customers, its central facility in Newark houses sophisticated, high-speed web offset presses; state-of-the-art personalization systems; and complex in-line equipment, used to incorporate the many features that go into successful and responsive direct marketing pieces.

Communicolor has a roster of 120 national clients, and the company works with each individually from project concept to show how its capabilities can best be used to achieve the customer's objectives.

CLOCKWISE FROM TOP:
MICHAEL SPAUL, SENIOR VICE PRESIDENT AND GENERAL MANAGER OF COMMUNI-COLOR, LEADS THE CONSISTENT QUALITY MISSION FOR DIRECT MAIL MARKETERS AT THE COLUMBUS-AREA HEADQUARTERS.

COMMUNICOLOR'S CONTINUOUS IMPROVE-MENT PROCESS IS IMPORTANT TO EVERY JOB WITHIN THE COMPANY.

THE REVOLUTION IN DESKTOP PUBLISHING HAS SPAWNED ELECTRONIC PREPRESS AS THE STANDARD INPUT TO PRESS PLATES OVER MECHANICAL ART BOARDS.

Communicolor offers an extensive range of advanced prepress, printing, data prep, and bindery services, and often mails the finished pieces. New capabilities and products are continually created by Communicolor's marketing, engineering, and even equipment operators.

"At the same time," says William Tracey, director of customer and technical services, "Communicolor works to educate the customer. The better a customer appreciates the requirements of the technology, the better result we can create. All companies strive for quality. At Communicolor, quality has many components, but one commandment—the job absolutely has to be delivered on time, and right the first time."

Substantial Growth

Communicolor has experienced substantial growth since 1971, when its parent company, Standard Register, became the first major business forms company to open a plant devoted exclusively to the production of direct mail components. In 1978, Communicolor opened a second plant nearby to house its variable image (personalization) system equipment and operations. A third facility, offering expanded printing capacity, was opened in 1984. Then in 1989, the company added 100,000 square feet to its original facility, consolidating

all printing and personalization equipment under one roof for optimum efficiency and handling.

In 1994, Communicolor acquired a 115,000-square-foot facility in Eudora, Kansas, which provides production backup and increased capacity in printing and personalization, while adding electron beam variable imaging to in-line collator products.

One reason for Communicolor's success and growth is its 600 employees, 400 hired mainly from the Newark area. "Communicolor," notes Phillip Annarino, division manager for human resources, "is the premier employer in town. Salaries are extremely competitive, and Communicolor offers careers, not merely jobs."

Job tenures are lengthy, in part because Communicolor avoids layoffs.

When business is slow—summer is often a weaker production time in the direct mail industry—the company takes the opportunity to provide additional training, as well as complete other tasks that cannot be accomplished during high-production times.

Communicolor also contributes to the community it calls home. Fully one-third of all employees, for example, participate in Newark's annual Corporate Challenge, with events ranging from volleyball to miniature golf, to raise funds for the local YMCA youth programs. Another contribution of the company is the yearly practice of giving every Communicolor employee a tree to plant. "Planting a tree annually," says Larry Kincaid, manager of quality assurance, "is just one more way in which we give something back and make our community a better place to live."

CLOCKWISE FROM TOP LEFT:
THE ELECTRONIC CONSOLE NOW COMPUTERIZES INK FOUNTAIN LEVELS AND REVIEWS BOTH SIDES OF THE WEB FOR CONSISTENCY OVER THE ENTIRE PRESS RUN.

COMMUNICOLOR'S CONTINUOUS ROLL-TO-ROLL PROCESSING REQUIRES THAT THIS WORK-IN-PROCESS MATERIAL BE AT HAND TO FEED THE HIGH-SPEED DAILY ACTIVITY.

THE AUTOMOTIVE INDUSTRY HAS EMBRACED PERSONALIZED DIRECT MAIL FROM COMMUNICOLOR AS A RELEVANT MEDIA TO REACH ITS CUSTOMERS.

TARGETED DIRECT MAIL PIECES ARRIVE AT MILLIONS OF MAILBOXES EACH DAY. COMMUNICOLOR PROVIDES THIS CAPABILITY TO MAJOR COMPANIES THROUGHOUT THE UNITED STATES.

Time Warner Communications, Columbus Division

THERE ARE TWO WORDS THAT BEST DESCRIBE TIME WARNER COMMUNICATIONS, Columbus Division—technology and innovation. From its beginnings as a cable system called Warner Cable Communications Inc., the Columbus Division has been known as a leader in the industry. ✦ Since the founding of the

Columbus location in 1971, its historic innovations have included pioneering QUBE, the nation's first interactive cable television service, which gave consumers a voice and allowed communities to conduct polling. In the 1980s, the division was the first in the area to provide push-button, pay-per-view service. MTV and Nickelodeon also trace their roots to the division.

COMMUNICATIONS PROVIDER
Today, while cable television remains a core business, the nearly 500-person division is a full-fledged communica-

tions provider, offering a wide range of services to more than 194,000 customers in 38 Central Ohio communities.

The Columbus Division of Time Warner gives customers access to 60 channels, plus eight premium and eight pay-per-view channels. Its network, in terms of channels offered, has always been in the top 10 percent of the country, and accesses a 700-mile, state-of-the-art, fiber-optic cable network. This network has been continuously upgraded over the years at a cost of more than $157 million;

in 1994, Time Warner's network design won the first national Emmy engineering award ever presented. The design has been adopted by other cable and telephone companies nationwide.

Time Warner also provides the latest in access to entertainment, news, and information through computers and its on-line computer service. Called Road Runner, the first service of its kind in Central Ohio provides customers with high-speed access to the Internet and other commercial on-line services at speeds of up to 100 times faster than today's standard telephone computer modems. Also important is Road Runner's local content. Consumers can check out details on a variety of subjects including entertainment, schools, museums, and government. Other Road Runner features include its user-friendly design, which appeals to Internet novices; a clearer, more vivid picture; and quicker download time.

Time Warner offers superior customer service that surpasses industry standards. The division is the only local communications provider in Columbus to guarantee on-time service. This means that if service appointments are not met, the customer's account is credited $20; if installation appointments run late, installation is free. In addition, the division was among the first to make customer service employees available 24 hours a day, year-round, and service appointments are scheduled in two-hour windows, so customers don't have to wait several hours. In recognition of its commitment to service, the company won the national Cable Television Administration and Marketing Society's 1994 Customer Is Key Award, an award based on customer surveys.

TIME WARNER WAS ONE OF THE FIRST COMPANIES IN THE COLUMBUS AREA TO OFFER CUSTOMER SERVICE 24 HOURS A DAY, 365 DAYS A YEAR. IT IS THE ONLY LOCAL COMMUNICATIONS PROVIDER THAT GUARANTEES ON-TIME SERVICE AND INSTALLATION.

BEXLEY MIDDLE SCHOOL STUDENTS TRAVEL TO THE RAIN FOREST OF COSTA RICA THROUGH AN ELECTRONIC FIELD TRIP SPONSORED BY TIME WARNER COMMUNICATIONS. THE SCHOOL RECEIVES MORE THAN 540 HOURS OF COMMERCIAL-FREE EDUCATIONAL PROGRAMMING AS PART OF CABLE IN THE CLASSROOM.

Ongoing Innovations

Time Warner customers can look forward to more innovations in the future. For example, the division's high-tech cable network has the capability of delivering telephone service. Other highlights on the horizon include digital compression, or compression of signals, which will ultimately allow the division to provide even more channels, choice, on-demand service, and convenience for customers. Instead of having to watch or record a particular movie at a set time, consumers will be able to choose to watch or record it whenever they want.

Helping to strengthen the Columbus division's operations is its affiliation with Time Warner Cable—the nation's largest cable television opera-

tor, serving 13 million customers in 37 states—and a unit of Time Warner Entertainment Co., L.P. Time Warner, which is responsible for providing *Time*; *Life*; HBO; Warner Bros. cartoons; and Little, Brown and Company books to customers, also is responsible for providing industry-leading vision and vast resources for the local division. At the same time, the local division enjoys the independence to make decisions that affect its market.

The Columbus Connection

Columbus' national reputation as a strong test market and hotbed of technology, along with encouragement from local government and local business, has played a role in

Time Warner's continued growth and investment in Columbus, says Terry O'Connell, division president. And the Time Warner company believes in giving back to the community. Community service projects that the company is proudest of include Cable in the Classroom, through which every school in its service area—273 public and private schools in 13 districts—receives free cable service from Time Warner Communications. More than 540 hours of commercial-free, educational programs are available to teachers to use in their classrooms. Such access provides educators with the opportunity to create video libraries to supplement their teaching materials.

Other community initiatives involve literacy and the arts. Each year, Time Warner conducts an installation campaign during which proceeds are donated to the Literacy Initiative of Central Ohio. Since 1990, its donations have totaled more than $175,000. Projects include media sponsorships, where Time Warner showcases events and community activities through public service announcements on its network and through its cable guide.

Whether it's on television, the Internet, or elsewhere, Time Warner's Columbus Division is committed to being one of the most advanced technology companies providing its customers the latest in communications.

BridgeStreet Accommodations

AN IDEA THAT BEGAN AS A LOSS-LEADER SERVICE TO REAL ESTATE CUSTOMERS IN need of temporary accommodations that grew into a $16 million enterprise— this is the story behind BridgeStreet Accommodations, formerly known as Temporary Corporate Housing. What started as an incidental service is now an industry of its own—the supplying of fully furnished apartment accommodations as an alternative to hotel living. With operations in four cities, Temporary Corporate Housing joined hands in 1997 with other companies in the business to become BridgeStreet Accommodations. By the end of that year, BridgeStreet had operations in 16 cities and was poised to become the premier national provider of corporate apartments.

For this reason, BridgeStreet Accommodations has opened a central reservation office and established a toll-free number. The company plans to grow by expanding in existing markets and establishing a presence in targeted metropolitan areas in the United States, Canada, and Europe. BridgeStreet recently completed a successful initial public offering, which will provide capital to support its expansion strategy. The stock trades on the Nasdaq market under the symbol BEDS.

Location, Location, Location

Topping its list of consumer-driven services, BridgeStreet Accommodations offers the most important aspect of temporary housing: location.

Important businesses are located throughout Columbus and its emerging suburbs. For this reason, BridgeStreet Columbus has more than 300 apartments in 16 complexes spanning the city. "Where hotels are restricted geographically, we offer the flexibility in location and lifestyle that customers demand," says Natalie Hickernell, general manager of the Columbus office. "We provide housing wherever our customers would like us to be, including access to reservations nationwide.

"We actually serve two customers," Hickernell continues. "We serve our guests, those who call our apartments their home, as well as the employer who has brought that individual into the Columbus market as a new employee, a consultant, a trainee, or a customer."

Columbus businesses have come to think of BridgeStreet Accommodations as a vital employee benefit and a crucial link in the delicate process of luring top professionals into their organizations. By using the flexible, comfortable, and personal services of BridgeStreet instead of the traditional hotel room, the employer actively demonstrates its commitment to its personnel and makes the transition experience as positive as possible.

"Corporations are telling us to 'take special care of this family,' much as they have in the past with their top clients or customers," observes Hickernell. "It is difficult to recruit the best talent. People are the most critical resource of the modern company, so everyone that is brought in is treated like family—by the employer and by us."

BridgeStreet Columbus' full-size apartments offer one-, two-, and three-bedroom floor plans in residential settings. These apartments are fully furnished and fully equipped,

BRIDGESTREET ACCOMMODATIONS COLUMBUS HAS MORE THAN 300 APARTMENTS IN 16 COMPLEXES SPANNING THE CITY (TOP AND BOTTOM LEFT).

WOOD-BURNING FIREPLACES CONTRIBUTE TO A QUAINTNESS AND CHARM NORMALLY ASSOCIATED WITH THE COMFORTS OF HOME (BOTTOM RIGHT).

including amenities such as house-keeping services, cable television, and local phone service.

SERVICE COMMITMENT

"Almost anyone can provide A+ housing with a complete array of amenities. And while many companies' primary focus is that of the material aspect, we channel our expertise into serving the human aspect of our customers," says Hickernell. Years of experience have cultivated a deep understanding of what is most important to BridgeStreet clients. "It's the little things that mean the most: Could someone let my dog out during the day? Would you be able to pick up a few staple items at the grocery store for me?" adds Hickernell.

For the relocating family, a temporary housing arrangement is still home for the weeks or months before permanent housing is secured. "It is always stressful to change jobs, sell and buy a home, and move your children," says Hickernell, "but we do our best to help families maintain their lifestyle. When your temporary housing is worry-free, you can concentrate on more important things, like helping your kids through the transition, finding schools and social outlets, and being productive in your job."

At the heart of the BridgeStreet philosophy is a commitment to service, demonstrated locally by its staff of more than 50 employees. While automation is key in helping the

operation run smoothly, a human being can always be reached when calling BridgeStreet offices, and reservations can be secured with one phone call. Daily, weekly, and monthly rentals are available with no lease to sign and no security deposit required.

Customer feedback—whether suggestions for improvement or gratitude for a job well done—is taken very seriously by the staff, and clients' likes and dislikes are very quickly incorporated into the overall service package. Housekeeping is performed by BridgeStreet Columbus staff—not contracted out. "Our hospitality staff literally touches our clients' lives every day," explains Hickernell. "They are always willing to go the extra mile for our guests. They play a vital role in ensuring our clients' satisfaction."

To provide a seamless continuum of quality services, BridgeStreet Accommodations develops relationships with customer-driven providers, like appliance and furniture companies who back up their quality products with responsive service. "We have assembled the right group of companies with the right outlook and the right attitude toward our customers," explains Hickernell. "We don't have vendors, but partners who share our same perspective on how to create value for our customer."

The housing may be temporary, but BridgeStreet's commitment to service is permanent. The firm's mission has been developed and honed over time to ensure that families are able to maintain their lifestyles and live in a place they can call home.

MPW Industrial Services Inc.

I N 1972, A YOUNG ENTREPRENEUR IN CENTRAL OHIO NAMED MONTE BLACK SET OUT TO establish his own truck-washing business. Black wasn't sure how far this new business, then called Central Ohio Mobile Power Wash, would go—there were plenty of skeptics along the way, including the financial institutions that were hesitant to supply

start-up capital for the venture. But from the beginning, Black adopted high standards to guide its growth. Black's goals—to be the best in offering quality, safety, service, training, and innovation—were ahead of their time, but have become prevalent throughout most businesses and industries today.

Being ahead of its time is nothing new for Black's company, now called MPW Industrial Services Inc., which recently celebrated its 25th anniversary. Today, it is recognized as one of the leaders in the industrial cleaning business nationwide, with more than 30 offices in 18 states, as well as in Mexico and Canada, and more than 1,200 pieces of equipment designed to meet clients' ever changing needs. A rising star in Central Ohio, MPW has been ranked as one of the top private companies in the area, based on an annual survey conducted by Arthur Andersen.

Industry Trendsetter

Driving MPW's success have been two key industry trends among U.S. businesses. One is the outsourcing of noncore business activities, which enables companies to become more focused, and the other is the creation of smaller vendor lists in order to ensure better consistency in service and quality.

MPW also has grown by adding complementary services, which have increased its customer base. In the

early days, Black's operation provided power-washing services for tractors, trailers, buildings, and heavy equipment. The company added industrial cleaning services in 1978 and purchased its first dry vacuum truck and water blaster. Chemical cleaning was added in 1981. Other additions included an industrial mobile water division, container cleaning group, air filtration, facility management and support services, and environmental services.

Fast-Paced Style

Some of the company's innovations are driven by industry changes and trends. For example, new environmental and safety standards often necessitate more specialized industrial cleaning methods. Such changes require that MPW must constantly search for new processes and procedures that will better serve its customers' needs. In addition, safety specialists from MPW conduct routine audits at clients' job sites to ensure that procedures are safe and that substances are being handled properly.

Waste reduction is becoming increasingly important in industry. In response, company engineers are

CLOCKWISE FROM TOP:
HEADQUARTERED IN HEBRON, MPW INDUSTRIAL SERVICES INC. HAS MORE THAN 30 OFFICES IN 18 STATES, AS WELL AS IN MEXICO AND CANADA.

THE COMPANY'S FLEET OF MORE THAN 1,200 VEHICLES IS KEPT IN TOP CONDITION.

MPW'S SHOP HAS A 15-TON OVERHEAD CRANE, MIG AND TIG WELDING, MILLING, TOTAL FABRICATION CAPABILITIES, AND ENGINE LATHE CAPACITY.

then require the services of chemical cleaning or industrial mobile water. Growth is unrestricted.

Many clients have MPW permanently on-site seven days per week. MPW is responsible for all industrial cleaning aspects of their businesses. For one particular manufacturer, on-site associates are specifically trained to clean and maintain automated robots.

It's all linked to partnering with customers and making them as much a part of the company as MPW is of theirs. Both companies reach for solutions together, whether problems are related to cost efficiency or some other area.

The company has an international presence as well. Overseas projects include cleaning turbines in Taiwan and an aluminum mill in Wales. Much of the company's international work has come from existing clients that have operations abroad.

MPW has traveled far since its early days as a truck-washing company. Based upon its past history of constantly rising to meet new challenges, the company is sure to experience new ventures, further innovation, and continued growth in its future.

MPW ASSOCIATES WATER BLAST VISCOUS MATERIAL FROM A BREECHING DUCT IN PREPARATION FOR STRUCTURAL RENOVATION.

focusing on ways to eliminate waste and to recycle reusable parts of substances. Customers also demand rapid response. If a client needs a piece of equipment that's not readily available, MPW can create it. There isn't any industry or customer that MPW can't accommodate. Skilled mechanics also remain on call, and can be immediately dispatched to make any necessary equipment repairs.

MPW's clients include utilities and many different types of manu-facturers, including those in the phar-maceutical, pulp and paper, steel, and automotive industries. MPW goes from grease pits to sterile environments. MPW may be called to wash boilers or clean drain lines at power plants. The same power plant may

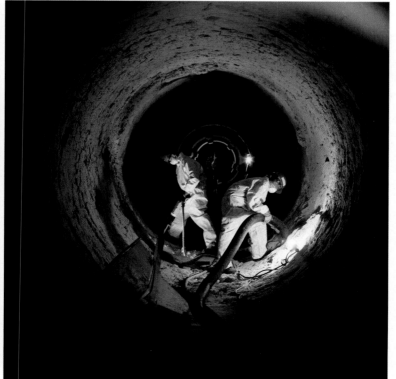

MPW's TRAINING DEPARTMENT DESIGNS AND DELIVERS ORIENTATION TRAINING, INITIAL SAFETY TRAINING, AND ONGOING OPERATIONS SKILLS TRAINING WITH ONE OBJECTIVE IN MIND—TO DO THE JOB RIGHT THE FIRST TIME, EVERY TIME (LEFT).

SAFETY PRACTICES ARE CRUCIAL IN CLEANING CONFINED SPACES. UNDER DIFFICULT CONDITIONS, MPW EMPLOYEES VACUUM LIME SLURRY IN A PAPER MILL (RIGHT).

RED ROOF INNS, INC.

ONVENIENT LOCATIONS, HIGH-QUALITY ACCOMMODATIONS, FRIENDLY SERVICE, reasonable cost—that's the guarantee Red Roof Inns delivers to guests seven nights a week. And to travelers, that's a welcome commitment. On any given night, Red Roof Inns serves thousands of individuals at its more than 250 properties located in over 33 states.

Red Roof Inns was incorporated in 1972 by company founder James R. Trueman, who opened the first inn in the Columbus suburb of Grove City, Ohio, on February 20, 1973. Since its establishment, the Hilliard, Ohio-based company's growth has been steady: In 1989, Red Roof Inns organized a 200-Roof Salute to mark the opening of its 200th inn. By 1997, the company was once more celebrating, this time marking its 250th inn opening with Red Hot Jazz. The event included 250 Phoenix-area high school band students participating in a concert at the Phoenix Red Roof Inn (the company's first all-interior-corridor building design) while attempting a world record as the largest jazz band.

ANNIVERSARY YEAR BRINGS CHANGES

In 1998, the economy lodging chain will mark its 25th anniversary year of the opening of its first inn. On February 1, 1996, the firm marked a significant milestone as it became a publicly traded company, with an initial offering of 10 million shares of common stock placed on the New York Stock Exchange. That same year, Red Roof Inns also announced plans to franchise.

"Franchising," says Red Roof Inns Chairman, President, and CEO Francis W. "Butch" Cash, "is an opportunity to really expand and grow the brand. How many inns should we have? A lot closer to 1,000 than 300."

ACCOMMODATIONS FOR THE BUSINESS AND LEISURE TRAVELER

From the start, Red Roof Inns has offered value-priced accommodations

to travelers. From late 1996 to mid-1997, the company completed a chainwide renewal program that encompassed more than 85 percent of its properties and cost in excess of $55 million. Today, each Red Roof Inns room, though economically priced, is furnished with a color television, Touch-Tone telephone, wall-to-wall carpeting, full tub and shower combination, and king-size or extra-long double bed. Each inn provides access to movies and games on demand through LodgeNet, as well as free CNN, ESPN, and Showtime. Each day, guests of Red Roof Inns also enjoy complimentary local telephone calls, coffee, and *USA Today*. In addition, universal rooms for physically challenged travelers and nonsmoking and smoking rooms are available at most inns throughout the chain. Also, most Red Roof Inns welcome pets.

The business traveler comprises about half of the guests served by Red Roof Inns. In large part, this is because of the extra steps Red Roof Inns takes to serve the needs of those whose work takes them on the road. Early on, Red Roof Inns became the first national economy lodging chain to offer both fax and copy machine services to guests at every property.

CLOCKWISE FROM TOP:
FRANCIS W. CASH, CHAIRMAN, PRESIDENT, AND CEO OF RED ROOF INNS, INC.

RED ROOF INNS OFFERS BUSINESS KING ROOMS, WHICH FUNCTION AS A VIRTUAL OFFICE ON THE ROAD. ALONG WITH A KING-SIZED BED, THE BUSINESS KING ROOM FEATURES A LARGE WORK AREA WITH A DESK, OVERHEAD LIGHTING, A RECLINER, MODEM JACKS FOR COMPUTER HOOKUP, AND TOUCH-TONE TELEPHONES WITH HOLD AND SPEAKER FUNCTIONS.

THE NEW RED ROOF INNS BUILDING FEATURES ALL INTERIOR CORRIDORS, NEW BATHROOM DESIGN, AND A REGIONALLY BASED DECOR PACKAGE.

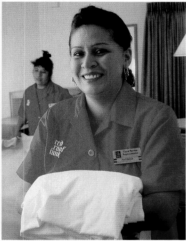

Today, Red Roof Inns offers business king rooms, which function as a virtual office on the road. Along with a king-sized bed, the business king room features a large work area with a desk, overhead lighting, a recliner, modem jacks for computer hookup, and Touch-Tone telephones with mute and speaker functions.

Along with increasing the comfort available to its guests, Red Roof Inns has been expanding the ease and convenience with which travelers may reserve and reach their accommodations. The company offers a 24-hour, toll-free phone number that connects guests to its central reservations center, which annually handles more than 2.6 million calls. The chain's totally integrated computer system capabilities also permit travelers to make reservations directly through their inn of choice. In addition, a special toll-free number has been established for group reservations when reserving 10 or more rooms.

Red Roof Inns has established itself as a leader in the economy lodging segment also through its innovative marketing and advertising programs. Over the past 10 years, the company has been supported in its television and print promotions by actor/comedian and spokesperson Martin Mull. In 1997, Red Roof Inns ran its first summer advertising campaign, Summer Money-Making Tips.

The company operates its inns with a view to offering inn locations and room quality comparable to many mid-price hotels at substantially lower room rates. Red Roof's inns are generally located near interstate highways, major traffic arteries, or major destination areas such as airports, universities, hospitals, or convention centers. The company is firmly established in most of its markets, and many of its inns are in locations superior to those available for development today. Each of the inns is well constructed and maintained, and all are attractively landscaped to enhance their appearance.

Howard Nusbaum, executive vice president of the Ohio Hotel & Motel Association, states, "Red Roof is an economy hotel that provides a quality room at a reasonable price . . . Others in the industry have followed its lead."

Red Roof Inns' combination of price, location, and consistent quality—the attributes that have driven its growth in the past—remain key to its success in the future.

CLOCKWISE FROM TOP LEFT:
EACH RED ROOF INNS ROOM, THOUGH ECONOMICALLY PRICED, IS FURNISHED WITH A COLOR TELEVISION, TOUCH-TONE TELEPHONE, WALL-TO-WALL CARPETING, FULL TUB AND SHOWER COMBINATION, AND KING-SIZED OR EXTRA-LONG DOUBLE BED.

SPOKESPERSON MARTIN MULL JOINS PHOENIX-AREA HIGH SCHOOL BAND STUDENTS AT THE 250TH RED ROOF INN OPENING CELEBRATION ON MAY 10, 1997.

GUEST SERVICE REPRESENTATIVES WORK HARD TO PROVIDE EACH GUEST WITH A COMFORTABLE STAY.

FRIENDLY FRONT DESK GUEST SERVICE REPRESENTATIVES ARE AVAILABLE TO OFFER ASSISTANCE TO THE GUESTS.

COMMERCIAL MOVERS, INC.

COMMERCIAL MOVERS, INC. (CMI) WAS ESTABLISHED IN 1973 TO PROVIDE A SPECIAL-ized moving service—office relocations. Today, the company is more than just a moving company supplying labor and trucks. Commercial Movers, Inc. now provides complete project management services plus a full array of related

services—all while maintaining leadership in the office relocation industry. The company's entire staff is committed to providing customers the highest-quality, most complete service available in the industry.

Moving an entire office is a challenge. A company's business and profitability can depend on minimizing its downtime. CMI's employees are experts at this complex task. CMI has developed a complete line of services designed to accommodate its clients' needs, reduce stress, and save money. "Our customers cannot afford for their business to be interrupted," says Dan Cordray, president of Commercial Movers, Inc. "They need more than someone with labor and trucks. They need a professional relocation and facility management organization with the experience, ability, and resources to provide quality services at a competitive cost."

VALUE-ADDED SERVICES
CMI's relocation experts schedule and accomplish its clients' relocations with careful and thorough planning. This process begins with an exami-

nation of the client's current offices, along with its future location, to determine the logistics of the move. Commercial Movers, Inc. has become the largest mover with the most resources to accommodate any size office move.

Commercial Movers, Inc.'s variety of services are a direct response to customers' desires to outsource services and utilize fewer vendors. From CMI's first telephone call until the move is

complete, clients can be assured of the company's total commitment and support. CMI provides a single source for information on every detail of the relocation process. "We provide many value-added services, such as facility management, design, project management, move management, product acquisition services, and others," says Cordray. "Providing these services allows the client to continue to do its business without having to dedicate someone on their staff to handle and oversee all of these matters."

Commercial Movers, Inc. has established a division exclusively devoted to relocation management. The company can design the customer's new space, monitor third-party vendors, and coordinate any possible aspect related to the relocation or internal facility management.

Commercial Movers, Inc. handles all phases of systems furniture reconfiguration and installation. Its certified office systems movers are trained and equipped to install or reconfigure any system. The skill of CMI employees in performing recon-

DAN CORDRAY, PRESIDENT AND CEO OF COMMERCIAL MOVERS, INC. (TOP)

IN AN INDUSTRY WHERE TIME IS MONEY, CMI IS PROUD OF THE DEPENDABILITY AND FLEXIBILITY OF ITS PROFESSIONAL FLEET AND CREWS (BOTTOM).

figuration means little down-time for the customer, increased productivity, and greater profitability, whether adjusting one work surface or installing 100 stations. Commercial Movers, Inc. has the know-how, flexibility, and staff to complete any size job.

Commercial Movers, Inc. can also recycle dated systems furniture. At its in-house facility, it can repaint and refurbish previously used systems furniture. CMI can also provide the same refurbished systems furniture at a fraction of the cost to purchase new.

Electronic systems are an integral part of business. Today, they are likely the most valuable thing a company possesses. Commercial Movers, Inc. can move sensitive computer equipment and similar high-value products with unmatched safety and experience. CMI delivers and stores as much as 200 million pounds of electronic and computer equipment per year. Commercial Movers, Inc. honed its experience handling computer equipment for such notable companies as IBM, AT&T, Digital Equipment Corp., and many other similar manufacturers, often making daily pickups and deliveries of equipment worth $3 million. Commercial

Movers, Inc. has gained the trust of those who manufacture computers and high-value equipment, and now has the trust of those who use them.

Storage of additional or surplus items at the customers' own facilities can be expensive and restrictive. CMI can solve many of its clients' overcrowding problems with its warehouse facilities and services that include furniture storage and asset management of inventory.

Commercial Movers, Inc. can also provide the simplest of moving

services required. Whether a customer's relocation needs dictate a crew of two or an entire force of moving professionals, CMI can handle the full gamut of relocation needs. Although based in Columbus with facilities in Cleveland, Cincinnati, and Indianapolis, Commercial Movers, Inc. has an unlimited range to its services.

Commercial Movers, Inc. means value-added services that save its customers time and money. Customer satisfaction is CMI's only measure of success.

TRACEWELL SYSTEMS

N 1973, LARRY TRACEWELL, RECOGNIZING A VOID IN THE ELECTRONIC PACKAGING industry, developed an injection-molded portable electronic enclosure that could be adapted to meet individual customer needs. With the development of this product, Tracewell established both his philosophy—"To achieve a technological advantage

through continuous, innovative product development"—and his company, Tracewell Enclosures, Inc. Throughout the 1980s, the product line was expanded, using such unique processes as die cast aluminum and injection molding, as well as the pioneering use of conductive plastic in systems enclosures.

In the two decades since its founding, Tracewell's company has evolved into a major manufacturer of network systems that lists many Fortune 500 companies among its customers. In 1991, the company name was changed to Tracewell Systems to better reflect the scope of its product line. Today, the company's 130 employees design and produce network computer systems, electronic bus packaging, backplanes, interconnect products, and standard and custom power supplies for an extensive array of applications.

CONTINUOUS, INNOVATIVE DEVELOPMENT

The Tracewell philosophy of continuous, innovative product development has been central to the company since its creation. Through the years, the company has continued to pursue production innovations. Tracewell has received patents on its VXI In-

telligent Mainframe and VME/VXI test platforms, and has other patents pending.

In creating these products, Tracewell's electrical, mechanical, and industrial design engineers use the latest in highly sophisticated design-to-production techniques. This includes the fully automated fabrication and assembly process that employs both surface mount technology (SMT) and standard thru-hole technology. Tracewell Systems also provides individualized support and service to each customer after the sale.

Tracewell has matched innovation with quality. In 1995, Tracewell Systems received ISO 9001 certification, the designation which signifies that a company does work of consistent quality, as verified by an international certification organization.

CONTINUOUS GROWTH

By 1982, Tracewell's sales had grown sufficiently to require doubling its manufacturing facilities. The company acquired new, automated manufacturing equipment and, in 1983, added another 5,000 square feet of space. In 1987, Tracewell moved to a 52,000-square-foot office and manufacturing complex in Westerville, where it is still located.

Two recent events help to underscore the company's growth. First, on December 20, 1996, Tracewell Systems acquired the engineering and manufacturing division of CompuServe. With the acquisition, Tracewell Systems reached its goal of becoming a total systems solutions provider.

Following the acquisition, Tracewell Systems divided its activities into two groups, the Computer Packaging Group and the Network Computer Systems Group. The Computer Packaging Group continues the design and production of a broad range of electronic packaging products. The Network Computer Systems Group—the former engineering and manufacturing division of CompuServe—specializes in the design and production of telecommunication and network systems, as well as interconnection products, custom circuits, and test and development units.

The vision, talent, and resources of this group created product solutions that contributed greatly to the reliability and profitability of CompuServe in its first 20 years. This commitment to excellence and quality makes the Network Computer Systems Group a perfect fit and a natural next step for Tracewell Systems.

IN JULY 1997, TRACEWELL COMPLETED A 46,000-SQUARE-FOOT ADDITION TO THE EXISTING BUILDING IN WESTERVILLE.

▼ WESTCAMP

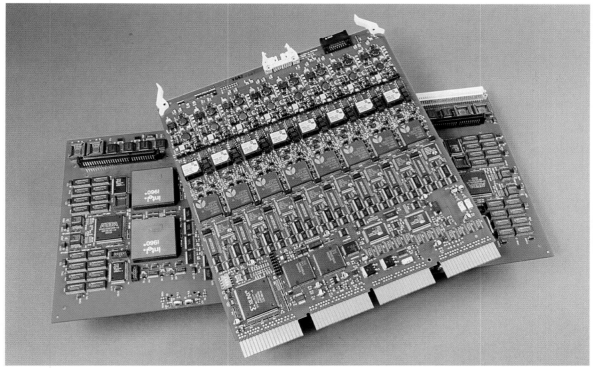

CLOCKWISE FROM TOP LEFT:
CUSTOM TELECOMMUNICATIONS BOARDS
BUILT BY TRACEWELL SYSTEMS ARE DE-
SIGNED BY COMPANY ENGINEERS TO MEET
CUSTOMERS' SPECIFIC REQUIREMENTS.

TRACEWELL SYSTEMS HOLDS A PATENT
FOR THE VXI INTELLIGENT MAIN FRAME.

THE STF ("STRAIGHT FLOW THROUGH"),
DESIGNED BY TRACEWELL POWER, USES A
UNIQUE COOLING SYSTEM WITH UNIMPEDED
AIR FLOW.

Second, in July 1997, Tracewell completed a 46,000-square-foot addition, including both office and manufacturing space. This addition, which nearly doubled the company's space, will accommodate its expansion into the future.

Tracewell Systems has built a reputation for unparalleled manufacturing standards, leading-edge design solutions, and incredibly reliable, customizable electronic packaging products. In the future, Tracewell Systems will focus its efforts on the telecommunications and network industries, and, with its recent growth, the company is well positioned to grow into these expanding markets.

TRACEWELL POWER

In 1995, a second company, Tracewell Power, was incorporated as an affiliate to Tracewell Systems. Tracewell Power specializes in the designing, manufacturing, and marketing of electronic power supplies (which convert available AC power into DC power) from 200 to 2,000 watts.

Tracewell Power is committed to innovative design, excellent quality, and rapid response manufacturing of high-performance power supplies. The company produces a broad spectrum of standard products, as well as customer designs for high quality power solutions.

Tracewell Power achieved ISO 9001 certification in 1995. Each step in the design and production process, from market concept to product design, is rigidly controlled to ensure high-quality and customer satisfaction.

Tracewell Power has developed many new and unique products through independent research and development, and in conjunction with partners. These products include the VME/VXI power planes and the STF series of power supplies. Tracewell Power has several patents pending as a result of this work.

Tracewell Power's engineering staff is experienced in a diverse range of power supply applications, and uses its research facilities, development labs, and CAD resources to apply advanced design concepts to each project. Engineering, manufacturing, and marketing teams work together to deliver standard and custom power solutions to original equipment manufacturer (OEM) companies in the computer, test, and telecommunications industries.

Tracewell Power provides power systems quickly and cost effectively

with end use in mind. This focus on end use ensures high performance and a seamless integration with the customer's existing systems.

Tracewell Systems and its affiliate Tracewell Power are both dedicated to the philosophy of continuous, innovative product development. With their growth, they will continue to provide a wide range of quality products for their customers in a variety of markets.

STERLING COMMERCE

STERLING COMMERCE IS ONE OF THE PIONEERS OF THE AGE OF ELECTRONIC COMMERCE— the new way of doing business in today's global community. Electronic commerce encompasses new technologies such as E-mail, E-forms, electronic funds transfer, and electronic data interchange to achieve the instant exchange of information within and between organizations. Sterling Commerce is helping to develop new business strategies, and the tools and technologies needed to accomplish them.

Founded as Informatics General in 1974, the company was a trailblazer in the development of electronic data interchange (EDI), and established proprietary EDI standards for various industry groups. In 1985, the firm was acquired by Dallas-based Sterling Software, becoming its electronic commerce group. The company quickly grew to become the world's largest independent vendor of business-to-business electronic commerce software and services. Then, in a public offering in 1996, the group spun off as Sterling Commerce. This was followed by a secondary offering in February 1997 that raised an additional $450 million to support the company's aggressive growth plans.

Sterling Commerce is growing at one of the fastest rates of any industry in Central Ohio as it helps companies worldwide conduct business electronically. Says Warner C. Blow, president and chief executive officer, "The bottom line is that every operation can be handled faster and more accurately by means of electronic commerce. There is no limit in sight to the continued growth of this form of communications."

AGGRESSIVE EXPANSION

Sterling Commerce has been experiencing revenue growth and pretax profits of 30 percent annually. In addition, the company recorded revenues of $350 million in 1997 and expects to be a billion-dollar company by the year 2000. Expansion will come from a few strategic areas at Sterling Commerce: international growth, development of Internet-related products, and acquisitions.

While North America is Sterling Commerce's largest market, the company is already capitalizing on the growth potential of international markets. Sterling Commerce has operations in approximately 70 countries through company-owned offices and distributorships. International expansion will come from existing domestic companies that have global operations, as well as foreign companies.

STERLING COMMERCE HAS OPERATIONS IN APPROXIMATELY 70 COUNTRIES, AND SERVES MORE THAN 40,000 CUSTOMERS WORLDWIDE. AT ITS CORPORATE COMPLEX AT TUTTLE CROSSING, THE COMPANY RECENTLY BUILT A NEW, 94,219-SQUARE-FOOT OFFICE BUILDING, ITS FOURTH IN COLUMBUS, TO ACCOMMODATE THE GROWTH.

BLT PRODUCTIONS

As more and more companies move onto the information superhighway to conduct business, Sterling is developing new products and solutions to help companies navigate their way. Some products are targeted toward smaller companies that do not have the resources to build an electronic infrastructure and, therefore, must use the Internet as their communications link.

In other markets, Sterling plans to acquire companies that offer geographic and technological benefits. To accommodate future expansion, the company, which currently employs 2,000 worldwide, plans to add approximately 600 employees during the next few years. Meanwhile, at its corporate complex at Tuttle Crossing in northwest Columbus, the company recently built a new, 94,219-square-foot office building on its campus, its fourth in Columbus, to accommodate the growth.

ASSISTING COMPANIES WORLDWIDE

Sterling Commerce serves more than 40,000 customers worldwide, including nearly all of the Fortune 500 companies, with products such as communications software, EDI and messaging software, banking systems software, value-added message processing, and consulting and outsourcing services. The company has also released a series of products and services aimed at helping business implement Web-based commerce solutions.

By eliminating the paper shuffle at companies, Sterling Commerce not only assists retailers with ordering merchandise automatically from their vendors and banks with moving funds electronically, but it helps other companies process accounts payable, purchasing, traffic management, and logistics electronically, as well as providing customers with the ability to order products through the World Wide Web. Ultimately, companies operate more efficiently and competitively, at reduced costs, and with the knowledge that their information is exchanged securely and reliably.

DOUG MARTIN

Sterling has developed the industry's most innovative products, all of which hold the number one position among comparable options. These products are grouped into four main families: GENTRAN, software that facilitates electronic gateway messaging and translation worldwide; CONNECT, products that help companies create an electronic commerce infrastructure for themselves and for external trading partners; COMMERCE, products that provide services and software to facilitate the electronic exchange of business transactions among multiple trading partners; and VECTOR, products that enable financial institutions to offer integrated payment processing services.

Sterling Commerce's broad range of products meets most electronic commerce needs and functions with any variety of computer systems, thereby making it the logical choice for businesses. United Parcel Service, for example, uses GENTRAN products for messaging, COMMERCE products for linking with partners, and CONNECT products as a bridge for linking its various worldwide systems.

PART OF THE COMMUNITY

Columbus has helped Sterling Commerce grow by providing a stable workforce that boasts a strong work ethic. In response, the company supports various arts and nonprofit organizations and schools in Columbus. Sterling Commerce also has taken an active role with the City of Columbus, Greater Columbus Chamber of Commerce, and Inland Port Commission to make the city competitive and to help local companies become larger, stronger, and more global.

Just as it pioneered electronic data interchange and electronic commerce, Sterling Commerce plans to remain on the leading edge of the industry, developing new electronic solutions to help companies do business more efficiently. And, as Blow concludes, "Sterling Commerce has to think globally—because the world is our market."

STERLING COMMERCE IS ONE OF THE PIONEERS OF THE AGE OF ELECTRONIC COMMERCE, OFFERING PRODUCTS SUCH AS COMMUNICATIONS SOFTWARE, EDI AND MESSAGING SOFTWARE, BANKING SYSTEMS SOFTWARE, VALUE-ADDED MESSAGE PROCESSING, AND CONSULTING AND OUTSOURCING SERVICES.

CENTRAL OHIO TRANSIT AUTHORITY (COTA)

STABLISHED IN 1974, THE CENTRAL OHIO TRANSIT AUTHORITY (COTA) CONTINUES to meet new challenges in an ever changing community. With a fleet of 303 buses, COTA provides more than 17.7 million passenger trips and travels 9.7 million miles annually. ✳ Founded by Franklin County and the municipal-

ities of Bexley, Columbus, Gahanna, Grandview Heights, Grove City, Hilliard, Reynoldsburg, Upper Arlington, Westerville, Whitehall, and Worthington, COTA is led by a 13-member board of trustees under the directon of Board President Philip W. Whitaker of Worthington. Eleven members are named by the mayors and approved by the city councils of the member cities, and two are appointed by the county commissioners. The board, whose members serve without compensation, set the policies and direction for COTA, while daily operations are handled by General Manager Glenna L. Watson.

MEETING TRANSPORTATION CHALLENGES

COTA is committed to serving all passengers in Central Ohio. Currently, more than half of the transit system's fleet is lift-equipped, providing passengers with disabilities an opportunity to use regular, fixed-route service. Passengers aged 65 and older, as well as passengers with disabilities, may obtain a special identification card that entitles them to ride at a reduced fare.

Project Mainstream, COTA's paratransit service, is available for

riders with physical disabilities who, without transportation, might otherwise be unable to hold a job, participate in social activities, or receive medical treatment.

COTA strives to creatively meet transportation challenges by providing better access to jobs, helping to fight traffic congestion, and improving mobility. Partnerships with businesses are continually being established to provide economic support for requested transit services, such as the 1997 partnership with students at the Ohio State University (OSU). This program allows OSU students to use

COTA's services by paying a nominal quarterly fee.

In 1997, COTA introduced vintage-looking, diesel-powered trolleys, which provide service on COTA LINK, the system's special weekday lunchtime service in downtown Columbus. The trolleys also are used for special events and occasions. The first trolley COTA received has been named Trolley 101-GLW in honor of Glenna L. Watson, who was instrumental in bringing the trolleys to Central Ohio.

COTA also was selected to participate in an innovative federal grant project called Livable Communities, which will bring a pilot transit center to the Columbus area, linking the burgeoning Easton development in northeastern Franklin County with nearby neighborhoods and the main COTA system. The transit center is expected to open in 1998.

As Greater Columbus continues to grow, COTA is committed to providing the best possible transportation system in Central Ohio. COTA's mission statement clearly defines its goals: "COTA's mission is to produce economic, environmental, and social benefits for the entire community by meeting the mobility needs of Central Ohio residents."

CLOCKWISE FROM TOP:
COTA GENERAL MANAGER GLENNA L. WATSON PROUDLY STANDS NEXT TO ONE OF THE THREE VINTAGE-LOOKING, DIESEL-POWERED TROLLEYS INTRODUCED TO CENTRAL OHIO IN 1997.

THE OHIO STATE UNIVERSITY (OSU) BUS IS ONE OF 24 PAINTED BUSES IN COTA'S FLEET. IT DEPICTS OSU ATHLETICS ON ONE SIDE AND ACADEMICS ON THE OTHER.

WITH A FLEET OF 303 BUSES, COTA PROVIDES MORE THAN 17.7 MILLION PASSENGER TRIPS AND TRAVELS 9.7 MILLION MILES ANNUALLY.

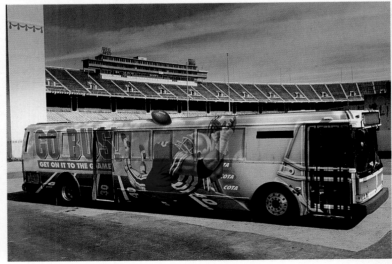

WYN MOLDED PLASTICS, INC.

IN 1977, WHEN THE PRECISION PLASTIC MOLDING COMPANY HE HAD BEEN HEADING moved out of state, Wayne Miller decided to remain in Circleville, Ohio. At the time, Miller hoped to bring to another local firm the years of experience he had acquired working for major corporations. He quickly realized, however, that he could serve Circleville in a better way.

"I went out and interviewed," Miller recalls. "Then, my wife and I talked. She said I'd been saying for years I could do a better job than the people I worked for, so now it was time to put up or shut up."

The Millers put up. With $500,000 worth of business lined up if they had a plant to do it in, they gained financing, purchased two molding machines, leased a building, and started Wyn Molded Plastics. It was a business the Millers more or less named for Wayne Miller: Wyn is Wayne with the vowels removed.

Wyn Molded Plastics focuses on thermoplastic injection molding, a technique that shoots thermoplastic materials into a mold cavity to produce a piece or part to exacting specifications. In addition to the latest in injection press technology, the company offers painting and high-temperature baking of the paint, postdecorating with screening, hot stamping, and assembly of dissimilar materials. Production is supported by a line of services—from product development to design assistance and product manufacture.

From that one small plant with two molding machines has grown a company with a major presence in Columbus and in the injection molding industry. Today, the Millers head an operation of 410 employees, with headquarters in Circleville and additional plants in Athens, Ohio, and Leeds, Alabama. The 130,000-square-foot Circleville facility now maintains 32 various-sized injection molding machines, while the 44,000-square-foot Athens operation has seven large machines.

Wyn's Circleville and Athens operations are closely tied to the Honda automotive plant in Marysville. Wyn supplies components both directly to Honda and to Honda suppliers. In Circleville, Wyn produces automotive door pockets and panels, speaker grills, seat backs, high-mount lenses used in the back of the window, and other auto interior items, as well as such exterior items as the housings for lights, lenses, and overlenses on the front of the car. And because Honda Tier One Suppliers stresses the just-in-time approach to inventory control, which directs that components reach its plant only as they are needed on the assembly line, Wyn operates a medium-sized trucking company of 28 trailers, seven tractors, and three straight trucks, which carry shipments to destinations within Ohio several times a day.

Such dedication to meeting the customer's needs is key to Wyn's success. The Millers say, "The cause of the company's growth is not anything secret. First, we recognize that the customer is at the forefront of the business: We will take the company and turn it inside out like a sock to accommodate the customer. And second, we recognize that it's our employees who keep us at that forefront." The Millers believe it is this philosophy that will ensure Wyn Molded Plastics' success far into the future.

WYN MOLDED PLASTICS, INC. WAS FOUNDED IN 1977 WITH ONE SMALL PLANT AND TWO MOLDING MACHINES; TODAY, THE COMPANY HAS 410 EMPLOYEES, WITH HEADQUARTERS IN CIRCLEVILLE AND ADDITIONAL PLANTS IN ATHENS, OHIO, AND LEEDS, ALABAMA. THE 130,000-SQUARE-FOOT CIRCLEVILLE FACILITY (BOTTOM RIGHT) NOW MAINTAINS 32 VARIOUS-SIZED INJECTION MOLDING MACHINES.

Tosoh SMD, Inc.

AUNCHED BY TWO PARTNERS IN 1975 IN A CONVERTED COLUMBUS BARROOM, BARELY a mile from its current site, Tosoh SMD, Inc. is a company that has come a long way without traveling very far. Founded as Specialty Metals and Alloys Company, Inc., its main activity was to supply materials to customers for coating

plastics, and the company started with just two part-time employees—a one-person office staff and a machinist.

From those humble beginnings, the company has grown to become one of the world's three major producers of thin film deposition materials, known as targets. In 1978, it was purchased by Varian Associates, Inc.; in 1988, it became part of the TOSOH Corporation, a $3 billion-a-year supplier of chemicals, high-purity metals, electronic devices, and scientific and diagnostic instrumentation. Today, Tosoh SMD employs 300 people, with about 35 percent of its production exported overseas.

FILM DEPOSITION

Tosoh SMD, Inc.'s dedication to completing all its tasks in the most efficient, highest-quality manner is perhaps best demonstrated by the cleanliness at its facility. It is immaculate and contains areas clean to a level known as Class 10, which means these areas have only 0.001 the quantity of airborne particulates as the average hospital operating room. Such cleanliness is required for the work of Tosoh SMD, a world leader in providing materials for depositing metallic films that are 0.02 times the diameter of a human hair.

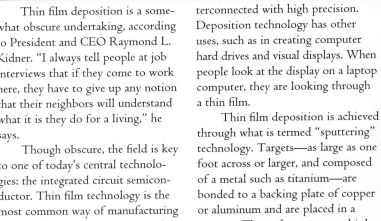

Thin film deposition is a somewhat obscure undertaking, according to President and CEO Raymond L. Kidner. "I always tell people at job interviews that if they come to work here, they have to give up any notion that their neighbors will understand what it is they do for a living," he says.

Though obscure, the field is key to one of today's central technologies: the integrated circuit semiconductor. Thin film technology is the most common way of manufacturing semiconductors; in fact, semiconductors are layers of thin film materials deposited over one another and in-

terconnected with high precision. Deposition technology has other uses, such as in creating computer hard drives and visual displays. When people look at the display on a laptop computer, they are looking through a thin film.

Thin film deposition is achieved through what is termed "sputtering" technology. Targets—as large as one foot across or larger, and composed of a metal such as titanium—are bonded to a backing plate of copper or aluminum and are placed in a vacuum. There, the targets are hit by ions created in a plasma; these ions erode the target surface, turning it

passed in the commercial real estate industry. Clients include a variety of well-known international corporations and Fortune 500 companies, such as AT&T; Cincinnati Bell Information Systems; Marriott; Kubota; BISYS Fund Services; General Motors; McGraw-Hill; Whirlpool; First USA, Inc.; Caterpillar Logistics Services; Seagate Software SMG; Ty Inc.; Partylite; Owens-Corning; The Limited, Inc.; Planet Hollywood; and Prudential Insurance. The company's growth has come from existing clients, which tap Pizzuti for additional projects, as well as a continuing stream of new clients.

Early on, Pizzuti acquired and redeveloped a wide range of commercial properties for its own portfolio. Over time, the company diversified its services and today provides clients with build-to-suit, development, asset and property management, and marketing services to cover any type of real estate project, including, but not limited to, warehouses, distribution centers, and manufacturing facilities; downtown and suburban office buildings; land development for mixed-use commercial and industrial projects; and specialized facilities for high-technology uses.

TREND-SETTING PROJECTS

Over the years, Pizzuti's portfolio has grown to include numerous high-profile, trend-setting projects, including SouthPark industrial park in Grove City. SouthPark is a 500-acre, master-planned business park, which has been recognized as a leading industrial complex in the region. Tenants include McGraw-Hill, Lennox, and Airborne Express. In 1997, the company began development of another premier master-planned industrial park in the Village of Obetz called CreekSide, which will duplicate SouthPark's amenities and features. Goodyear Tire and Rubber has signed on as the park's first tenant.

Pizzuti also recently announced plans for a multimillion-dollar, mixed-use project called Miranova in downtown Columbus. Miranova will feature more than 100 residential units, all

with river views; two office buildings; retail space; and accompanying parking facilities. Designed by world-renowned Arquitectonica, Miranova is located along the Scioto River and will serve as an important anchor in Columbus' downtown riverfront development.

In its hometown and in communities where it develops projects, Pizzuti stands out as a community leader, supporting various arts and nonprofit organizations. Associates follow the lead of the company's founder, who, in addition to his reputation as a business leader, is a well-known civic and community activist. Ron Pizzuti serves on numerous foundation, arts, and education boards. He also has been instrumental in the planning of riverfront development downtown and has played a key role in helping to attract major-league sports teams to Columbus.

When it comes to developing office and industrial sites, Pizzuti recognizes that giving back to a community is more than simply erecting a building to generate tax dollars and jobs. The process also involves designating land for residential development so associates can live close to

their new jobs, and adding new roads and other community services, such as fire stations. At SouthPark, for example, 20 percent of the land was set aside for residential development and another 5 percent was designated for community services and nature reserves.

In the future, Pizzuti will continue to focus on developing premier office and industrial sites in existing markets, which represent some of the strongest commercial real estate markets nationwide, and in new areas as opportunities arise.

PIZZUTI RECENTLY ANNOUNCED PLANS FOR A MULTIMILLION-DOLLAR, MIXED-USE PROJECT CALLED MIRANOVA IN DOWNTOWN COLUMBUS. THE $150 MILLION PROJECT, TO BE LOCATED ALONG THE SCIOTO RIVER, WILL SERVE AS AN IMPORTANT ANCHOR IN COLUMBUS' DOWNTOWN RIVERFRONT DEVELOPMENT.

PIZZUTI'S CLIENTS INCLUDE A VARIETY OF WELL-KNOWN INTERNATIONAL CORPORATIONS AND FORTUNE 500 COMPANIES, SUCH AS AT&T; CINCINNATI BELL INFORMATION SYSTEMS; MARRIOTT; BISYS FUND SERVICES; GENERAL MOTORS; McGRAW-HILL; THE LIMITED, INC.; PLANET HOLLYWOOD; AND PRUDENTIAL INSURANCE.

SCHULER INCORPORATED

ITH THE PRESSURE OF ONE'S FINGERTIPS, THE IMAGE OF THOMAS JEFFERSON CAN be transferred from a nickel onto a square of aluminum foil. In a similar fashion, but requiring extreme precision and force measured in tons, a piece of sheet steel can be shaped into the roof or door panel of an automobile.

Schuler Incorporated, one of the world's leading suppliers of state-of-the-art metal-forming machine tools, is equipped to provide the exact amount of force and precision required to handle the job.

Schuler can build machine tools to the largest scale, including automotive presses that are 112 feet long and weigh more than 3,750 tons. At the other end of the scale, 80 percent of the world's coinage—including the nickel in the above example—is produced on Schuler minting presses.

Schuler Incorporated is part of Schuler Presses, which was founded near Stuttgart in 1839. Schuler Presses now employs 3,500 people worldwide, with major manufacturing facilities in Europe, Brazil, and China. The company's North American corporate headquarters was established in Columbus in 1978, and the 80 employees located in Columbus provide sales, service, project management, and engineering services to North American customers.

SUPPLIERS TO THE WORLD

Schuler's main product line is mechanical and hydraulic presses used for sheet and solid metal forming, particularly for the automotive industry. Schuler supplies presses to European, Asian, and South American automobile manufacturers, as well as to the American Big Three—General Motors, Chrysler, and Ford. Schuler minting presses manufacture coins in national mints throughout the world, and Schuler forging presses are used to make products like socket wrenches and constant velocity joints. The company also has expertise in high-pressure tube hydroforming, a process that creates a stronger lightweight component in fewer operations by using pressurized water to shape metal tubing.

With all its products, Schuler brings to market the advantages of German engineering and its reputation for excellent service. Presses such as those Schuler builds are critical pieces of equipment; should one fail for long, an entire assembly line can be

brought to a halt. From Columbus, a dozen Schuler technicians are on call to respond quickly to any problem.

Schuler is also developing an expanding business in the rebuilding and remanufacturing of large presses. Rebuilding makes a press new as of its construction date; remanufacturing upgrades the press to current standards. Through such upgrades, Schuler can add new capabilities, such as quick die-change capability, allowing operators to change press dies in minutes rather than hours, thus significantly improving flexibility and productivity.

In 1997, Schuler demonstrated its commitment to the Columbus area by completing a high bay expansion to help meet the growing demand for press repair and rebuilding, and to manufacture subassemblies for other member companies of the Schuler Group. The expansion added 11,000 square feet in manufacturing and assembly space, and includes several large machines, a 100-ton crane capacity, and a paint booth. The expanded capabilities of the Columbus group guarantee that Schuler will be a valuable member of the community for many years to come.

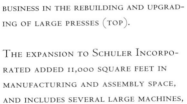

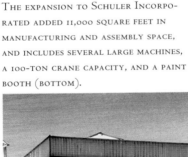

SCHULER IS DEVELOPING AN EXPANDING BUSINESS IN THE REBUILDING AND UPGRADING OF LARGE PRESSES (TOP).

THE EXPANSION TO SCHULER INCORPORATED ADDED 11,000 SQUARE FEET IN MANUFACTURING AND ASSEMBLY SPACE, AND INCLUDES SEVERAL LARGE MACHINES, A 100-TON CRANE CAPACITY, AND A PAINT BOOTH (BOTTOM).

LCI INTERNATIONAL

EW INDUSTRIES HAVE CHANGED AS DRAMATICALLY AS THE TELECOMMUNICATIONS INdustry. Once a field sluggishly dominated by a single giant, today, telecommunications is an arena in which newer, more competitive firms are staking out larger and larger claims. LCI International, a Fortune 1,000 company that is one of the fastest-growing major telecommunications companies in the nation, is among those aggressive players.

Founded in Columbus in 1983, LCI International provides voice and data transmission services to residential and business customers, as well as to other carriers. LCI serves customers throughout the United States, providing connectivity to more than 220 countries worldwide.

PRESENCE IN COLUMBUS

Although LCI relocated its corporate headquarters to McLean, Virginia, in 1991, Columbus remains a major center for the company's operations. LCI employs 1,200 people at its three operational facilities in the Tuttle Crossing area of Dublin. These facilities include LCI's Network Control Center, which provides around-the-clock monitoring of its 280 million circuit miles of digital fiber-optic capacity, and one of LCI's two national customer service call centers, which provide around-the-clock support to commercial and residential customers. In addition, LCI maintains sales operations, information systems functions, several administrative services, engineering and operations offices, and provisioning support in Columbus.

BROAD-BASED GROWTH

In the complicated and ever changing telecommunications market, LCI has experienced exponential growth, thanks to its straightforward offer of flat-rate services that are simple, fair, and inexpensive. From 1992 to 1996, company revenues jumped from $260 million to $1.1 billion, and customer "minutes of use" increased nearly fivefold to 8.2 billion. And LCI's growth is broad based: The company is expanding both as a result of across-the-board gains in all business segments

and through strategic acquisitions, as well as through the continued development of new and additional services.

When LCI was founded in Columbus as LiTel Telecommunications Corporation, its goal was to be a regional long-distance carrier. After the 1991 move to McLean, the company changed its name to LCI International to reflect its new ambitions: to expand into a full-service, nationwide carrier and to take on the Big Three long-distance carriers—AT&T, MCI, and Sprint.

LCI is continuing to expand its range. With the passage of the Telecommunications Act of 1996, the company entered the new local services market, and by mid-1997 was already providing local services to business

customers in 22 markets in 10 states on a resale basis.

Today, LCI's goal is to continue gaining market share in the telecommunications industry. Chairman and CEO H. Brian Thompson states: "Looking ahead, we have every reason to believe that our market position, technologies, people, strategies, and balance sheet strength will continue to make us one of the industry's outstanding success stories."

A BASE OF HIGH-QUALITY CLIENTS. A CULTURE ROOTED IN THE COMMUNITY. AND A refreshing approach to client service. These are the attributes that have enabled the Columbus office of Baker & Hostetler LLP, to write an extraordinary chapter in this national law firm's history of success, service, and accomplishment.

CLIENT RELATIONSHIPS

Baker & Hostetler is built upon client relationships. It was true when Newton Baker, Joe Hostetler, and Tom Sidlo founded the firm in 1916, and it's true today. The firm is proud of its quality legal work, its involvement in the communities in which it does business, and the many advances it has made as it has grown into a national firm of nearly 500 attorneys. Adhering to the principles of its founders, Baker & Hostetler credits its success to the quality of its relationships with clients.

As the firm has listened and responded to clients' needs, it has developed the people, the resources, and the technologies to provide legal services in virtually every area of law, nearly anywhere in the country. Baker & Hostetler has established the systems and organization to handle the legal affairs of some of the country's largest corporations and many of its fastest-growing smaller enterprises. In every case, the firm's relationships with clients, as people and as partners, has determined the course of its growth.

SUCCESSFUL CLIENTS

The Columbus office of Baker & Hostetler is fortunate to enjoy pro-fessional relationships with many of the city's successful businesses and individuals, as well as an array of national companies based in Columbus and elsewhere. The firm is associated with such clients as American Dental Partners, Inc.; Boeing, the largest aerospace company in the world; and Emery Worldwide, one of the leading expediting companies in the United States, as well as such national companies as Miller Brewing Co., Ford Motor Co., and Shell Chemical Co.

Baker & Hostetler, in Columbus, regularly services clients in a wide array of industries, including health care, mutual funds, automotive, retail food services, insurance, banking, education, and real estate, to name only a few.

Whether working on a union organizational campaign in Seattle for Boeing, attending to the legal needs of Team Rahal while it concentrates on its Indy car racing program, or guiding OhioHealth and Doctors Hospital through the ongoing changes in health care competition and regulation, Baker & Hostetler's attorneys consistently strive to form partnerships with its clients and to solve problems effectively and efficiently. The firm's attorneys are committed to understanding clients' needs, the

CLOCKWISE FROM TOP:
RICHARD A. VINCENT, PRESIDENT AND CEO OF DOCTORS HOSPITAL, AND WILLIAM W. WILKINS, PRESIDENT AND CEO OF OHIOHEALTH (SEATED, LEFT AND RIGHT), BOTH LONG-TERM CLIENTS OF BAKER & HOSTETLER, ARE PICTURED WITH ATTORNEYS (FROM LEFT) ROBERT W. MCADAMS JR., GEORGE W. HAIRSTON, RICHARD W. SIEHL, AND TIMOTHY B. MITCHELL.

(FROM LEFT) GEORGE H. BENNET JR., ESQ., EXECUTIVE VICE PRESIDENT AND GENERAL COUNSEL FOR CARDINAL HEALTH INC., AND ROBERT D. WALTER, CHAIRMAN AND CEO OF CARDINAL, ARE JOINED BY ALEC WIGHTMAN, HEWITT B. SHAW JR., AND BARRY R. ROBINSON, ATTORNEYS WITH BAKER & HOSTETLER.

CHARLOTTE AND JACK KESSLER (SEATED) ARE PICTURED WITH BAKER & HOSTETLER ATTORNEY GARY A. WADMAN.

Lima Engine Plant

complexities of their businesses, and the industries in which they operate.

Cardinal Health, Inc., one of the nation's largest pharmaceutical services providers and a corporate leader in the Columbus community, has used Baker & Hostetler for nearly 20 years for a wide array of legal services. During that period, Cardinal Health grew to become one of the largest companies in the country. Baker & Hostetler supported this growth with its commitment to understand the health care industry, in order to help Cardinal achieve its objectives.

CLIENT SERVICE

The Columbus office of Baker & Hostetler is a full-service office with resident practitioners in major specialty areas, including corporate, securities, commercial, real estate, bankruptcy, employment law and benefits, estates and trusts, litigation, tax, environmental law, and health care. Additionally, the intellectual resources, problem solving ability, and geographic presence of legal professionals in 11 offices nationwide are available to clients based in Columbus.

In addition to serving clients in the Columbus corporate community, Baker & Hostetler is a resource to many of the city's leading families for sophisticated estate and personal planning services and a provider of legal services in the public and quasipublic arena. Baker & Hostetler

has served as general counsel to Rickenbacker Port Authority (RPA) for more than 12 years. Rickenbacker International Airport is a national model for successful conversion from a military base to an international freight airport and air industrial park. Baker & Hostetler assists the City of Columbus in the negotiation of its labor contracts and the City of Worthington as its general counsel, as well as a number of other municipalities, school districts, and public institutions. Likewise, Baker & Hostetler has served as general counsel to the Central Ohio Transit Authority (COTA) since its inception.

Baker & Hostetler's national presence, size, and diversity of experience enable its attorneys to respond to client needs whenever and wherever they arise. Recently, the firm deployed an around-the-clock crisis management team to help a national

company deal with the aftermath of a chemical plant explosion.

CULTURE AND THE COMMUNITY

Baker & Hostetler recognizes the importance of supporting the community and encourages employee involvement in professional and community organizations. The firm supports numerous charitable organizations that promote the social and cultural life of the Columbus community.

Baker & Hostetler is proud of the reputation it has earned as a strong, national law firm, believing that its attorneys are among the best. The firm's culture is marked by integrity, civility, sensibility, and professional excellence. But what the firm values most are the close relationships its attorneys share with clients. These relationships are considered the foundation and the future of Baker & Hostetler.

CLOCKWISE FROM TOP:
PICTURED AT FORD MOTOR COMPANY ENGINE PLANT IN LIMA, OHIO, ARE BAKER & HOSTETLER ATTORNEYS (FROM RIGHT) NANCY ENGBERS FALK, OTTO BEATTY III, AND ELLEN J. GARLING, WITH RICHARD M. HEMKER, SUPERVISOR OF LABOR RELATIONS IN LIMA.

PICTURED WITH MAYOR GREGORY LASHUTKA (RIGHT) IS BAKER & HOSTETLER ATTORNEY RONALD G. LINVILLE.

GEORGE W. HAIRSTON, MANAGING PARTNER OF THE COLUMBUS OFFICE (BOTTOM CENTER), IS PICTURED WITH DANIEL J. GUNSETT, ASSISTANT MANAGING PARTNER (BOTTOM RIGHT), AND PRACTICE GROUP COORDINATORS GEORGEANN G. PETERS, THOMAS L. LONG, MARK D. SENFF, AND RICHARD L. BIBART (CLOCKWISE FROM BOTTOM LEFT).

Honda of America Mfg. Inc.

HONDA OF AMERICA MFG. INC. HAS TRAVELED FAR SINCE IT BEGAN PRODUCING motorcycles in its first U.S. manufacturing facility in 1979. That first plant, located in Marysville and started with 64 associates, today has the capacity to manufacture 150,000 motorcycles and utility vehicles annually, is an

industry leader in production efficiency and flexibility, and is the number one U.S. producer of ATVs and motorcycles for export.

In 1997, a J.D. Power & Associates quality study ranked Honda of America Mfg. Inc.'s Marysville Auto Plant best in the world, and the Accord it produces was ranked the number one premium midsize car on the market. The award is only the latest in a long list of accomplishments for the company, which has established itself as one of the world's premier automobile manufacturing operations.

Overall, Honda of America Mfg. has more than 12,000 associates working at four plants in Central Ohio. They are responsible for manufactur-

ing cars, motorcycles, engines, and all-terrain vehicles, which are exported to more than 60 countries. Last year, automobile production for Accords, Civics, and Acura CLs alone was 640,000 units.

Among the best-selling automobiles nationwide each year, the Accord and the Civic have been named in *Car and Driver* magazine's annual list of 10 Best Cars, and the Civic has received *Automobile* magazine's Automobile of the Year Award. Honda cars are also recognized as leaders in terms of owner loyalty and customer satisfaction.

GROWING CAPABILITIES
Honda's Central Ohio operations encompass manufacturing, research

and development, engineering, and administrative functions located within an approximately 8,500-acre area near Marysville, northwest of Columbus. In addition, the company operates an engine and drivetrain components plant in Anna, Ohio, that has the capacity to manufacture 900,000 engines per year.

All these functions are part of the Honda of America Mfg. goal of establishing self-reliance, and the company has made great strides in reaching that goal. Unlike the early days, when Honda operations in Japan did all the design and tooling, as well as supplying most of the parts for the cars built in Ohio, many models today are totally designed, engineered,

CLOCKWISE FROM TOP LEFT:
HONDA'S CENTRAL OHIO OPERATIONS ENCOMPASS MANUFACTURING, RESEARCH AND DEVELOPMENT, ENGINEERING, AND ADMINISTRATIVE FUNCTIONS LOCATED WITHIN AN APPROXIMATELY 8,500-ACRE AREA NEAR MARYSVILLE, NORTHWEST OF COLUMBUS.

WITH A HISTORY OF GROWTH AND AN INCREASING EMPHASIS ON SELF-RELIANCE, HONDA OF AMERICA MFG. WILL CONTINUE TO BE A MAJOR PART OF THE CENTRAL OHIO COMMUNITY, WHILE PRODUCING SOME OF THE WORLD'S FINEST MOTOR VEHICLES.

TODAY, HONDA OF AMERICA MFG. HAS THE CAPACITY TO MANUFACTURE 150,000 MOTORCYCLES AND UTILITY VEHICLES ANNUALLY.

HONDA OF AMERICA MFG. HAS TRAVELED FAR SINCE IT BEGAN PRODUCING MOTORCYCLES IN ITS FIRST U.S. MANUFACTURING FACILITY IN 1979.

and manufactured exclusively in the United States.

In recognition of its growing self-reliance and increasing prominence in the industry, Honda of America Mfg. has been given enormous responsibility in the Americas, includung helping to develop plants in countries such as Mexico and Brazil.

A Cut Above

In addition to its reputation for quality and reliability, Honda stands out among the competition due to its commitment to continuous improvement. The company's strong relationships between suppliers and associates help ensure this commitment is met.

Company associates work closely with suppliers to maintain high quality, productivity, and safety standards, as well as to meet cost goals. Suppliers are involved early on in the model-development process to help ensure the best product possible. Suppliers also help provide superior products by participating in quality circles, a concept that Honda of America pioneered among United States automakers in the mid-1980s. There are more than 4,000 quality circles among the company's domestic suppliers.

Honda of America Mfg. has a firm understanding that it takes more than high-tech equipment and machinery to build state-of-the-art vehicles. Top-rate associates also are needed, as well as training and incentives to help associates excel. The company's successful use of team-working environments, which involve associates at all levels of company operations,

are legendary. Associates earn points for ideas about various types of improvements, and awards include automobiles and motorcycles.

Honda of America Mfg. is well-known for pioneering various manufacturing techniques and concepts in the automotive manufacturing industry. Those include rolling model changes, where production on one model stops and another starts on the same shift without stopping production. The company conducted the first such model change in the United States, and has achieved six highly complex model changes over the past 10 years. Honda of America Mfg. also maintains flexible manufacturing techniques that allow it to respond quickly to market changes without having to incur any downtime.

Support from the Central Ohio community is recognized by Honda of America Mfg. as an integral part of its successful growth track, and the company has been generous in giving back to the community by

creating new jobs and supporting volunteerism. U.S. investments total nearly $4 billion, with much of that spent in Central Ohio. There were 2,400 jobs created in the area during the past two years without adding new plants, and there have been no layoffs since operations began in 1979.

Each year, hundreds of associates get involved in their communities through the company's Honda Hero Volunteer project. Associates who volunteer 50 hours of service annually to a nonprofit organization qualify for a $200 grant for that group. Recently, the company and its suppliers committed $1 million over five years to the Center of Science and Industry (COSI) to fund an exhibit that will highlight the latest in manufacturing technology.

With a history of growth and an increasing emphasis on self-reliance, Honda of America Mfg. will continue to be a major part of the Central Ohio community, while producing some of the world's finest motor vehicles.

Clockwise from top left: In recognition of its growing self-reliance and increasing prominence in the industry, Honda of America Mfg. has been given enormous responsibility in the Americas. That includes helping to develop plants in countries such as Mexico and Brazil.

Support from the Central Ohio community is recognized by Honda of America Mfg. as an integral part of its successful growth, and the company has been generous in giving back to the community by creating new jobs and supporting volunteerism.

Honda of America Mfg. maintains flexible manufacturing techniques that allow it to respond quickly to market changes without having to incur any downtime.

Honda has created 2,400 jobs in Central Ohio during the past two years, and there have been no layoffs since operations began in 1979.

Squire, Sanders & Dempsey L.L.P.

A SENIOR ATTORNEY FROM SQUIRE, SANDERS & DEMPSEY RECENTLY SPENT TWO DAYS visiting a new client. But the time was not spent discussing litigation, because none was pending. Instead, the visit was made to allow the attorney to become familiar with the client's particular operations, needs, history, and agenda.

Such visits, undertaken at no expense to the client, are standard procedure with the century-old firm, where the practice of law is rooted in a thorough understanding of its clients. "Every client has their own traditions, their own feel," says Alex Shumate, managing partner at Squire, Sanders & Dempsey. "You have to absorb this. You have to learn each client's separate personality to represent their needs and interests well."

Top-Tier Practitioners

In Columbus, Squire, Sanders & Dempsey is acknowledged to be among the city's handful of top-tier legal practitioners. From its offices in the Huntington Center, the firm sits opposite the Ohio Statehouse, where it is often engaged in legislative matters on behalf of clients. The firm is close to a number of the corporate and public clients that it serves, and at the heart of the Columbus community to which its attorneys contribute their time and talents.

Beyond Columbus, Squire, Sanders & Dempsey has more than 400 attorneys practicing in offices in eight major U.S. cities and in the international cities of Bratislava, Brussels, Budapest, Kiev, London, Moscow, Madrid, Prague, Taipei, and Hong Kong.

The activities of Squire, Sanders & Dempsey are far reaching. For example, following the fall of the Berlin Wall, the firm began working extensively in eastern Europe to establish a basis for commercial law practice in those nations. The firm is nationally prominent in the United States: according to *The Bond Buyer*, the municipal bond industry's newsletter, it has consistently ranked among the top national firms in the number of issues in which it participates—including the bond issue for the Riffe Center for Government and the Arts in downtown Columbus.

A Varied Practice

In Columbus, the tasks undertaken by Squire, Sanders & Dempsey encompass the range of the world's work. On any given day, its attorneys may be handling a corporate merger, meeting with health care providers to advise how they may best deal effectively with the challenges of managed care, providing advice on diversity management, working through international contacts to identify business opportunities for a client, acting as bond counsel to the State of Ohio, litigating a complex case of computer software piracy, or assisting with an environmental audit.

Squire, Sanders & Dempsey is a cutting-edge firm—one that handles cases and transactions that turn on recent legal developments or that are likely to break new legal

A HELIX-SHAPED STAIRCASE CONNECTS THE MAIN RECEPTION AREA OF SQUIRE, SANDERS & DEMPSEY L.L.P. TO THE LIBRARY. (FROM LEFT) PARTNER CRAIG WOODS, MANAGING PARTNER ALEX SHUMATE, AND PARTNERS CATHERINE ADAMS AND DAVID YOUNG

THE BRUSSELS OFFICE OF SQUIRE, SANDERS & DEMPSEY L.L.P. IS IN A BUILDING ON THE BELGIAN CAPITAL'S AVENUE LOUISE, AN UPSCALE SHOPPING MECCA IN THE UPPER CITY.

ground. Its practice includes a distinctive blend of public and private clients. The resulting expertise in both the public and private sectors is an advantage to all clients.

The Columbus office's expertise is broad—with 75 attorneys who are divided into the specialties of business, litigation, public, environmental, labor and employment, health care, banking and finance, and real estate law.

Whatever their practice area, attorneys at Squire, Sanders & Dempsey strive to represent their clients by anticipating issues and initiating measures to prevent problems. The firm's attorneys seek solutions that are practical and result oriented.

FOCUSING RESOURCES

Perhaps Squire, Sanders & Dempsey's key strength is its ability to draw upon the resources of the entire firm, then direct those resources to the requirements of a particular case. Today, the complexity of the law

and of the issues bearing on a single case often require the involvement of attorneys with varied specialties to achieve the best results.

In handling cases, the Squire, Sanders & Dempsey philosophy is to engage those individual attorneys within the firm most qualified to achieve the desired result in the most cost-effective manner. Teams of attorneys are assembled from the relevant practice areas regardless of the individual attorney's office location, and the client is provided that service as though the attorney were at the nearest office.

The firm conducts its practice guided by two fundamental principles—to serve its clients effectively, and to maintain the professional standards that for more than a century have distinguished the firm and its people.

Just as any client has its own personality, so, too, does any law firm. Squire, Sanders & Dempsey, says Shumate, is composed of "people

who live in the community, work in the community, and give back to the community." As a result, the firm and its lawyers are extensively involved in the arts, education, and other activities of Columbus. The firm's culture, Shumate adds, creates attorneys who are well rounded as individuals, and can offer clients both knowledge of the law and knowledge of the world the law exists to serve.

CORE MATERIALS CORPORATION

WHEN MANUFACTURERS REQUIRE FIBERGLASS-MOLDED PRODUCTS AND SHEET-MOLDED composites (SMC) for their business needs, many turn to Core Materials Corporation. One of the top SMC producers nationwide, Core Materials annually produces approximately 35 million pounds of structural, cosmetic,

and specialty SMC materials at its plant on Manor Park Drive. Most of this material is used by Core Materials (CMC) to manufacture fiberglass body parts for the automotive and trucking industry, recreational vehicles, and commercial products, while the remainder is sold to other compression-molding companies.

CMC utilizes some of the industry's largest SMC compression-molding presses (up to 4,500 tons), highest-strength resin systems, and most advanced robotic equipment, all of which provide extensive production flexibility. The company has the capability to manufacture fiberglass-molded products that weigh anywhere from five to 150 pounds.

THE CORE ADVANTAGE
The demand for CMC's molded products and SMC material is linked to what company officials call the company's competitive edge, or core advantage. It includes a reputation for unsurpassed customer service, innovation in design and engineering, a commitment to continuous improvements in operations and efficiency, and superior-quality products.

"Quality assurance has always been an integral part of Core Materials' corporate philosophy. As a result, one of our core values is to exceed our customers' objectives in the quality, design, and cost effectiveness of our products and processes," says Jarvis Pigge, Core Materials' product development manager. Internal and external audit teams ensure that the company meets its high standards.

Other competitive advantages include the ability to manage customers' products from concept to production, the capability to perform low-volume, manual assembly or high-volume, highly automated assembly; state-of-the-art equipment and presses

to ensure superior products; entrepreneurial employees, who have top-notch credentials and industry knowledge; continuous research to ensure constant technical advances; and an established just-in-time manufacturing system that ensures customer orders are delivered on time.

A LONGTIME PRESENCE IN COLUMBUS
Growth has been a hallmark of CMC since it opened for business in Columbus in 1980 as Columbus Plastics, a 270,000-square-foot facility with nine compression molding presses. The first expansion occurred in 1988 and included the addition of 50,000 square

feet, as well as a 2,500-ton and a 3,000-ton press. In recent years, other expansions have added seven more presses and 30,000 square feet to the company's operation. In 1997, the company acquired a new facility in South Carolina.

In 1997, the company changed its name to CMC and announced plans to pursue new market opportunities in additional industries. To accomplish this goal, Core Materials added a 24-inch SMC machine, increasing its compounding capacity by 30 percent. "The additional machine opens up the door to more diversification, in both product and materials," Pigge says.

From CMC's perspective, the benefits of being located in Columbus are numerous. Because of the city's central location, the company is only a 10-hour drive or a 90-minute flight from more than 50 percent of the U.S. and Canadian manufacturing capacity and retail purchasing power. "The logistical benefit of our location is that we're able to reach more U.S. markets in 24 hours than any other region in North America," says Pigge.

In addition, the city's highly developed transportation infrastructure—two international airports, three major railroads, more than 130 trucking lines, 38 freight forwarders, and more than 86 million square feet of warehouse and distribution space—helps the company ensure on-time distribution of its products.

MAKING IMPROVEMENTS ITS MISSION

Since Columbus has been good for CMC, the company has worked to give back to its community through growth and dedication to continuous improvements. The company's mission statement sums it up best: "Through the working together of all employees of Core Materials Corporation, our objective is to produce the highest-quality products using the most cost-effective means in a workplace that is safe and environmentally compliant and that continues to provide challenging opportunities for all of our employees. As a team, we will focus

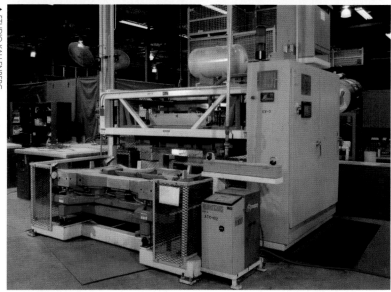

on continuous improvements in all that we do to consistently exceed our customers' expectations and requirements."

CMC also prides itself on its commitment to environmentally sound manufacturing processes and consistently utilizes the best available pollution abatement technology. The mission statement continues: "We are committed to adhering to high standards of environmental quality

and to providing a workplace that protects the health and safety of our employees and the communities surrounding our facility."

Core Materials' dedication to continuous improvement and environmental quality benefits customers, employees, and the people of Columbus. It is this dedication that ensures that Core Materials will be an important part of the Columbus community for many years to come.

CMC UTILIZES SOME OF THE INDUSTRY'S LARGEST SMC COMPRESSION-MOLDING PRESSES, INCLUDING THIS 4,500-TON PRESS.

CMC HAS THE ABILITY TO MANAGE CUSTOMERS' PRODUCTS FROM CONCEPT TO PRODUCTION, AND THE CAPABILITY TO PERFORM BOTH LOW-VOLUME, MANUAL ASSEMBLY AND HIGH-VOLUME, HIGHLY AUTOMATED ASSEMBLY.

STUDIO KALLENBERG

STUDIO KALLENBERG

APPLIED INNOVATION INC.

PPLIED INNOVATION INC. (AI), THE TELECOMMUNICATIONS INDUSTRY'S LEADING expert in producing data communications products, is known for keeping pace with technology and anticipating customers' needs for the future. AI is known for creating solutions and products that provide telecommunications companies with the data-switching, monitoring, and other management tools they need to operate their rapidly expanding networks.

AI's focus on customer service has helped it gain a competitive edge. "We very closely tune our products to the requirements of the telephone industry and not to thousands of customers," President Gerry Moersdorf says. "They ask us for products unique to their business and we respond."

Based on Moersdorf's philosophy and on quality, cutting-edge products, Applied Innovation (ranked 10th among the top 200 small businesses nationwide in 1994 by *Forbes* magazine) supplies products to the major interexchange carriers and access providers, including MCI. In addition, the company serves all seven regional Bell operating companies and, with further deregulation of the telecommunications industry, expects to add even more customers in the future.

PRODUCT EXPANSION

To better serve its current customer base, Applied Innovation is expanding its product line to ensure long-term growth for the company. As more businesses and consumers use the Internet as part of their daily routine, they create a burden for the telephone systems. Applied Innovation's new product series will help telephone companies keep up with the burgeoning customer demand for efficient Internet access, while at the same time preserving its current systems.

Applied Innovation is also exploring enhanced sales of its current product series through international expansion. Many developing countries, including those in Asia and Latin America, are pursuing the development of telephone infrastructure. China provides the greatest potential for Applied Innovation's products. As it builds the equivalent of a five-state U.S. telephone system every two years, China's goal is to grow from one telephone per 1,000 people to one telephone per 100. (In the United States, the rate is 1.5 telephones per person and growing.)

Applied Innovation is partnering with international telephone suppliers in such countries as Australia, Mexico, and the Czech Republic, to assist with its international expansion. Other global telecommunications alliances and acquisitions are forthcoming.

CONSTANT INNOVATION

To ensure that AI maintains skilled and qualified associates and continued success with its product lines, the company has established a state-of-the-art research and development facility in Raleigh, a leading telecommunications hub. In addition, the company continues to shorten development cycles and is constantly working to keep up with the rapidly changing technological advancements in the telecommunications industry—some of which have a life span of only 18 months. Other recent upgrades include the adoption of a market-oriented approach to product development. Marketing and engineering teams work together to ensure that products have a market before large R&D investments are made.

"WE VERY CLOSELY TUNE OUR PRODUCTS TO THE REQUIREMENTS OF THE TELEPHONE INDUSTRY AND NOT TO THOUSANDS OF CUSTOMERS," SAYS APPLIED INNOVATION PRESIDENT GERRY MOERSDORF.

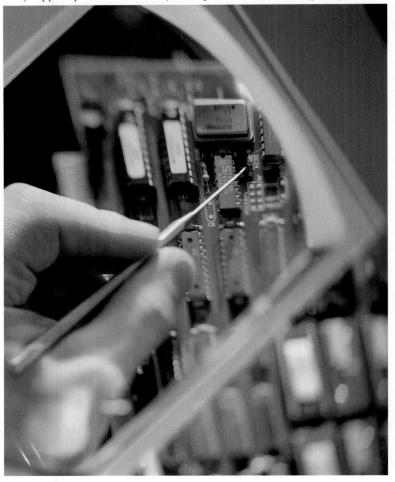

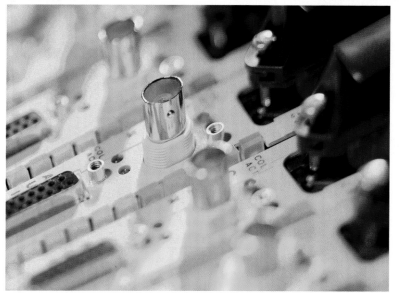

Applied Innovation's successful track record has not gone unnoticed by its competitors. "There are so many companies in electronics that come and go. We had a chance to be acquired or become the Columbus manufacturing arm for a large company, but I still appreciate and enjoy the independence," Moersdorf says.

Among the company's key accomplishments is building a world-class company in middle America, out of the limelight of technology hubs on the coasts. "I am very proud of building the company in Columbus with Columbus people," Moersdorf says. "We have built world-class pieces of engineering in Central Ohio." The company's central geographic location proves to be a selling point to customers as well.

Also notable are AI's high-profile applications, including BellSouth's use of Applied Innovation equipment to monitor data communications at the 1996 Olympic Games in Atlanta. Other AI products were used to survey the data communications network providing television stations with video and audio transmissions.

In 1996, Applied Innovation had $41 million in revenues. The company, which went public in 1987, should pass $100 million in revenues by early 1998, as it adds products and expands into new markets. Given its track record, Applied Innovation is sure to reach that target, and then exceed it, as the company continues to keep pace with technology and anticipate its customers' telecommunications needs into the 21st century.

CLOCKWISE FROM TOP LEFT: APPLIED INNOVATION INC., THE TELECOMMUNICATIONS INDUSTRY'S LEADING EXPERT IN PRODUCING DATA COMMUNICATIONS PRODUCTS, IS KNOWN FOR KEEPING PACE WITH TECHNOLOGY AND ANTICIPATING CUSTOMERS' NEEDS FOR THE FUTURE.

APPLIED INNOVATION'S NEW PRODUCT SERIES WILL HELP TELEPHONE COMPANIES KEEP UP WITH THE BURGEONING CUSTOMER DEMAND FOR EFFICIENT INTERNET ACCESS, WHILE AT THE SAME TIME PRESERVING ITS CURRENT SYSTEMS. AI INCLUDES ITSELF AS AN INTERNET CUSTOMER WITH AN ADDRESS OF WWW.AIINET.COM.

APPLIED INNOVATION SUPPLIES PRODUCTS TO THE MAJOR INTEREXCHANGE CARRIERS AND ACCESS PROVIDERS, INCLUDING MCI.

CROSSMANN COMMUNITIES OF OHIO, INC./ DELUXE HOMES

ACHIEVING SUCCESS IN THE HOME-BUILDING INDUSTRY REQUIRES LONG-term planning, hard work, and patience—all qualities that have helped Deluxe Homes become the fifth-most-active home builder in Central Ohio. Deluxe Homes, based in Westerville, entered the Central Ohio

market in 1983, and now employs 37 people.

In its first year, the company closed on 10 houses. At the time, Steven M. Dunn, president of Deluxe Homes, was not only running the home-building side of the company, he was also serving as its sales manager. From these humble beginnings, the company steadily grew.

In 1986, the company completed about 90 homes; for the next seven years, it averaged between 100 and 140 homes a year. "It's been planned, steady growth rather than coming in and wanting to go from zero to 500 homes in a year," says Dunn. "We've gone out and selected good, desirable locations, and we've tried to provide what customers want."

Finding a good location is a primary desire of home buyers, regard-less of their price range, and helping them fulfill this desire is a goal of Deluxe Homes. The company's first project was the Madison Mills sub-division in southern Franklin County, a location already selected for a hous-ing development by another company. When that developer left the planned 320-house neighborhood two-thirds incomplete, Deluxe Homes acquired the site and completed it.

Deluxe Homes also began build-ing in Westerville, a popular housing location in the county's north end. The company has remained active in that suburban Columbus community, while also launching projects in other housing hot spots such as Grove City, Hilliard, and Reynoldsburg, as well as within the city of Columbus.

About 80 percent of Deluxe Homes' customers are first-time home buyers. To serve that market, the com-pany builds affordable homes, priced between $90,000 and $150,000. Deluxe Homes also builds for the "move-up market," with houses priced between $140,000 and $200,000. Servicing this market has proved to be a natural fit for Deluxe Homes, which has a grow-ing repeat and referral business.

EXPANDING PRESENCE

In 1993, Deluxe Homes merged with Crossmann Communities, Inc., Indi-ana's largest home-building company, which provided Deluxe Homes with a means for growth. Relying upon the financial strength of its partner to secure land in Central Ohio for new development, the company com-pleted 250 homes in 1996.

Due to the fact that more and more people are being drawn to out-

DELUXE HOMES HAS REMAINED ACTIVE IN THE SUBURBAN COMMUNITY OF WESTERVILLE, WHILE ALSO LAUNCHING PROJECTS IN OTHER HOUSING HOT SPOTS SUCH AS GROVE CITY, HILLIARD, AND REYNOLDSBURG, AS WELL AS WITHIN THE CITY OF COLUMBUS.

THE COMPANY INTENDS TO ADHERE TO THE FUNDAMENTALS THAT HAVE HELPED IT BECOME AND REMAIN A SUCCESSFUL HOME BUILDER IN CENTRAL OHIO— STEADY, PLANNED GROWTH AND SERVICE TO ITS CUSTOMERS.

lying areas, the company now has projects planned or completed in Delaware, Licking, Madison, Pickaway, and Union counties. But attention hasn't been drawn completely away from areas with which it's already familiar, as Deluxe Homes maintains several projects under development within the city of Columbus.

To secure future growth and success, Deluxe Homes is diversifying in order to take advantage of changing demographics and buying trends. This includes condominium development as well as a 50-lot, private-gated community project near Dublin. The target markets for this project are empty nesters or professionals who want the features of a home with condominium amenities such as snow removal and landscaping.

BUILDING RELATIONSHIPS

Despite this diversification, the company will remain committed to building affordable homes for the first-time home-buying market. Deluxe Homes is proud that it adds to the local

economy by making home ownership possible. The company also works to contribute to the community in other ways. For example, Deluxe Homes helped raise $6,000 for the Special Olympics through its Go for the Gold promotion, designed to take advantage of the excitement generated by the 1996 Summer Olympics. Employees also are involved in various community causes of their own.

And Deluxe Homes intends to adhere to the fundamentals that have helped it become and remain a successful home builder in Central Ohio— steady, planned growth and service to its customers.

"We're still providing the same level of service we've always provided," Dunn says. "I don't ever see that changing. We want to continue to build relationships, not just houses."

ABOUT 80 PERCENT OF DELUXE HOMES' CUSTOMERS ARE FIRST-TIME HOME BUYERS. TO SERVE THAT MARKET, THE COMPANY BUILDS AFFORDABLE HOMES, PRICED BETWEEN $90,000 AND $150,000.

BISYS® FUND SERVICES

THE LARGEST INDEPENDENT ADMINISTRATOR AND DISTRIBUTOR OF MUTUAL FUNDS in the country, BISYS Fund Services performs every back-office function a mutual fund complex requires—from fund accounting to transfer agency and compliance support, as well as strategic planning, marketing, and wholesaling.

BISYS Fund Services provides distribution and administration services to more than 60 mutual fund complexes, encompassing more than 700 individual portfolios with a market value exceeding $170 billion in assets.

Founded in Columbus in 1984 as The Winsbury Company, it was acquired in 1993 by The BISYS Group, Inc., which is headquartered in Little Falls, New Jersey, and is a leading provider of outsourcing solutions for banking, mutual fund, insurance, and retirement plan services. BISYS Fund Services also maintains offshore facilities in Dublin, Ireland, and the Cayman Islands to provide both domestic and international financial institutions with the complete array of services necessary to successfully compete in the offshore funds market.

A FULL RANGE OF SERVICES

BISYS Fund Services' menu of services and its technical expertise encompass every facet of this burgeoning industry. More than 500 professionals, headquartered in the heart of Columbus' Easton development, perform all of the services associated with manufacturing and distributing mutual funds with two critical exceptions: they do not perform investment management, and they do not provide custody of securities services for their partners' assets or the securities in their customer accounts. BISYS is unique in that it performs both high-level and task-oriented functions, rendering valuable support to its clients, the intermediaries that sell these services, and their fund shareholders. These groups rely on BISYS Fund Services to handle the behind-the-scenes roles associated with building

and growing a successful mutual fund complex.

BISYS' role as distributor means that it serves as the legal functionary charged with facilitating the purchase and sale of its clients' mutual funds to their customers, as well as the marketing expert to whom its clients turn for both strategic and tactical sales support to gather new assets for their complexes.

As mutual fund administrator, BISYS' role entails a variety of complex, technical services that range from legal and compliance support to day-to-day business management, transfer agency, fund accounting, and shareholder servicing. BISYS is responsible for maintaining the records and processing thousands of daily transactions for its combined investment partners.

Key to BISYS' success as an outsourcing partner is the posture it adopted early on as a growth-enabling resource. BISYS operates strictly as a business partner—never as a competitor. As the industry's leading outsourcing specialist, BISYS is uniquely positioned to support each client with a true business alliance. This operating discipline completely eliminates any possible corporate conflicts of interest, and is a critical distinction in today's global marketplace, which is inundated with aggressive firms competing for investors.

"By outsourcing, banks and investment management firms have access to the best possible mutual fund services without making a large investment in people and infrastructure to provide these services themselves," says J. David Huber, president of BISYS Fund Services. "Partnering with outside experts also allows them to concentrate on the most economically and strategically advantageous components of their mutual fund business."

THE LARGEST INDEPENDENT ADMINISTRATOR AND DISTRIBUTOR OF MUTUAL FUNDS IN THE COUNTRY, BISYS FUND SERVICES PERFORMS EVERY BACK-OFFICE FUNCTION A MUTUAL FUND COMPLEX REQUIRES—FROM FUND ACCOUNTING TO TRANSFER AGENCY AND COMPLIANCE SUPPORT, AS WELL AS STRATEGIC PLANNING, MARKETING, AND WHOLESALING.

TOMASCO MULCIBER, INC.

FOUNDED IN 1986, TOMASCO MULCIBER, INC. WAS THE FIRST U.S. OPERATION of Masuda Manufacturing Company Ltd., a leading Japan-based manufacturer of automobile and motorcycle parts. Created to supply parts to Honda of America Manufacturing, TOMASCO began production with 19 associates

on September 21, 1987. Today, there are more than 450 associates, and the original building has been expanded three times. Continued company growth was assured in 1987, when Masuda shared ownership of TOMASCO with North American Honda, Bestex Kyoei Company Ltd., and Marujun Seiki Industrial Company Ltd.

A Unique Corporate Culture

Using a blend of the best of Japanese and American management and manufacturing practices, TOMASCO associates perform metal stamping, welding, assembly, injection molding, and painting operations. More than 30 million parts are manufactured annually, and include fuel filler lids, hood and truck hinges, air-conditioning shrouds, hood lock assemblies, engine mounts, and steering hanger beams as the major products. They are then delivered mainly to the Honda plants located in North America and to Isuzu U.S. TOMASCO produces parts that are shipped to nine different countries other than the United States.

All production at TOMASCO is conducted using carefully engineered equipment specifically designed for each production application. TOMASCO is currently operating 40 metal stamping presses that range in capacity from 45 tons to 800 tons, and, to maintain a competitive edge, robotics is used in a wide variety of welding processes.

Also key to TOMASCO is quality control at all levels and a commitment to training through the efforts of a diversified workforce. TOMASCO recognizes the invaluable contributions its associates have made to its success, and encourages and rewards suggestions to improve efficiency and quality. In recognition of TOMASCO's attitude and com-

mitment to equality, unity, and teamwork, associates at all levels wear the same uniform.

As a symbol of the melding of two cultures and the company's nurturing spirit toward associates, TOMASCO's grounds are landscaped with more than 100 Japanese cherry trees. Originally, a tree was planted for each new associate— a custom that had to be suspended with the phenomenal growth of the building structure.

Deep Connection to the Local Community

TOMASCO strives to bring Japanese and American cultures together on the community level, as well. Through its Adopt-a-School program, TOMASCO established a school exchange partnership between Leawood Elementary School in Columbus and Shinjo Elementary School in Yamagata, Japan; Yamagata is the site of one of Masuda's three plants. Recognizing that the elementary-school-age children are the leaders of tomorrow, the company's dream is to encourage their abilities to understand, communicate, and conduct business with each other in the future.

TOMASCO associates are setting goals to ensure the company's

future. Recent corporate goals include improving customer service, further expansion of TOMASCO, and maintaining a clean, organized, and safe working environment.

In this spirit, TOMASCO associates can be seen wearing buttons with the company's recently established mottoes: Start Smooth, Finish Strong, and Total Preparation—Nothing Less. It is a strategy that assures TOMASCO's continued growth and success for many years to come.

FOUNDED IN 1986, TODAY TOMASCO HAS MORE THAN 450 ASSOCIATES.

TOMASCO IS CURRENTLY OPERATING 40 METAL STAMPING PRESSES THAT RANGE IN CAPACITY FROM 45 TONS TO 800 TONS.

TOMASCO MULCIBER, INC. ASSOCIATES OPERATE STATE-OF-THE-ART EQUIPMENT TO PERFORM WELD PROCESSES CONSISTING OF RESISTANCE SPOT/PROJECTION AND A COMBINATION OF 52 SPOT AND CO_2 ROBOTIC MACHINES.

DOWNTOWN AND THROUGHOUT THE CITY, COLUMBUS IS BEING REVITALIZED. Star Banc Corporation, a multistate banking company that has served Ohio for more than 134 years, is part of the reason. Star Banc has been serving Central Ohio since 1985, operating originally as The Ohio State Bank.

Listed on the New York Stock Exchange, Star Banc is the 57th-largest bankholding company in the nation. With 1997 assets of more than $10 billion, Star Banc ranks in the upper echelon of banks in the United States in profitability, revenue growth, customer service, efficiency, and shareholder returns.

Star Bank—Star Banc Corporation's largest subsidiary—is a major regional banking presence in Ohio, Kentucky, and Indiana. In Columbus and Central Ohio, its expanding presence comprises more than 60 locations, including traditional branches, in-store branches, Super ATMs, and a Virtual Banking-Video Banking center at Ohio State University (OSU).

EXCELLENCE IN FINANCIAL SERVICES

Commercial banking has been at Star Bank's core since its founding. Today, technological advances help support those characteristics essential to sound commercial banking that endure at Star Bank: knowledgeable and experienced lenders, industry and market expertise, tenacious calling efforts, and prudent underwriting standards. In Columbus, this quality of service is delivered through Star Bank's regional commercial banking office and its on-site staff.

Star Bank offers complete cash management services: balance reporting, ACH (automated clearing house), account reconciliation, controlled disbursement, EDI (electronic data interchange), wires, and lockbox. The bank's corporate cash management programs are attuned to the objectives of its clients—from major corporate firms to small businesses—to manage, control, and invest available funds, while reducing administrative expense and increasing on-line management information. In 1996, Star Bank launched StarView, a state-of-the-art, Windows-based fund and account management workstation, and TaxComm, a Touch-Tone phone tax payment service that enables businesses to deposit all state and federal taxes.

Columbus, with its central location, has long been a center of trade. More recently, that trade has become international. Star Bank, through the skill and experience of its international bankers, is a leader in the specialized field of international trade services and international corporate banking. Star has received recognition from both the U.S. government and the State of Ohio for excellence in this area.

Expanding its international network, Star Bank established a trade service arrangement with the HongKongbank of Hong Kong in 1996. This alliance broadens the range of trade services Star Bank can offer corporate clients with dealings in the Asia-Pacific region. It also initiated an automated Canadian cash manage-

STAR HAS MORE THAN 270 BRANCH OFFICES AND MORE THAN 450 SUPER ATMS THROUGHOUT ITS MARKETING AREA. CONSUMER BANKING JOINS COMMERCIAL BANKING AND TRUST AS LEADING FINANCIAL SERVICES IN STAR'S MARKETS.

ment system, a benefit to bank clients dealing with Ohio's largest trading partner.

Star Bank engages in extensive trust activities; by the end of 1996, its trust assets under management or administration totaled $30 billion. Star Funds, a family of nine proprietary mutual funds, for which Star Bank is investment adviser, have been very successful. The Star Funds Relative Value mutual fund was recognized by the *Wall Street Journal* and *Morningstar*, and both the Relative Value and Star's Growth Equity funds were recognized by Lipper Analytical Services, Inc.

In 1996, two innovative offerings were established for Star Funds investors. The first, called Star Points, rewards new investors in Star Funds with one frequent flier point for every dollar invested. In addition, VOICE—Vision for Ongoing Investment in Charity and Education—allows those establishing new agency trust accounts with Star to designate an institution to receive a contribution from Star, based on a percentage of the amount in the account.

EXPANDED CONSUMER OFFERINGS

To match its strength in trust and investment services and commercial banking, Star Bank has placed renewed emphasis on consumer banking operations. Central to this effort is Star's 24-Hour Banking program. Although other banks have adopted certain components of remote banking, Star was the nation's first to offer the service as an integrated package. The 24-Hour Banking program offers seven integrated features—traditional branch banking, Super ATMs, voice banking by telephone, computer banking, screen phones, video banking, and Internet banking.

Through Star's 450 Super ATMs, customers can buy postage stamps, make withdrawals in foreign currency, obtain detailed account statements, order checks, and request copies of canceled checks. With Star's 24-hour banking by telephone, customers may pay any bill, using a voice recognition system that provides complete security.

Customers with personal computers can simply point and click to execute dozens of banking transactions, from anywhere in the world, any time of day. Those without a PC may use special screen phones—a cross between a PC and an ATM—that put customers on-line without using a computer. On the OSU campus, a touch-screen video kiosk allows Star customers to perform many tasks they would normally complete at a branch office.

In addition, Star's Internet home page allows customers to access their accounts immediately at no charge; others may request the company's computer banking software, send E-mail messages, and request information from Star.

Star's 134-year record of paying dividends and its 25-year record of dividend increases reflect Star's focus on the customer. Star's unique Five Star Service Guarantee backs up the bank's guarantee of quality service with cash.

As the 20th century draws to a close, the U.S. banking industry is being transformed by continuing consolidations and government deregulation. Star is poised to take advantage of those changes. Through an aggressive pursuit of new technology, new customers, and new markets, and a commitment to guaranteed customer satisfaction with its many banking services, Star Bank will continue its tradition of service and success into the next century.

24 Hour Remote Banking

Branch Banking | Super ATM | Voice Banking | ScreenPhone | PC Banking | Video Banking | Internet Banking

THE 24-HOUR BANKING INITIATIVE HAS PLACED STAR AT THE FOREFRONT OF THE NATION'S BANKING INDUSTRY IN PROVIDING INNOVATIVE SERVICES WHEN AND WHERE CUSTOMERS WANT THEM. IT CONSISTS OF FULLY INTEGRATED ELEMENTS THAT GIVE CUSTOMERS MAXIMUM CHOICE IN BANKING—24 HOURS A DAY, SEVEN DAYS A WEEK (TOP).

CUSTOMERS WITH PCS CAN SIMPLY POINT AND CLICK TO EXECUTE DOZENS OF BANKING TRANSACTIONS—FROM ANY TIME ZONE IN THE WORLD AT ANY HOUR OF THE DAY (BOTTOM).

TS Tech North America is a major supplier of seating and interior component parts to the automotive industry, with 10 facilities located in North America. Four of these are located in Ohio—one in Athens and three in the Columbus area. TS Tech's primary customers are Honda manufacturing plants in Ohio, Canada, Mexico, and Brazil.

TS stands for parent company Tokyo Seat, which has a long relationship with Honda going back to the early motorcycle days in Japan, and has evolved into a worldwide company producing seats and accessories for a variety of transportation models. In 1986, Tokyo Seat established TS Trim Industries in Canal Winchester to support Honda operations located in Marysville. This was followed with an additional TS Trim plant built in Athens, Ohio, that began operations in 1988. During 1995, the company acquired a long-vacant building in Reynoldsburg and began a new plant called TS Tech USA. Also at this time, North American headquarters and research/development were established at the Reynoldsburg site.

DAVE HENRY

A Blend of the Best

TS Tech engineering combines state-of-the-art technology with the ultimate in comfort and safety. The company's products include door and roof liners, seat cover trim and welded frames, and recreational seating for motorcycles and jet skis. The company's humanistic philosophy emphasizes respect for every individual, and recognizes that every associate is part of a team contributing to the quality of the products. The team concept is underscored by the uniforms that are worn by everyone in each plant, without exception. This reinforces that each associate, regardless of job function, is an important part of the process that has led to the company's international reputation for excellence.

At TS Tech, there are no private offices, no reserved parking, and everyone dines in the same cafeteria. The removal of these artificial barriers results in vastly improved accessibility and communications. Additionally, a "blended" management style incorporates the best of Japanese and American principles into a singular concept that provides both cultures an environment of cooperation, teamwork, and continued success.

Although foreign-owned, it is important to note that the TS Tech organization is very much an American company. In Ohio, 1,400 American associates produce American-made parts for vehicles made in Ohio and exported to more than 60 countries worldwide.

The company and its affiliates are exemplary corporate citizens, involved with schools and universities, local chambers of commerce, charities, and the international business community. TS Tech North America is a success story—resulting from Ohio's efforts to recruit foreign businesses to the state—which has created jobs, taxes, and good corporate neighbors.

Clockwise from top:
During 1995, TS Tech North America began a new plant called TS Tech USA in Reynoldsburg. The company's North American headquarters and R&D are now located at the Reynoldsburg site.

In 1986, Tokyo Seat established TS Trim Industries in Canal Winchester to support Honda operations located in Marysville.

TS Tech products include door and roof liners, seat cover trim and welded frames, and recreational seating for motorcycles and jet skis.

ROGER RILL

L-S II Electro-Galvanizing Company

A LEADING PROCESSOR OF CORROSION-RESISTANT STEEL, THE L-S II ELECTRO-Galvanizing Company in Columbus is also known for its success in another area—the company has produced a working example of a better approach to workplace management. ✴ It's an approach that won praise from U.S.

Secretary of Labor Robert Reich, who visited L-S II's forerunner operation, L-S Electro-Galvanizing, in Cleveland, Ohio. Reich called it a high-performance workplace that passed the "pronoun test"—where workers referred to management as "we," not "they."

New Technology, New Rules

L-S II's story began in the mid-1980s, when the U.S. auto industry announced plans to extend auto life by using more corrosion-resistant steel. To acquire needed technology, Cleveland-based LTV Steel, the nation's third-largest steelmaker, formed a joint venture with Sumitomo Metals of Japan. David Murdock, L-S II's director of human resources, explains, "We said that as long as we are pursuing this new technology, let's go the extra step and create a new and different organization."

The new system, created jointly by management and the workforce, places emphasis on education and participation. Over time, plant personnel, known as technicians, are expected to develop knowledge and abilities in each of the plant's six key operating areas, along with numerous maintenance and support skills. Technicians rotate jobs regularly, doing maintenance one day, production the next, then possibly inspecting or shipping huge rolls of steel to a customer's plant.

Pay is pegged to how many skill areas a technician has mastered.

The plant also has a no-layoff policy; workplace problems focus on problem solving rather than on grievance procedures; and work scheduling is handled by an employee committee. The aim is to replace the traditional, rigidly defined, less productive workplace with one where workers are empowered and productivity-oriented—where teamwork, the total company, and the customer are all very important.

Innovation in Columbus

With the success of the Cleveland operation, ground was broken in 1989 for a second plant on a 75-acre site in south Columbus, which was selected because of the city's convenience to major transportation lines that serve automotive stamping plants, and because of the support of the

city and state. Opened in 1991, the 300,000-square-foot plant represents a $200 million investment that today processes 360,000 tons of corrosion-resistant, electro-galvanized flat rolled steel coils a year. Within the plant, a 72-inch-wide, 1,000-foot-long line uses proprietary Sumitomo electrolytic plating technologies to deposit corrosion-resistant coatings on cold rolled steel produced at LTV Steel's Cleveland Works. The coatings can be pure zinc, zinc/nickel alloy, zinc/nickel alloy with protective organic paint, or pure zinc with specialty paints.

The goal of L-S II Electro-Galvanizing Company, Murdock says, is to be the premier electro-galvanizer in the world. "People have said we adopted Japanese-style management. We didn't. The style we chose represents the best that Americans can be."

OPENED IN 1991, THE 300,000-SQUARE-FOOT PLANT REPRESENTS A $200 MILLION INVESTMENT THAT TODAY PROCESSES 360,000 TONS OF CORROSION-RESISTANT, ELECTRO-GALVANIZED FLAT ROLLED STEEL COILS A YEAR.

THE WIDE, VERTICAL STRIP BETWEEN THE L BEAMS AND CROSS BEAMS IS ELECTRO-PLATED AS IT PASSES THROUGH ONE PORTION OF THE 1,200-FOOT ELECTRO-GALVANIZING LINE (LEFT).

THE TAKE-UP REEL AT THE END OF THE ELECTROPLATING LINE REWINDS THE FINISHED ZINC- OR ZINC/NICKEL-COATED STEEL INTO A COIL. THE AVERAGE FINISHED COIL IS 58 INCHES WIDE, 5,000 FEET LONG, AND 40,000 POUNDS IN WEIGHT (RIGHT).

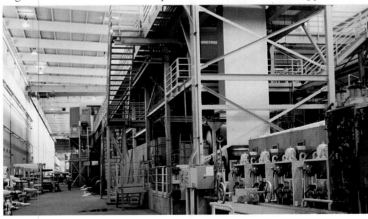

THE NEW ALBANY COMPANY

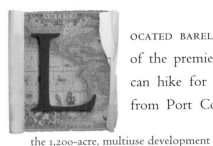

OCATED BARELY A DOZEN MILES NORTHEAST OF COLUMBUS, NEW ALBANY IS ONE of the premier residential areas in all of Central Ohio. It is a place where one can hike for miles through woods and meadows, and still be just 10 minutes from Port Columbus Airport. New Albany is only a few miles from Easton,

A BRAND-NEW, 180,000-SQUARE-FOOT MIDDLE AND HIGH SCHOOL OFFERS STUDENTS STATE-OF-THE-ART TECHNOLOGY AND UNRIVALED ART AND MUSIC STUDIOS (LEFT).

WITH APPROXIMATELY 700 LOTS ALREADY DEVELOPED, NEW ALBANY WILL EVENTUALLY HAVE SOME 1,300 UPSCALE HOMES IN ITS COUNTRY CLUB DEVELOPMENT (RIGHT).

the 1,200-acre, multiuse development that combines retail, office, recreation, and entertainment facilities. With approximately 700 lots already developed, New Albany will eventually have some 1,300 upscale homes in its country club development, and, even though the community is quite young, it is already the regional leader for houses priced at more than $500,000 and for families relocating to the area. Its varied neighborhoods include homes starting at $300,000.

Described as "very beautiful" by *Town & Country* magazine, New Albany is defined by its land, its architecture, and the talents of its master planners—elements that offer a style of living that is at once modern and

gracious. It is singularly impressive for the strength of its vision and for its meticulous execution.

REALIZING A VISION

The community is the realization of a long-held dream of Leslie Wexner's, the visionary founder of the Limited, Inc. retailing empire. Wexner envisioned a new kind of country living, with open spaces, trees, barns, rolling pastures, and streams, but also a place with every modern convenience. To help him shape the idea, Wexner formed a development company and engaged the interest and the talents of the nation's best designers and architects. Collaborating on the project were Dr. Gerald McCue, retired dean of the Harvard University Graduate School of Design; Laurie Olin, former chairman of Harvard's Department of Landscape Architecture; renowned Georgian architect Jaquelin Robertson; interior designers Keith Irvine and Tom Fleming; and, to design the golf course, acclaimed golfer and course architect Jack Nicklaus.

In New Albany, community life revolves around the golf and tennis complex, a spectacular Georgian manor

designed by Robertson. An elegant clubhouse with antique treasures from around the world, it is warm and inviting, and an excellent place to meet for wine tastings, book clubs, and cooking classes. New Albany also features a world-class tennis facility, two Olympic-sized swimming pools, and a first-class health and fitness club.

Like the rest of New Albany, the unique, 27-hole golf course makes great use of the character of the land. Says Nicklaus, "New Albany has some great natural advantages: good movement to the terrain, large trees and water, and a variety of open areas. In consequence, several holes have the open feel of the Scottish links; others, the lush look of the Carolinas."

ARCHITECTURAL GRACE

New Albany is a place where land and life are tied together through the rooted tradition of American Georgian architecture.

Robertson states, "If one were going to build a fine country community, the most trusted style to turn to would be American Georgian. There is in American Georgian architecture a harmonious relationship between

buildings and the land that everyone seems drawn to, as any trip to the Virginia tidewater and piedmont areas will confirm."

To date, more than 70 Georgian homes, valued in excess of $1 million each, have been built in New Albany. This is a remarkable accomplishment, considering the lack of homes selling at that price in the region. In addition, more than 400 other beautifully detailed Georgian homes have been completed and are now occupied.

Town & Country points to New Albany's architectural guidelines as a primary reason for its attractiveness. But it is more than an aesthetic choice. A home is both a place to live and an investment, and by assuring that each home contributes to the overall beauty of the community, New Albany protects the investment each family has made in its home.

Some 600 acres of permanent green space has been left in New Albany's neighborhoods. Through this land, there are meandering streams, inviting meadows, hedgerows, and 40 miles of white-painted fencing. The community is also laced with leisure paths in a network of six trails that run from neighborhood to neighborhood, leading to parks and the clubhouse.

New Albany is also creating a new standard for education, one which—like the rest of the community—combines the best of the old and the new. Schoolchildren partici-pate in hands-on learning, studying tadpoles and frogs in a 30-acre nature preserve located a mere 100 yards from their classroom. There is a brand-new, 180,000-square-foot middle and high school, with state-of-the-art technology and unrivaled

art and music studios. It is certainly one of the most beautiful schools, public or private, ever built, and the curriculum is designed to prepare students for the challenges of the 21st century.

REASONS FOR SUCCESS

Wexner credits the success of New Albany to the public's rediscovery over the past decade of long-held traditional values, including concern for the environment, appreciation for craftsmanship, and the desire to live in beautiful, natural settings—all while maintaining the advantages of modern suburban living.

Says Olin, "The real test, years from now, will be when people who know nothing about how New Albany started look at it and say, 'This is wonderful. This is a fabulous community.' "

EXECUTIVE OFFICE PLACE

A VISIONARY ENTREPRENEUR PERCEIVES A NEED AND SETS OUT TO FIND A SOLUTION. Such a definition befits Frank and Gail Fabish, who, after hearing about the dilemmas that confront businesses when it comes to leasing traditional office space, sought to alleviate such problems by entering the shared office space industry.

Frank Fabish had used the concept in Cleveland, and drew on his experiences to tailor the new business to the needs of the Columbus marketplace. In 1989, Fabish and his wife, Gail, launched Executive Office Place, leasing commercial office buildings and subletting the space to businesses. With a high proportion of service industries, a low unemployment rate, and a reputation as a regional distribution hub, Columbus was the ideal location for their company, and has provided a steady client base from the beginning.

Initially offering a total of 34 offices in two locations, the Fabishes quickly realized that if they added more locations, they could not only offer clients more options, but would be able to leverage overhead, marketing, and advertising costs. As a result, Executive Office Place now has 195 offices in four locations, giving the company control of approximately 35 percent of the total shared office space in Columbus. The company's occupancy rate is at 95 percent, the highest ever in its history.

The four sites—at 65 East State Street in downtown; at 2720 Airport Drive; at 438 East Wilson Bridge Road; and at 1335 Dublin Road—cover nearly all quadrants of Franklin County. The only quadrant in which Executive Office Place has yet to estab-lish a presence is Dublin, and an agreement has been signed to open a 65-office location at Tuttle Crossing in the fall of 1998.

FILLING A NICHE

To a company that is expanding, consolidating, or relocating to Columbus, sharing office space is an appealing concept for a number of reasons. While clients have their own office space, they share access to conference rooms, state-of-the-art telecommunications systems, and such support services as word processing, faxing, and copying. "We free people up to focus on what they do best—sales and service—and to focus almost 100 percent of their time on that, so they become more productive," says Frank Fabish.

Another key benefit is flexibility. "We are able to give clients the flexibility of starting with an individual office and adding offices when they are ready," Fabish adds. Executive Office Place's size and multiple locations can also fill the need of a tenant that requires more than one office. The company's largest client leases 10 offices.

That flexibility also extends to staffing and technology. If a client company only needs part-time support staff or part-time graphics assistance, it is able to select the amount of services that it requires. Although there is a fee for utilizing Executive Office Place's services, it is typically less expensive than the cost of employing a full-time staff person.

Many standard leasing arrangements require a tenant to sign a long-term lease, with no guarantee that additional space will be available when expansion becomes necessary. At Executive Office Place, lease arrangements, like other services, are designed to fit a client's individual needs. The company offers month-to-month leases

IN 1989, FRANK FABISH AND HIS WIFE, GAIL, LAUNCHED EXECUTIVE OFFICE PLACE, LEASING COMMERCIAL OFFICE BUILDINGS AND SUBLETTING THE SPACE TO BUSINESSES.

LARRY HAMILL

for up to three years. And if a company needs to expand, the staffing and technology services are already in place.

KEEPING PACE WITH TECHNOLOGY

Tenants of Executive Office Place span a wide variety of businesses. Fabish estimates that approximately 45 percent are locally based entrepreneurs and regional businesses, while some 55 percent are large companies, representing a mix of such local and national firms as Motorola, Nestlé, Oracle, and Amdahl Corporation.

As the rapidly changing business market evolves, one goal of Executive Office Place is to remain on the cutting edge of technology. "You have to be able to provide the same level of communications that are available in the headquarters of a large company," says Fabish.

Several years ago, because many tenants did not have personal computers, Executive Office Place's support staff provided computer services. Today, every tenant has a PC, and technical services such as chart and graph production and database management are provided. Other recently added services include videoconferencing, local area networks, E-mail and Internet access, and high-speed data transmission.

As companies have become more global, Executive Office Place has expanded its presence worldwide through membership in the Executive Suite Association, which provides tenants with access to offices in 550 U.S. locations, and in the Alliance Business Centers Network, which provides 200 additional locations worldwide.

Reflecting on its years in business, Fabish says his company's repu-

tation as a top provider of shared office space in Columbus is linked to high-caliber associates and hands-on ownership and management. "A lot of companies have the objective of providing quality, but don't hire quality people. That's the only way to do it. We feel proud of what we've been able to do. We feel we're providing a good set of services to the business community."

THE FOUR EXECUTIVE OFFICE PLACE SITES—(CLOCKWISE FROM TOP LEFT) 65 EAST STATE STREET IN DOWNTOWN; 2720 AIRPORT DRIVE; 438 EAST WILSON BRIDGE ROAD; AND 1335 DUBLIN ROAD— COVER NEARLY ALL QUADRANTS OF FRANKLIN COUNTY.

EXXCEL Contract Management

IF YOU LOOK AT THE LIST OF CONSTRUCTION PROJECTS COMPLETED BY EXXCEL CONTRACT Management, you'll see something unique: the same clients appear over and over. But repeat customer business is only one measure of EXXCEL's success. Further proof is the fact that the company has handled construction projects totaling more than 8 million

square feet—a space equal to 170 football fields—since it was founded in 1991.

Headquartered in Columbus, EXXCEL Contract Management provides design and construction services, including design/build, general construction, and construction management, for office buildings, distribution centers, and manufacturing facilities throughout the United States.

Every EXXCEL project demonstrates a mastery of detail and overall coordination. The company offers a full range of capabilities, including state-of-the-art real estate analysis, site search and assistance with acquisition, master planning and conceptual

development, building design and engineering, procurement of contractors, and management of actual construction. And, as an added convenience to the customer, it offers these services as a package, or in any combination that suits the project at hand.

COMMITMENT TO EXCELLENCE

EXXCEL operates under the belief that excellence is voluntary. A company cannot force its employees to have a commitment to creativity, responsibility, and quality—characteristics at the heart of excellence. Instead, the company must strive to attract individuals who view excellence as

a personal commitment. These individuals then operate through high-performance teams, using their expertise to undertake and complete a given project.

Because EXXCEL Contract Management is managerially lean, not only is overhead reduced, but authority is placed in the hands of each high-performance team. As a result, team members have the latitude and authority to accomplish their responsibilities within EXXCEL's corporate goals and objectives, and in turn, they receive the support they need. For example, all project teams are in constant communication with the professionally managed information systems in the main office, which provide immediate access to EXXCEL's computerized estimating system, computerized scheduling documentation, and other capabilities.

Such excellence translates into EXXCEL's work. For example, the company conducts thorough site searches: In addition to figuring the cost of running in utility lines or constructing access roads, it considers such issues as local housing availability. In addition, EXXCEL's procurement methodology ensures quality work and timely completion by prequalifying potential contractors—each of which is assessed for its safety record, quality, financial stability, experience, and ability to comply with schedules—and by holding mandatory prebid meetings, which ensure complete understanding of the proposed project.

In the end, this commitment to excellence has readily apparent results: a growing list of construction projects completed to high professional standards, measurable client satisfaction, and obvious industry success. And EXXCEL Contract Management can claim all these qualities in full.

EXXCEL CONTRACT MANAGEMENT PROVIDES DESIGN AND CONSTRUCTION SERVICES, INCLUDING DESIGN/BUILD, GENERAL CONSTRUCTION, AND CONSTRUCTION MANAGEMENT, FOR OFFICE BUILDINGS, DISTRIBUTION CENTERS, AND MANUFACTURING FACILITIES THROUGHOUT THE UNITED STATES. EXXCEL DESIGNED AND BUILT THIS OFFICE WAREHOUSE, LOCATED IN SOUTHPARK, FOR PIZZUTI DEVELOPMENT, INC.

THIS BULK WAREHOUSE BY EXXCEL WAS AWARDED THE METAL BUILDING OF THE YEAR AWARD FROM MBMA.

◀ BRAD FEINKNOPF

PHOTOGRAPHERS

IAN ADAMS is an Akron-based environmental photographer who has traveled throughout the eastern United States, documenting its natural, rural, and historical areas. He leads outdoor photography workshops, seminars, and photo tours. Adams' Ilfochrome color prints have been widely exhibited and are included in many corporate and private collections. His work has also been featured in *Avenues, Better Homes and Gardens,* and *Country,* as well as on 18 covers of *Ohio Magazine,* for which he is a contributing editor.

ERIC ALBRECHT, who has been named Photographer of the Year three times by the Ohio News Photographers Association, has also received numerous awards from the National Press Photographers Association. He has exhibited his work in a one-man show at the Canton Art Institute and at the Great Southern Hotel's *Seven Lenses, Seven Visions* exhibit. His work has been featured in many publications, including *A Day in the Life of America, Day in the Country, USA, The Art of Seeing, The Best of Photojournalism,* the *Columbus Dispatch,* and *Ohio Magazine.*

GEORGE C. ANDERSON, a native of Champaign, has lived in Columbus since 1975. He is a self-employed photographer who specializes in taking pictures of people.

GREG BARTRAM, originally from Pittsburgh, moved to the Columbus area in 1980. He is a self-taught photographer who specializes in portraiture and images of sports, bar and bas mitzvahs, and weddings. Bartram has worked for several local sports teams including the Chill, the Crew, and the Xoggz. In addition, he enjoys playing bass guitar.

ROD BERRY, a native of Columbus, owns and operates Rod Berry Photography, a stock photo agency covering a range of subjects from landscape and architecture to recreational activities. His largest files include images of Ohio, especially Columbus skylines, attractions, and events. Berry does freelance assignments and fine art photography, and his work is currently represented in a number of galleries in the Midwest.

ROGER BICKEL, a Bingham Farms, Michigan-based freelance photographer, specializes in travel and nature stock photography. His travel photos cover most of the 50 states, and his nature photos feature the flora and fauna of Michigan. Bickel's work has appeared Towery Publishing's *Cincinnati: Crowning Glory* and *Greater Detroit: Renewing the Dream;* such periodicals as *National Geographic Traveler, Better Homes and Gardens, Woman's World,* and Delta Air Lines' *Sky;* and books published by Houghton Mifflin, Barnes & Noble, Insight Guides, and Children's Press.

JAY BROWN is a native Ohioan who graduated from the Ohio State University with a bachelor's degree in biology. He is a freelance photographer who specializes in shooting live punk and alternative bands. Brown's work has been featured in the *New York Times Magazine, Spin, Alternative Press, Columbus Monthly,* the *Columbus Free Times,* and *Columbus Alive.*

JANET CENTURY has been producing black-and-white and color photography for a wide range of corporations, publications, agencies, and universities for more than 15 years. Her work has been published in *Images from the Heart: A Bicentennial Celebration of Cleveland and Its People; To Heal a Nation,* a book about the Vietnam Veterans Memorial; and *The Beacon* magazine, in a story about Vietnam veterans returning to Vietnam. The recipient of numerous industry awards, Century recently was commissioned to photograph workers for USS *Kobe's Steel Town Story.*

SCOTT CUNNINGHAM earned a bachelor's degree from Bowling Green State University and a master of fine arts in photography from Long Island University before moving to Columbus in 1992. The co-owner of Cunningham/Feinknopf Photography, he specializes in lifestyle and fashion photography and has won three Addy Awards for his work. His clients include The Limited, HMS Advertising, and Easy Rider. Cunningham is also represented by Gamma Liaison Stock, and is currently working on an exhibition titled *The Côte d'Azur.*

BRAD FEINKNOPF, a lifelong Columbusite, earned a bachelor of science in design from Cornell University and worked for several years in New York City as a photographer's assistant. The co-owner of Cunningham/Feinknopf Photography, he specializes in architecture, interiors, and corporate photography, as well as portraiture. Feinknopf's work has been published in *Architecture* and *World Architecture,* and he has won two Addy Awards. His clients include Karlsberger Cos., NBBJ Architects, URS Architects, and Smoot Construction Co.

KEN FRICK is a self-employed photographer whose work has been featured in *Newsweek, Smithsonian, Financial World, PC World, Nature Conservancy Magazine,* and the *Farm Journal National Edition.* Having earned a bachelor of fine arts in photography from Ohio University in Athens, he is currently a commercial photographer who divides his time between corporate, industrial, and editorial photography. Originally from Zanesville, Ohio, Frick moved to Columbus in 1984. He enjoys sports, motorcycling, and restoring his 100-year-old Victorian cottage.

LARRY HAMILL, a freelance photographer since 1973, graduated with a bachelor of fine arts in painting and drawing from the Ohio State University. Hamill's clientele includes AT&T, Bank One, IBM, and Kenyon College. Based in Columbus, Hamill travels the world shooting images for his stock photography files. Represented by agencies in Japan, Germany, and India, his work has appeared in national and international publications. Expansion into computer graphics has allowed Hamill to integrate his talents with painting, photography, and design. This technological creative outlet recently led to the publication of his work in Japan's premier magazine, *MacIntosh designers Network (MdN).*

TOM HOGAN, a graduate of the Ohio State University with a bachelor of fine arts in photography, has been a commercial photographer in Columbus for more than 20 years. His clients include Nationwide Insurance, CompuServe, Lucent Technologies, Victoria's Secret, Bath & Body Works, The Limited Too, and Blue Cross/Blue Shield of Ohio.

THE IMAGE FINDERS, founded by Jim Baron in 1986, is a stock photography company located in Cleveland. Its files cover a broad range of subjects, including agriculture, animals, butterflies, families, food, sports, travel, transportation, trees, and western states.

ED KREMINSKI is a freelance commercial photographer who grew up in the Midwest and studied mechanical and electrical engineering in college. While living in Seattle, he was inspired by the beauty of the Pacific Northwest to become a photographer. In 1987, Kreminski and his wife, Tina, returned to Columbus, where he currently specializes in location photography.

ROBERT E. LANDRUM first became interested in photography in 1974. A self-taught photographer, he learned the art of taking pictures by reading numerous books and experimenting on his own. A lifelong Columbusite, Landrum specializes in landscape photography and children's portraits.

JODI MILLER, a graduate of the Ohio State University, is a staff photographer for her alma mater's department of communications and technology. Miller's work has appeared in numerous publications, including *Ohio Magazine*, Greater Columbus Convention & Visitor's Bureau publications, *OhioPass*, and *Farm Journal*.

DALE NIELSON, originally from Phoenix, moved to Columbus in 1993. A flight attendant and photographer, he enjoys taking pictures of pets and travel scenes. In 1996, the Columbus Art League selected one of Nielson's travel photos for a juried show. His work was also featured in Planet Pet's *Dog Daze* exhibit.

RICK A. PREBEG, a native Ohioan, works on the television series *Jack Hanna's Animal Adventures*. A specialist in wildlife photography, Prebeg has an extensive collection of African photos. In addition to providing all of Hanna's publicity photography, Prebeg has supplied images for video box covers, books, posters, magazines, and postcards. His clients include many businesses in the Columbus area and around the country.

RANDALL LEE SCHIEBER is a Columbus-based photographer who studied photography and art and earned a bachelor of arts from Kent State University. His work has appeared in numerous publications, such as *Ohio Magazine*, *OhioPass*, Delta Air Lines' *Sky*, and *EcoTraveler*. Schieber's images have been used on posters and postcards, and he currently has calendars out on Columbus and Ohio.

RENÉE K. VELKOFF, a native Columbusite, is a horticulture consultant and an experienced photographer, specializing in musicians, wildflowers, plants, and family and friends. Her work has been exhibited at the Ohio State Fair and the Fort Hayes Visual Arts Gallery. Velkoff's images have been published in the *Columbus Dispatch* and on album covers for several local bands.

PAMELA J. WILLITS, the owner of PJ Communications, combines her writing and photographic abilities to meet clients' needs in marketing, communications, and public relations. Willits has written brochures, profiles, feature articles, ad copy, and news releases. Her photographs have appeared in brochures, audiovisual productions, travel guides, newspapers, and textbooks, as well as in regional and national magazines. Pursuing postgraduate studies in environmental law and natural resources, Willits has been active in the Society of Environmental Journalists and Women in Communications, Inc. She has also served as a volunteer literacy tutor through the Literacy Initiative.

Other photographers and organizations that contributed to *Discover Columbus* include Jim Baron, Michael Evans, William Holmes, the Muirfield Golf Club, Paul Natkin, the Ohio State University, the Thurber House, Dan Tyrpak, Wagner Photo, and Jerry Wisler.

INDEX OF PROFILES